Instructor Big

TEACHER'S ACTIVITY CALENDAR

Oodles of Bulletin Boards, Plays, Stories, Songs, Teaching Units, and Ideas for Every Month of the School Year

★

SCHOLASTIC INC., 2931 East McCarty Street, Jefferson City, MO 65102
Or call (800) 325-6149 between 7:30 a.m. and 5 p.m. Central Time. In Missouri, call (800) 392-2179.

ISBN 0-590-49010-9

12 11 10 9 8 7 6 5 4 3 2   0 1 2 3 4/9
                                                                              43

Printed in the U.S.A.

The material in this book, some in its original form, other in an adapted version, is taken from articles published in INSTRUCTOR magazine and in Teacher magazine during the years 1971 to 1981.

This book was compiled and edited by Instructor's associate editors Debra Martorelli and Susan Hood, with assistance from Instructor staffers Mary Dalheim, Susan Gaustad, Nancy Palubniak, and John Heisner. Charles Cary is designer and artist.

CONTENTS

SEPTEMBER

Happy new year! We may officially celebrate the new year on January 1, but every teacher and every student knows that the new year really begins in September. And what a great month it is! From Labor Day to Native American Day, special dates and exciting events keep coming your way. On the opposite page, we've selected red-letter days you'll want to highlight in class. After that, you'll find the best of INSTRUCTOR'S Bright Ideas for September, a story to start the year, and back-to-school activities designed to help kids brush up on skills they may have neglected over the summer. Plus, there are welcome-back bulletin boards to make, reading games to play, and much more. So what are you waiting for? Here's a salute to September!

Red letter days

SEPTEMBER SPECIAL EVENTS
These special events usually occur in September, but the exact dates may vary from year to year.
Labor Day (first Monday)
National Grandparents Day (first Sunday after Labor Day)
National Hispanic Heritage Week (beginning with the second Sunday)
Responsible Pet Care Week
Native American Day (fourth Friday)
Rosh Hashana (usually in September or October)
Yom Kippur (usually in September or October)

1 **Edgar Rice Burroughs,** author of the Tarzan books, was born in 1875. Read some in class to celebrate!

3 **The Treaty of Paris,** ending the American Revolutionary War, was signed in Paris in 1783. Benjamin Franklin, John Adams, and John Jay represented the United States. Great Britain recognized America's independence (with the western boundary set at the Mississippi River) and gave Florida to Spain.

4 Extra! Extra! Read all about it! In 1833, 10-year-old Barney Flaherty was hired as the **first newspaper carrier** in the United States after answering an ad in the *New York Sun.*

6 **Jane Addams,** pioneer social worker and winner of the 1931 Nobel Peace Prize, was born in 1860 in Cedarville, Illinois.

7 "Uncle Sam" was born. "Uncle Sam Wants You," the familiar Army recruiting poster, features a character who originated in 1813 when a Troy, New York, newspaper coined his name to stand for the United States. The real "Uncle Sam" was allegedly Samuel Wilson of Troy, who stamped "U.S." on military provisions during the War of 1812.
Also, American painter Anna Mary Robertson, better known as **Grandma Moses,** was born in 1860. Famous for her primitive paintings, she began her artistic career at age 78. Her 100th birthday is proclaimed Grandma Moses Day in New York State.

8 Are your kids *Pink Panther* fans? If so, they'll want to know that **Peter Sellers,** the British comedian and actor who played the bumbling Inspector Clouseau, was born on this day in 1925.
Also, today is the day schoolchildren first read the **"Pledge of Allegiance"** in *The Youth's Companion* in 1892.

9 Happy birthday, **California!** On this date in 1850, the "Golden State" was admitted to the Union.

10 The **sewing machine** was patented in 1846.

12 **Jesse Owens,** a run-away great in track and field, was born in 1913. Owens ran off with the world record for the running broad jump, a record that stood for 25 years. He also won four gold medals in the 1936 Berlin Olympics hosted by Adolf Hitler.

13 In 1814, by the dawn's early light, Francis Scott Key, who was being held prisoner aboard a British ship, was inspired to write the **"Star Spangled Banner."** His song later became our national anthem in 1931.
Also today, **Margaret Chase Smith** was elected senator in 1948. She was one of the first women to hold that office.

15 There's a bit of mystery in the air! That great lady with the whodunit flair, **Agatha Christie,** was born in 1891. Also born on this date in 1934 was children's book author and illustrator, **Tomie de Paola.**

16 *Q:* If April showers bring May flowers, what do May flowers bring? *A:* Pilgrims! In 1620, the Pilgrims set off from Plymouth, England, bound for the New World. Today, we commemorate the event with **Mayflower Day.**

17 Run up the flag! Strike up the band! It's **Citizenship Day,** celebrated in honor of the day in 1787 when our country's leaders signed the U.S. Constitution at the Constitutional Convention in Philadelphia, Pennsylvania.

19 Here's an unlikely crew! A rooster, a duck, and a calf crewed on the **first hot air balloon,** flown over Versailles, France, in 1783.

20 In 1519, Portuguese explorer **Ferdinand Magellan** set out to see the world with five ships and 270 sailors. One of his ships was the first to sail all the way around the globe.
Also in 1884, women formed the **first Equal Rights Party** and set out to get the right to vote.

21 Forty-nine stars made room for one more when **Hawaii** became the fiftieth state to join the union in 1959.

22 **Hobbit Day** celebrates the birthday of J.R.R. Tolkien's characters, Bilbo and Frodo Baggins.

23 What's black and white and read all over? In the 1830s it was the McGuffey Readers, that's what! **William McGuffey,** self-taught educator and author of these famous school books, was born in 1800.
Also, sculptor **Louise Nevelson** was born on this date in 1900.

24 The **U.S. Supreme Court** was created in 1789.

25 **Vasco Nunez de Balboa,** Spanish conquistador, became the first European to look upon the Pacific Ocean in 1513. He took possession of it in the name of Spain.

26 John Chapman, better known as **Johnny Appleseed,** is believed to have been born on this date in 1774. He was known as a planter of orchards, and a friend of wild animals.

28 **Frances E. Willard,** American educator and women's rights leader, was born in 1839.

30 **James Meredith** won a victory for civil rights when he became the first black student admitted to the University of Mississippi.

SEPTEMBER: Bright Ideas

BEAUTIFUL BOOKMARKS
Use those colorful and attractive postcards you receive in the mail as bookmarks so you can share them with your students. Leave them on the library table or on the bookcase. Or, make pockets to hold the cards and pin them to the bulletin board. Since kids may read the cards, be discreet and make sure all the messages are acceptable. Laminate them for extra durability.
SHIRLEY SHRATTER

A GET ACQUAINTED SONG
Use this song at the beginning of school. One child begins singing with the teacher. On the words "We are friends," the child points to a classmate. They dance or skip in a circle while the class sings the song again. The third time, the two children point to two more students, join hands and skip. Continue until all are dancing.
MARY MATTHEWS

You like me, I like you
We are friends, just we two.

	NUMBER OF SIDES	NUMBER OF CORNERS	NUMBER OF equal SIDES	NUMBER OF RIGHT ANGLES
●				
▬				
▮				
▲				
●				
▪				
◢				
▬				

NAME GAME
Help kids learn one another's names quickly. Seated in circles of six or more, students give their names and favorite activities. The child at the right must repeat what the child before has said, then tell about himself. If the class finds this too easy, make the groups larger. After the game, children jot down as many names and associated activities as they can remember. EDWARD WALSH

SOUNDING OFF
Have kids fill in each blank with the word that tells what sound the mentioned animal or thing makes. The answer rhymes with the last word of the previous sentence:
1. "I'd like to have some food right now."
Is the meaning of our cat's ...... (meow)
2. Do horses have a word to say?
The answer to this one is ...... (neigh)
3. Ask the cow, "Bess, how are you?"
Her answer will be simply ...... (moo)
4. Listen to any bird you meet.
It will twitter or it will ...... (tweet)
5. However, what the big bee does
Is zoom up with a steady ...... (buzzz)
6. What are the two words of a clock?
That's easy--just tick and ...... (tock)
7. Across the street you'd better scoot
When you hear the auto horn ...... (toot)
8. When it's so cold your fingers tingle
That's when you hear sleigh bells ....(jingle)
9. It's a very soothing matter
To hear rain go pitter ...... (patter)
10. The cork that's in the bottle top
Comes out with a great big ...... (pop)
A. S. FLAUMENHAFT

FIRST-DAY ICE BREAKERS
The first day of school is unsettling for many children. Use these activities to help kids break the ice and get to know one another.
1. Divide the class into pairs and have kids make nametags for their partners, using letters cut from magazines. To encourage exchange of addresses and phone numbers, make sure this data appears on each tag.
2. Have students write descriptive paragraphs about classmates whose names they draw from a hat. Ask the kids to state their names so everyone can identify the person they've selected. Descriptions should include physical

attributes and clothing but must be limited to positive comments. Kids can take turns reading them while the rest of the class tries to guess who is being described.
3. Activities involving small groups often foster friendships. One such activity is pantomime. Together, pairs or trios of kids choose an animal and decide on a pantomime to represent it. The class must try to guess the animal being mimed.
4. Another game that's great for the first day is "Barnyard." Write the names of farm animals on slips of paper (repeating each animal several times) and have students draw for a name. Blindfolded and on hands and knees, kids must imitate the sounds their animals make and try to find other students who are imitating the same ones.
MARGARET E. MCINTOSH

SEQUENTIAL MEMORY CARDS
Stimulate the slow learner by using visual memory cards that you can make yourself. Collect pictures of different objects and glue them to tagboard strips, five on each. To use, hold up one strip and let the child see and pronounce the names of the objects, going from left to right, as you uncover them. When all objects have been named, turn the strip over and ask the child to try to remember the objects in the order

they appeared. As the child's skill increases, show the entire strip at once. Next, use numbers and letters of the alphabet instead of pictures.
PAMELA KLAWITTER

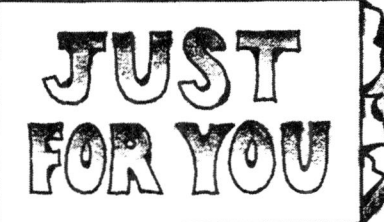

PUZZLES JUST FOR YOU
The first day of school is always hectic. Make students feel special and keep them busy while you handle that first half hour by giving each one a puzzle. You can make them easily by tearing pages from coloring books and gluing them onto construction paper. Cut pictures into large pieces and put them into an envelope marked "Just For You." Once they're assembled, kids can color the puzzles and take them home as a memento of their first day. What a great take-home surprise!
DIANE GETZ

CHART YOUR COURSE
Want a unique way to investigate shapes? Make a chart of them. List characteristics you wish students to find at the top of the paper and draw shapes at the side. Kids fill in the spaces with their answers.
RICHARD LATTA

ARE YOUR BATTING 1000?
Use the approaching World Series and your bulletin board to motivate better work habits. On a green background representing a baseball diamond and playing field, print the question, "Are you batting 1000?" Copy a large baseball player with the aid of your opaque projector and give him a bat made from wood-patterned wallpaper. Use any of the baseball shapes--balls, players, caps, and so on-- to display excellent written work or work habits you would like your students to develop. In no time at all, everyone will bat 1000! CLAUDIA WILCOX

BIOGRAPHICAL BOOKLETS
Teachers in the primary grades can promote kids' self-concepts by writing biographies of them early in the year. Start by conducting individual interviews. Take notes on special things about the child, his family, hobbies, and ambitions. Type out the items about each child, one to a page, and staple them together, book-fashion. Have the kids design their own covers and illustrate each page. These books should be available in the classroom all year long so kids can learn more about their classmates and reinforce their understanding of themselves and their own backgrounds as well. At the end of the year, they can take the books home to share with family and friends. Kids love being in the spotlight!
MARY LOU MURPHY

SEPTEMBER: Bright Ideas

BEHAVIOR POSTER

Make a self-discipline poster for students. Print good-behavior traits such as "Save shouting for outdoors" and "Bounce balls in the gym." Number each trait so when a student forgets one of them, you can gently remind him to notice that number. Watch as behavior improves in your classroom!
GERTRUDE WITTENBERG

CANNED ACTIVITY CENTERS

Here's an idea to perk up your curriculum in no time. These easy to make tiny activity centers work anywhere in the room. Start by collecting small cans. Cut out 10-15 discs from tagboard slightly smaller than the diameter of the cans. Color code sets of discs to match each container. List instructions on one disc and use the others for numbered activities. Laminate the discs and drop them into the cans.

Now you have miniactivity cards that are durable and have no corners to bend!
Strive for unusual, thought provoking activities. Here are a few to get you started:
1. Cover can with a collage of pictures of famous people and label it "Who Am I?" The numbered discs contain pictures of famous people, the instruction card directs kids to find some interesting facts about the celebrities.
2. Cover another can with a map and label it "State of Confusion." Outline different states on the numbered discs. The instruction card tells kids to identify the state, its capital, and list facts about it.
3. Decorate a can with geometric shapes and label it "Imagine That!" Draw random sets of lines or figures on the discs. Then, instruct students to transfer sets onto a sheet of paper and use them to create a picture,
PAMELA KLAWITTER

ROLL-ON GLUE

Here's an idea that puts an end to the messy chore of refilling glue bottles. Save your empty roll-on deodorant bottles. Ask kids to bring them from home, too. Wrap the bottles in layers of masking tape (in case of falls) and fill with glue. Not only will glue roll on easily, it won't spill out if the bottle tips over. DIANE KAUFMAN

LEARNING CENTER TIPS

Learning centers are as much fun to make as they are to work with. Use these pointers to guide you:
1. Gear centers to students' interests. Use a central theme.
2. Keep format simple. Avoid using too many words.
3. Use only one concept and state it at the top of the center.
4. Illustrate the concept with examples.
5. Provide activities for kids to practice the concept.
6. Limit use of the center to the number of students who can effectively work there at one time.
7. Provide a checklist to show students have completed work and that it was reviewed by you.
8. Be sure to instruct the class about the center, its purpose, and how it should be used.
EILEEN CATALANO

PERSONAL TIME LINES

The beginning of school is a time to make new friends. Help kids reflect on their own lives and become acquainted with their classmates by making autobiographical time lines.
Using paper about four feet long, have students draw a line across the width. Then, they divide the line into sections to represent each year of their lives. Kids must decide on a major event to mark each year and

illustrate them in the appropriate section. As time lines are finished, students can share them within small groups. Display the time lines until the kids are better acquainted. Bring them out again at year's end so students can reappraise the important events in their lives. BETH DIAZ

NAME-O-GRAMS
Here's a creative way for kids to express themselves by using the letters of their names. Have students look through magazines for photos representing things they like: foods, sports, holidays, clothing, and so forth. From these pictures, kids can cut letters to spell their names and glue them to tagboard. Short explanations like "I love wearing sneakers" can be printed beneath each one.
CAROLYN M. WILHELM

My name is tom

TOM

I like swimming in the ocean.   I like red.   I like the woods.

HAVE A BALL IN YOUR CLASS
Get a large ball and a box to put beneath it. Place open end of the box on the floor and cut a hole in the other end just large enough to

anchor the ball. Use the ball to depict such characters as a doctor, policeman, fireman, Santa, George Washington, or any other person. Make and attach characteristic hats, scarves, beards, and so forth. Add removable facial features by using soluble glue or tape. Arms, buttons, vests and other accessories can be added to the box. Children soon learn how to change the ball into their favorite personalities. This activity will help you develop ingenuity and imagination in your students.
FLORENCE RIVES

SEARCH AND ENJOY
Try this fun way to introduce reference books to your class as well as motivate students to use them. Have a variety of sources available in the room such as an atlas, an encyclopedia, a TV guide, a dictionary, a phone book, the Reader's Guide to Periodical Literature, and so on. Discuss each reference aid with kids then hand out index cards

with problems on each. Students must read their problems to the class and suggest the source from which they might obtain an answer.
MARGARET SULLIVAN

SAVE THAT NAME!
Stop! Don't throw away those name tags you make at the beginning of school. Use them when you invite a resource person to your class so that students can be called by name. Tell substitutes where to find the tags and instruct kids to wear them when you're not teaching class. Substitutes and resource persons will thank you!
RUTH TOWNSEND

GRAPHING BIRTHDAYS
Draw 12 inch-wide columns on tagboard, leaving about an inch between each. Give kids one-inch squares of gummed paper on which to write their names and birthday months. Have children guess which months will have the most birthdays. Then, as you point to each column, they can come up and stick their squares on the board. Use the completed graph in a learning center.
LILLIAN RUEBECK

SEPTEMBER: Bright Ideas

A BRAINY EXERCISE
A mind-stretching exercise can get your class into gear for the day. Here are some unusual names. What are their owners' occupations?
Phil O'Dendron (florist)
Frank Sandbeans (runs a hot dog stand)
Leo Tard (male ballet dancer)
Jack Inthepulpit (pastor)
Homer Unking (famous baseball player)
This activity is sure to give every brain in your classroom a workout!
BERNICE COHAN

SEPTEMBER GREETINGS
If you've got a bulletin board that you'd like to decorate, try this idea to welcome students on their first day of school. Cut bows and life-size face shapes from construction paper. Print students' names on each bow and tack them to the board. On the first day, give kids shapes to draw their faces on. They can match faces with bows already displayed. Bows can represent neckties or ribbons.
MARY JO HUISMAN

ALL TIED UP
Learning to tie shoelaces is no small feat for little kids. The process can be frustrating; so help kids practice the task by making lacing boards. Using 8½" x 11" tagboard, draw two lines 2½" from each side. Fold along the lines so that flaps turn in toward each other. Then punch parallel rows of holes along the edges of each flap. Finally, add a heavy shoelace that kids can easily manage. Let students work with the boards in their free time and take them home at night to practice with parents. LILLIAN KOSLOVER

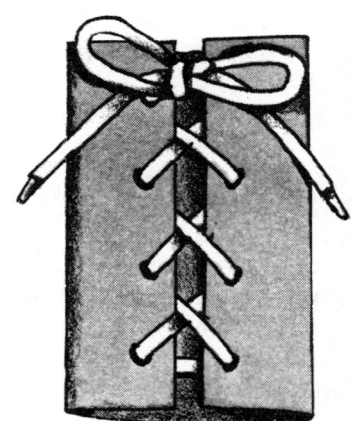

PUT-UPS
Constant criticism can really damage kids' egos. Put an end to put-downs in your class by introducing put-ups. Have the class make a list of common put-downs then tear up the sheet. Make a second list of put-ups, things that make people feel good about themselves, and post it for everyone to see. Give students a class list and encourage them to write put-ups next to each name. This activity not only helps language skills and increases vocabulary, it will make students aware of the good in their fellow classmates.
JANE MANRING

HOME ADDRESSES
Help children learn home addresses by making houses from shoe boxes. Make roofs by folding sheets of paper in half and stapling them along the fold. Line sides with paper and draw windows and doors. Write students' addresses on strips of paper and paste onto the houses. Use the houses to motivate kids to study their community and different aspects of their neighborhoods.
LORRAINE LEE

KEEPING IN TOUCH
Communication between parents and teachers should enhance any child's learning. Once you've had the chance to meet with parents, keep them informed of their

children's progress. A good way to keep in touch is through a weekly report. Send home a packet with students each Friday. It can include class and homework assignments, a skills checklist, and a brief note from you. Have students return the checklists on the following Monday, signed by a parent.

Create the checklist by modifying the standard report card, making it less formal. Add items that are important to you such as class participation and getting along with others. Adopt your own scoring system using grades like "Terrific," "Better," "Needs Work." Duplicate each list to use over a period of time so changes will be apparent.

Include positive comments as well as constructive criticism in your notes to parents. Try to highlight student accomplishments and suggest home activities to reinforce or supplement their regular school work.
PATRICIA D'AMARIO

MAKING CONTACT
The more you find out about your new students, the better you can help each child throughout the year. A home visit is a good way to ensure you and the student won't be strangers when you meet in class. It will also give you an idea of the child's family life.

Make the appointment for the visit far in advance. Schedule trips to two parent homes when both parents can meet with you. Talk with them separately and with the child. Ask them about the child's strengths, weaknesses and interests. Also, find out about the talents or skills of parents or siblings that might be shared with your class. Keep the visit as informal as you can. Don't take notes during the meeting; afterward jot down some highlights of the visit for future reference. JANE K. PRIEWE

CUEING UP
Here are 10 different ways to have a class line up for recess.
1. Assign letters A-Z. Call out given names of students at random. If assigned letter is in the name, line up.
2. Call letters. If letter is in child's first name, line up.
3. Call colors of clothes being worn.
4. Call letters. This time, kids get in line when their middle initials are called.
5. Name teachers. Kids can line up when the

name of a previous teacher is called.
6. Students put heads down. Select a child to tap heads of classmates. Once tapped, children may line up.
7. Call out kinds of pets (including no pet at all). Kids line up when their pet is called.
8. Assign letters A-Z. Students with a letter in the name of the day of the week line up first.
9. Number off by 6s. Give simple math problems that match the numbers. Leave by corresponding numbers.
10. Kids total the number of letters in their full names. They line up from smallest to largest numbers.
ROSALIE MILLER

THE BEAD BOX
Teach multiplication facts with the help of several strings of plastic curtain beads and a nine-drawer tackle box or hardware cabinet. Label each drawer separately with the numbers 2-10. Cut curtain beads into appropriate lengths for each group of times tables. (The drawer for the 5s table would have sets of five beads each, and so on.) Kids having difficulty with a particular times fact go to the drawers, take out the number of bead sets needed, and solve their problems. A work sheet with randomly selected facts can be used in conjunction with the "Bead Box."
LINDA NICHOLS

SEPTEMBER: A story to start the year

Billy learns his lesson

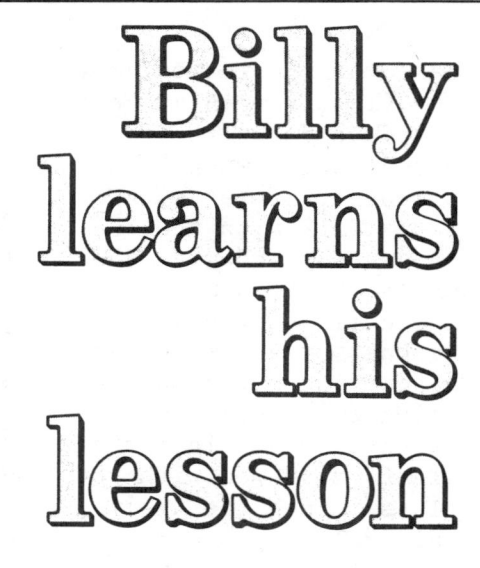

BILLY BULLFROG leaped high in the air and landed on a large white water lily. He felt good because he'd finally lost his polliwog tail. He was on his way to becoming a full-fledged bullfrog. Proudly Billy puffed himself out. At last he was big enough to go with his friend Ralph.

Just as Billy was ready to slide into the water to find Ralph, his mother called to him.

"Billy, come here with your brothers and sisters and cousins. It's time for school to start. Big John Bullfrog is waiting."

Billy sighed a great big sigh and joined his family. He sure didn't want

Ron and Hilda Stahl

to go to school and listen to Big John Bullfrog. He wanted to go with Ralph to the south side of the pond and swim around the tall cattails and slide in the mud.

Along with the other frogs Billy climbed up on the fallen log and hid behind a small branch. He watched from behind his branch as Big John hopped up on the log.

"Young bullfrog," said Big John in his deep, deep, deep voice. "Come right up here with the others. It's time to start lessons."

Big John waited until Billy was sitting exactly the way he wanted Billy to sit. Then he said, "First you

must learn to sing like this." Big John sat just right and held his head just right and sang in his deep, deep, deep voice.

"Churrummmm. Churrummmm."

Billy wriggled with excitement. It was the best song he'd ever heard. He listened as the girls tried to copy Big John. "Teedledeedeee. Teedledeedeee." Billy laughed so hard he almost fell off the log. Big John looked at Billy sternly and frowned.

"Boys, you try now," said Big John.

Billy puffed out his chest and sat just right. "Kneedeep. Kneedeep." He closed his mouth tight, feeling very silly as the girls laughed.

Big John quieted the frogs, then started teaching them how to find things to eat in the pond. Later as Big John talked about the enemies in the pond, Billy's mind wandered to Ralph at the south side of the pond. The warm sun made Billy sleepy and he fell right off the log with a loud SPLASH.

"Young bullfrog," said Big John, looking right at Billy as his head poked out of the water. "Come right up here in the front row."

Billy wanted to dive under the water and swim away fast, but he climbed up on the log and sat quietly through the rest of the lessons. Big John told how the snapping turtle would swim just under the water and grab tasty little bullfrogs for his supper. Billy shivered. He didn't want to be anyone's supper.

"The sniggily, sniggily snake is the worst enemy," continued Big John. "He hides in the tall grass and glides through the grass when he spies bullfrogs. He swallows a bullfrog before the frog can hop away."

Billy looked around in fright.

Big John explained how to watch out for the snake and other enemies. He explained the best ways to escape. Billy listened carefully until Big John started talking about hibernation. Then Billy thought again about Ralph.

Finally, school was out. Billy hopped off the log and swam toward the shore.

"Billy," his mother called.

Impatiently Billy hopped up on a water lily pad and waited for Mother.

"Billy, your father saw the sniggily, sniggily snake on the south side of the pond this morning. Don't go there to play."

Billy drooped down on the lily pad as his mother swam away. All day he'd planned on going to the south side of the pond to play with Ralph.

Billy sat up tall and pushed out his chest. Big John had taught him how to take care of himself. He could go anywhere he wanted to go and do anything he wanted to do! He hopped off the lily pad and swam to the south side of the pond and Ralph.

"Glad to see you, Billy," shouted Ralph, sliding across the mud.

"Glad to be here," said Billy, leaping out of the water and sliding along in the mud with Ralph. What fun!

They played until they were hungry. Then they hopped into the tall grass where they sat quietly, waiting for an insect snack. A rustling sound made Billy shiver with fright. He leaped closer to Ralph.

"Ralph," whispered Billy nervously. "Did you hear that? Could it be the sniggily, sniggily snake?"

Ralph shrugged. "No. I haven't seen the sniggily, sniggily snake around here in a long time."

"But my dad saw it here this morning," said Billy, shivering.

"Don't worry," said Ralph.

Billy listened again. The rustling sound came closer. What would he do if it was the sniggily, sniggily snake? What if the snake got him? What had Big John told him about getting away? Billy couldn't remember a thing.

"I'm getting out of here," cried Billy, hopping out of the grass. Just as he plopped down in the mud the sniggily, sniggily snake grabbed for him. Billy slid across the mud away from the snake. Ralph slid along beside him. When they reached the safe part of the pond, Billy and Ralph crawled up on a log, puffing and panting.

"I guess I'm not a full-fledged bullfrog yet," said Billy. "Maybe when I learn to obey Mother and remember Big John's lessons I will be." Then he slid into the pond and swam home. □

SEPTEMBER: Brushups and boosters

Most kids are rusty in basic skills after the long summer vacation. Here, Nicholas Criscuolo and Patricia Koppman suggest some painless ways to get them rolling again.

How do you get your kids back in shape for school after the long, lazy summer? How do you sweep out the cobwebs, grease the wheels, and get things rolling? Easy! Use the games and activities listed here as warm-ups to get your kids off to a running start and up over the hurdles this September. Or use them as backups to your lesson plans all year. With this bevy of back-to-school activities, you're ready for anything!

A capital idea During the first days of school, make a ditto for each child with 26 circles on it. Have each child write or print the capital letters in the circles, one per circle. Put these papers into individual folders. Repeat the activity in two months and let the kids compare their papers to see their improvement in handwriting. This warm-up activity can be done with lower-case letters, too.

Picture that! Collect magazine pictures—one for each student. Then cut each picture in half. Keep one set of the halves and distribute the other set to your students. Have each child paste his or her half to a piece of drawing paper and try to complete the picture. After they are finished, share the original pictures with them. They'll have fun comparing their impression with that of the original artist.

You're the teacher Develop your students' abilities to ask good questions by letting them imagine they are the teacher. Give them a list of statements—possible answers to questions—and have them think of a question for each. For example, one statement might be, "Sacramento is the capital city." The question would be, "What is the capital of California?"

A delicious kangaroo Try this warm-up exercise to acquaint yourself with your children's handwriting and punctuation skills, and to test their creativity. List five unrelated words on the chalkboard, such as *closet, delicious, kangaroo, snowstorm,* and *energetic.* Ask your students to study the words and then write a creative story

using all five words. Result? You'll have some interesting stories as well as a better idea of the language arts abilities of the children in your class.

Paint by number Reinforce your children's recognition of numbers while they have fun with art. Cut a black and white picture from a magazine or newspaper or make a simple line drawing of a picture or a design. Number the various parts of the picture. At the bottom of the page write a color key for your children to follow: 1—brown, 2—yellow, 3—red, 4—green, 5—blue, and so on.

What's missing? Write a paragraph on the board, leaving out the punctuation marks. Divide the class into two teams. Ask each team to get together and write the paragraph on a separate sheet of paper, filling in the correct punctuation. If one team has more correct answers than the other, it gets to choose a member to punctuate the paragraph on the board and then write another paragraph on the board minus the punctuation for the next round.

Wishful thinking Ask each student to think of one wish that he or she would like to have come true during the year. Have students draw or write their wish. Make a mobile or booklet containing the wishes. At the end of the year students will have fun reflecting on their wishes. Did they come true? How would they change their wishes now?

The name game List each child's first name on an index card. Ask students to perform the following tasks using the name cards: alphabetize the cards; find rhyming names; find names with the same beginning sound; find names with the same ending sound; find names with the same vowel sound; find the longest name; find the shortest name; try to think of other persons with the same name. For a variation on the game use last names or middle names.

Get the picture Sharpen your kids' observation skills by taking them on a walk

around the neighborhood and asking them to focus their eyes on the everyday things they see. When you are back in class, ask your children to list everything they saw on a specific corner or in a specific store window. Read the lists aloud and compare the different perceptions. Younger children may give you their perceptions orally or pictorially.

Our town On a large sheet of butcher paper let students draw their community, including important places such as the school, library, fire department, and churches. Draw each street in the community on your map and have each child draw his or her home on the proper street. After the map is completed it can be used with small cars, trucks, and trains to practice left-right orientation, to follow directions, to determine distances, and to learn other map-oriented skills.

Shape up! On a duplicating master, draw many different shapes of all sizes. Distribute copies and have your students cut out the shapes. Then ask them to use as many shapes as possible to create a picture—if they like, they can color the shapes. Later, they can glue the shapes on a piece of drawing paper and write stories about their creations.

Crisscross math puzzles Make up blank crossword puzzles, but instead of filling in words from definitions, have your children fill in numbers from equations. Your kids will love puzzling them out.

Got your number Make up a word-search puzzle that uses numbers instead of words. Ask your children to circle numbers going horizontally, vertically, or diagonally that add up to a specific sum. For example, you can ask them to circle all the numbers that add up to ten. They might circle a 2 and an 8 horizontally; a 1, 2, 3, and 4 diagonally; and so on. You can also practice subtraction, division, and multiplication skills using the number search.

I spy To give your kids more practice using adjectives, have each one silently select an object in the room. Then ask each pupil to describe the object without naming it and see if the others can guess what it is. For example, one child might say, "I spy a large, round, colorful ball." The child guessing the correct object goes next.

Making headlines Primary children will enjoy using the newspaper to learn their letters. Give each child a page of a newspaper with large letters and numbers on it, such as the headlines printed in grocery ads. Ask each child to cut out the letters and numbers he or she knows and paste them on tagboard. Words may be reviewed in the same way.

All mapped out Use the daily newspapers to collect weather maps for each member of your class. Pass them out and have each child paste his or her map to the top of a large sheet of paper. Write questions on the board, such as "In what parts of the country is it raining?" "What sign in the legend tells you it is snowing?" "Where is it the coolest?" "Can you name two other things the map tells you?" Have the children write their answers under their maps.

Letter-perfect letters Watch for illegible letters in each student's handwriting. Show the child how to form these letters correctly and encourage him or her to practice writing them. When the child has perfected the letters, tell him or her to choose three letters and make them into a design to display on the bulletin board.

Frame up Give each student a small frame made from a square of construction paper. The inside of the square has been cut out and laminated so it is transparent. To make a handle for the frame staple it to an ice cream stick. Duplicate a sheet of letters, numbers, or words you want to review for each child in your class and you're ready to begin. Call out a question, such as "What is 3 + 5?" or "What letter comes after *e* in the alphabet?" Your students should then place their frames over the correct answer on their papers. This is a quick and easy way for you to determine whether your students know the skill.

Going somewhere? Children are intrigued by maps. Encourage them to keep a scrapbook of maps cut out of old newspapers and magazines. Ask them to compare the similarities and the differences between their maps. For example, you might ask what is the purpose of each map and who might need to use it? You might even try this game: Cut out small sections of different maps and paste them on a separate piece of paper. Each section should include at least one major clue as to the location shown on the map such as a major river, town, or landmark. See if your children can pick out these clues or put two clues together to tell you what country, state, or city is shown on each map section.

A state of mine Here's an easy way to help your children review the names of the states and give them practice writing abbreviations. Ask each student to imagine a state where he or she would like to live. Then have each child write the name of that state and its correct abbreviation on the chalkboard. You might then ask your children to see if they can find other fascinating facts about their states to share with the class.

Play it again, Sam Does anyone in your class play a musical instrument? Start music class off on the right note by asking your young musicians to explain and demonstrate their instruments to the class. The others can research the origins of the instruments or draw pictures of them to be displayed on the bulletin board.

What's inside? For this activity, you'll need a tin can without a top. Make sure there are no rough edges on the can. Place a small item such as a feather, a rock, a cotton ball, a piece of candy, and so on inside the can. Then put a large sock in the can, stretching the top of the sock over the edges of the can. Have a student put his or her hand inside the sock and feel the item in the bottom of the can. (The child will not be able to see the item.) Then the child should describe the item he or she feels without naming it. From the description, the rest of the class tries to guess what it is. Record the child's description on a chart or on the chalkboard for language activities later.

Take a number Write a list of 10 to 15 words on the chalkboard and number them. Then write the numbers on index cards, one number per card, and drop them in a bag or box. The first player closes his or her eyes, draws a number, and then reads the word on the chalkboard that corresponds with the number he or she has chosen. To practice definitions, the child should not let anyone see the number he or she has drawn. He or she finds the number and the corresponding word on the chalkboard and gives its definition. The other children attempt to guess the word that fits the definition. The one who guesses the correct word goes next.

Purple pizza Your kids will love illustrating funny phrases like this one. Make a set of noun flash cards and another set of adjective flash cards; the more unusual the words, the funnier the results! Pass the cards out so each student has one adjective and one noun. Have each child put the two words together and try to illustrate the phrase. When the class is finished, ask each child to hold up his or her picture and see if the other children can guess from the picture what adjective and noun phrase is being illustrated.

The domino effect Playing dominoes is a fun way to review numbers. Once children have mastered the basic game (placing dominoes with the same number of dots end-to-end), have them move on to more complicated games. For example, you might play so that only two pieces that add up to the number 10 can be placed end-to-end.

Use your thinking cap! For this game you'll need to make a headband or hat. Depending on your group's interests, you might make a ten-gallon hat, a fire fighter's helmet, or an elf cap. Place two paper clips on the front of the hat and you're ready to play. Have one child come to the front of the room and stand facing the class. Place the thinking cap on the child's head and have the child close his or her eyes as you insert a flash card under the paper clips. Another student from the class says the word on the card, and the child wearing the thinking cap tries to spell the word correctly. To practice word meaning, a child from the class gives the definition of the word and the player tries to guess what the word is. Now that's what we call using your head!

Shopping spree! Pass out paper and old store catalogs. Have students think of hypothetical situations such as going to Hawaii for a vacation, moving to Alaska, or being chosen to go on the next trip to the moon. Have them write their situation at the top of their paper. Then the fun begins! Tell your students they will each have $500 to use to go shopping for what they will need for the trip. They are to cut and paste items from the catalogs and write the cost on their papers. Once they have selected everything they'll need, have them add up the cost of all the items. If the total cost is more than $500, ask them to choose items

SEPTEMBER: Brushups and boosters

on their list they could do without. After the shopping spree, have your students tell the class why they purchased the items they did.

Who is it? Have students go through magazines and find words that tell about themselves. After the words have been cut out and glued to a sheet of paper, the papers can be distributed and the other students can try to guess which person is described on each paper.

What comes next? Here's an easy way for your children to practice putting things in sequential order. Tell them you are going to read a story and they should think about what happens first, second, and so on. For example, read a story about a birthday party and write questions on the board such as, ''Who gave the party?'' or ''When did they open the presents?'' Or you can write statements from the story on the board and ask your children to copy them down in the order in which they happened.

How would you like to buy a used car? Encourage spontaneous and fluent expression by having your children draw something they would like to sell such as a car, a boat, a bicycle, or a new invention. Each child should then describe its best features to the class and explain why it is better than the same item being sold by someone else.

What's the word? To encourage students to use correct grammar, print verbs such as *work, works, working, isn't, aren't,* and so on, on oak tag cards. Give each child a card and ask him or her to use the verb on the card correctly in a sentence. Ask the other children to raise their hands if they detect an error.

Monster mix Ask each child to fold a piece of drawing paper into three equal parts; then draw a monster's head on the top of the paper, the body in the middle, and the tail on the bottom. Then have each child cut his or her monster into three pieces on the folded lines, and exchange pieces with the other children to form new monsters. A bulletin board can be developed with a new monster every day!

Give me ten Give each student a card with a noun on it and ask the student to write down on a separate sheet of paper 10 adjectives that describe his or her noun. Exchange lists of adjectives and have the other children try to guess what noun goes with each list.

That's a fact! Or is it an opinion? Let your kids decide! Make up a number of sen-

tences, some stating facts and others stating opinions. Put each sentence on a card and have each student draw one. Each child should take turns reading the sentence on his or her card aloud and telling whether the sentence is a fact or an opinion. Then you might ask each child what would have to be changed in order to make his or her fact an opinion or vice versa.

All the news that's fit to print Newspapers are supposed to tell only the facts. Talk about objectivity, and then have students read a story from a newspaper. Give the students two different-colored felt pens. Ask them to underline each fact in one color and each opinion in another. You might also compare ads in the newspaper. Which ones use more opinions than facts to sell their product?

Tic-tac-toe Have each child select a partner. The pair draws a tic-tac-toe diagram on a sheet of paper. The teacher then gives each pair of students a group of self-correcting flash cards reviewing vocabulary words, math facts, or letters. If the child can answer the question on the flash card, he or she is allowed to place an *x* or *o* on the diagram. Play continues until one child has three in a row.

Dial-a-question Make a spinner large enough for all students to see from their desks. Cut a circle two feet in diameter and another circle that is one foot in diameter out of oak tag. Next make a large arrow out of oak tag. Place the large circle on the bottom, the small circle in the middle, and the arrow on top. Fasten them together in the center with a brad. Divide each circle into ''pie pieces'' and write a number on each section. Hang the spinner on the board and you're ready to play. The first child comes up to the spinner and spins the arrow while the other children call out a math skill such as addition, subtraction, multiplication, and division. The child at the front then tries to use that skill with the two numbers the arrow lands on. If the child is correct, he or she spins again. If not, the next player gets a turn.

Be an architect Draw several different shapes on a duplicating master and run off enough copies for everyone in your class. Have your children cut out the shapes and write math equations on the back of each shape. Collect the shapes, mix them up, and you're ready to play. Call out one of the equations. The child who can answer the question correctly gets to keep the

shape. As your children collect the shapes, each child tries to use his or her shapes to build a house. For example, one child might use a square for the house, a triangle for the roof, a smaller rectangle for the door, and so on. The first to build a house wins!

Tell me about it Give each student a card with an adjective written on it. Then ask students to use magazines and catalogs to find examples of their adjectives. For example, if a child has the adjective *green,* he or she could cut out pictures of grass, pickles, frogs, trees, and so on. The students can glue their pictures onto a sheet of paper and have the other students try to guess from the picture what adjective they are holding.

Be reasonable! How do you develop your kids' reasoning skills? Easy! Write several sentences on the board, such as, ''Lonnie's mother scolded him when he came home from the movies.'' Or, ''Off in the distance we heard a terrible roar.'' Ask each child to write his or her interpretation as to why these events may have occurred.

Which way is up? Do your children understand *left* and *right?* How about prepositional phrases? Can they follow oral instructions? Find out with this easy game. Just write rows of letters on a sheet of paper and duplicate enough copies for everyone in your class. Then see if your children can follow your directions to place an *x* on the third letter in the second row; place a + under the last letter in the first row; place an *x* to the left of the letter *m;* and so on.

Screen test Before assigning your children to reading groups, have them try out for your very own Hollywood screen test. Ask each child to select a library book to read for pleasure. As they read the book, ask them to pick out one paragraph they'd like to read for the tape recorder and their stage debut. After each child reads his or her paragraph into the tape recorder, play the entire tape back for the class to enjoy. Children will love hearing themselves on tape, and this exercise will give you a good idea of each child's oral reading skills.

Good news Here's a get-acquainted activity that's sure to bring out the best in everyone! Have your students create self-portraits by folding a paper into four equal parts and drawing one good thing about themselves in each space. Place the self-portraits in a booklet that can be shared with the entire class. What better way to start the new year than to spread the good news?

Ten times the fun Have a math relay race and watch the fun multiply! Draw two large blank multiplication tables on the chalkboard. Write the numbers 0—12 across the top and down the left side. Divide your class into two teams and have them line up in front of the board. Then the race is on. The first child on each team steps to the board, picks two numbers on the table to multiply and fills in the blank. Then the child tags the next player in line. That child must go to the board and fill in another blank. If the second child sees a mistake already on the board, he or she must use his or her turn to correct the mistake. The first team to fill in the whole chart correctly wins.

Calendar bingo Pass out an old calendar to each child in your class. Call out an equation with an answer between 1 and 30. Children silently cover the answer on their calendar with a button or small square of paper you have supplied. The first child to have all the numbers covered in a row going across, down, or diagonally wins.

Roots Your kids can learn more about themselves by doing some simple research into their family backgrounds. Have each child draw a tree with leaves, branches, and roots. Ask the youngsters to write their family name on the trunk of the tree, their mother's name on the branch to the left, and their father's name on the branch to the right. On the leaves of the tree they can write their own name and those of their brothers and sisters. When the youngsters find out where their forebears originated, have them write it on the roots of the tree. This activity can be varied by using the names of aunts and uncles, cousins, and guardians.

Go west, young man Here's an easy way to have your children practice beginning map skills. Have your students draw a black star in the center of a piece of paper. Then have them write *north* at the top of the paper, *south* at the bottom, *east* at the right, and *west* at the left. Give directions such as, "Put your pencil on the star and draw a line to the word *north*. Draw a line from the word *north* to the word *east*." *Northeast, southwest,* and so on may be discussed when the simpler directions are mastered.

Buzz off Buzz is a great game to get your kids thinking about numbers and multiples

of numbers. Have your children sit in a circle and start counting around the circle. When a child comes to the number seven, any number that has a seven in it, or any multiple of seven, the child must say "buzz." Anyone who forgets and says the number is out. The last player left in the game is the winner.

Top secret information Children love codes and secret messages so why not use them to teach math? One of the easiest codes to use simply substitutes numbers for each letter in the alphabet.

Give each child a decoder card. The card should list the letters of the alphabet and each letter's code number. For example, A—1, B—2, and so on. Then give your students math problems. The children solve the problem and then look for the answer on their decoder cards. For example, the first problem might be 2-1 =? The answer is 1. The child looks on his or her card, and sees that the number 1 is equivalent to the letter *A. A* is the first letter in the secret message.

Putting it all together Take three large (3-lb.) coffee cans and cover them with adhesive-backed paper. Make a set of flash cards with beginning sounds, middle or vowel sounds, and ending sounds. Place the cards into the three cans, separating the three different kinds of sounds. Ask a child to draw one card from each container. The child then places the cards and thus the sounds together, and attempts to blend a word. Often the word will be a nonsense word, but the child still receives a point if he or she can pronounce the word phonetically. If the word is a real word, and the child can blend it and then use it in a sentence, two points are awarded.

Try this game using prefix, root word, and suffix cards. If the students are less sophisticated in their skill development, you may wish to use only two cans and two sets of cards, such as root words and word endings. This game can be adapted to review math skills as well.

Matchmaker, matchmaker, make me a match! Reinforce word recognition with this easy activity. Staple two rows of pockets horizontally on a piece of oaktag to hang up on the bulletin board. Then make a collection of spelling word flash cards with a duplicate of each card. Place one set of words in the top row of pockets and the other in a pile on the table. Let your children match the words in the pockets by

placing each word's duplicate in the pocket underneath.

Presto-chango! What's the difference between a car and a small wagon? The letter *t*! Reinforce your kids' memory of common spelling words with this simple game. Write the word *car* on the board. Ask your children what letter they should add, subtract or replace to turn *car* into a small wagon (*cart*). How can they turn *cart* into a sharp instrument used to play a game (*dart*), and turn *dart* into an adjective meaning "not sweet" (*tart*), and so on.

On your mark, get set, make a word! Divide the chalkboard into two or more parts. Divide the class into teams. The teams line up in front of the chalkboard. The first member of each team steps to the chalkboard and writes a letter on the board, the beginning of a word. The next person on the team steps to the chalkboard and adds another letter, and so on until (1) the word has been completed and can be extended no further, or (2) a word cannot be formed using the existing letters, at which time the team may begin a new word. Teams get one point for each letter in a completed word plus an additional five points for each completed word. No points are awarded for incomplete words.

Tell me a story Ditto a sheet of vocabulary words from last year's list or new words to be introduced this year. Ask students to cut out the words. Then have each child construct a story by arranging the words on a piece of paper and filling in the proper punctuation.

Tattle-tale titles Have you ever noticed the number of movies, TV shows, books, and songs that use numbers in their titles: "Eight is Enough," "Three's Company," "The Twelve Days of Christmas," "Ten Little Indians," and so on. Use these titles as clues to the answers of math equations. Write a math equation for each number in the titles you want to use. List titles in one column and math equations at random in another column on a piece of paper. Then have children draw a line from the equation to the title that contains its answer. For example, children would match the title "Snow White and the *Seven* Dwarfs" to the equation, ___ $\times 3 = 21$.

Dr. Nicholas P. Criscuolo is the Supervisor of Reading at the Strong School in New Haven, Connecticut. **Patricia S. Koppman** is an education consultant on leave from the San Diego Unified School District in San Diego, California.

SEPTEMBER: Start a reading center

READING IS A THREE-RING CIRCUS

"Step right up, folks, and see the pheeenomenonnn of the century! It walks, it talks, it . . ." Well, what it does is intrigue kids with reading and with books and with literature of all kinds. What it is, is a "Three-Ring Reading Circus." In Belmont, California, some 500 students and 100 teachers attended an after-school afternoon. Here's how it happened.

First, there was a brainstorming session, held by the San Mateo County Reading Association's executive board. At this time a location was decided upon, teachers contacted, plans laid for obtaining parental assistance, a student-teacher ratio fixed, and a time schedule planned. A notice was then sent to all schools in the county announcing the event.

Then the three "rings" were established. Ring one, held outside, introduced characters from children's literature, physical fitness a la reading, K-3 movement exploration, square dancing, listening and singing, reading through magic and mime, and drama. Ring two, included author Dale Fife, workshops in classrooms, a quiz show about books and stories, listening to poetry, puppetry, reading, creative writing, and bookbinding. Ring three, held in the multipurpose room, permitted some 200 participants to leisurely examine displays made by students, view slide and film shows, sing folk music with dulcimer accompaniment, discuss books with a librarian, and browse through two "stores" handling commercial reading games and aids.

All groups, registered ahead of time, could roam about within their "rings" for 45 minutes until a bell sounded, signifying movement time.

Belmont teachers agreed that all the planning and work was worth it. Try holding your own circus, as your needs prescribe, and elevate interest in reading among not only your students, but their parents as well.

Howard F. Kraus and Ellen Haas

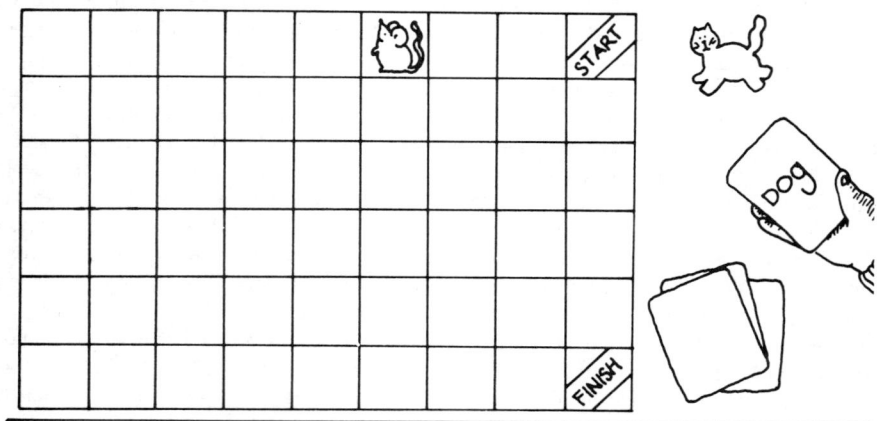

Nursery Rhyme Lessons

Teach young students nursery rhymes, then let the rhymes teach them. Here's how three old standbys can help youngsters with reading:

Where, oh where has my little dog gone?
Where, oh where can he be?
With his tail cut short and his ears cut long,
Oh, where oh where can he be?

Write the words to this familiar rhyme on the chalkboard. Read them aloud to the children and then ask them to read it along with you several times until the words are well established. Then make a word card for each word in the rhyme.

Shuffle the cards and spread them facedown on a table. The children take turns choosing a card, turning it over and reading the word. The child who finds and correctly pronounces *dog* is the winner. If a player misreads a card, he or she must keep it until the next round and read it correctly before turning over another card.

After the children play the game a few times add new sight words, using another key word as the object of the search.

Pussy cat! Pussy cat! Where have you been?
I've been to London to visit the Queen.
Pussy cat! Pussy cat! What did you there?
I frightened a little mouse under a chair.

Using the same procedure as above, read this rhyme to the children and have them recite it along with you several times. Again, make a card for each word. For this game, you'll also need a board like the one shown and two markers—one representing the cat, one the mouse. The markers can be cut from paper or posterboard, or you can use cat and mouse figures from a toy store.

Place the cards facedown in a pile. One player (or team) represents the mouse; the other player (or team) the cat. The mouse gets a three-step head start, then the players take turns picking cards and reading the words. If a word is read correctly, the appropriate marker is moved one step. The object: The cat tries to catch the mouse before it reaches the end of the board. Again, new words can be added occasionally to maintain interest—and to increase vocabularies.

Jack be nimble! Jack be quick!

Roll On

Put your new reading words on these cars and you'll be capturing the rapt attention of your class' racing fans.

Cut out the body of a streamlined racer from black construction paper, then glue it on a piece of white paper. For the wheels, cut two circles from plain white paper and draw lines of "spokes" to make word wheels containing six or eight segments. Then write in the words.

You might glue these word wheels on slightly larger circles of colored construction paper to give the appearance of tires. Then draw on lug bolts to make the wheels especially snazzy. Attach the wheels to the car with paper fasteners so they'll really spin.

The children can study these words as they admire the car. Then you can have them construct their own cars and help them when the time comes to "change tires."—*Shirley Weston, Fair Play, MO*

FRANK BRADBURY

Jack jump over the candlestick!

This game combines reading practice with physical activity—a happy combination for restless students. Have the children learn the rhyme as was done in the first two games and, again, make a card for each word.

For this game you will also need a mock candle and candlestick—you might try using a wooden dowel or long piece of chalk for the "candle" and a plastic cup with a hole punched in the bottom for the "holder."

Place the "candlestick" in the middle of the floor and ask the children to line up in front of it. Then have them take turns reading the words as you flash the cards. When a student correctly reads a word he or she jumps over the candle. Any child who misses a word takes the card to the back of the line. When that player arrives at the front again, he or she again tries to read the word and jump the candle.

When all the players have had a turn, place a book under the candle and work through the line again. Repeat the process until the children can no longer clear the candlestick. The excitement rises along with the pile of books.—*Jackee Day, Bedford, Ohio*

Skeleton Notes. Evaluate your children's note-taking ability by assigning a passage from any classroom textbook for silent reading. Then distribute strips of paper about 4.5 centimeters (2″) wide to the group. Ask students to jot down brief notes on one side of the strip while they reread the selected passage. With books set aside, have them use only their notes to rewrite the textbook material in their own words. Invite volunteers to read their notes and reconstructions aloud to demonstrate variations in recall and style. Then suggest that the group discuss each work with reference to accuracy and the retention of the main idea.

Condolences! New vocabulary, word recognition and enunciation are all part of the learning and fun of "Condolences," a card game. The deck consists of 53 playing cards, pairs of 26 cards duplicating current reading sight words, plus one card labeled *Condolences*. Four players can participate. Following "Old Maid" rules, the dealer distributes all cards. Each player draws one card from the person on the right, places matched pairs on the table and reads the words aloud. If a word is read incorrectly, the player retains the pair. The first child to match all cards in his or her hand wins. Play continues until only *Condolences* remains.

SEPTEMBER: Bulletin Boards

LET a double ice-cream cone (single if you teach alone) invite your kids to "drip" into your classroom as one of your flavors for the year. Cut out cone, name tags, and number of flavors from colored paper. Assemble (as above) and tape to hall-side of your room's door. **Jane Lamkin** and **Judy Finehirsh**

LAMKIN-FINEHIRSH

(22) FLAVORS

Peter	Jeffrey	Jason
William	Elvira	Dana
Jennifer	Sally	Michael R.
John	Jamie	Kelsey
Emily	Nicole	Chad
Michael C.	Celia	Chip
Nicky	Amy	Kimberly
	Alla	

RUFF, the classroom mascot, welcomes your kids to their new room. Create a cut-paper or cloth dog and attach to door. Each cut-out, brown-paper bone has a child's name printed in white. "Welcome!" is cut yarn or cutout paper letters taped in place.
Gail C. Einerson

WELCOME!

Vince · Rudi · Amy · Kim · Sol · Pam · Pat · Ruth · Ann · Ellen · Ken · John · Bill · Mary · Jason · Kyle · Ray · Terri · George · Phil · Cindy · Diane · Jack · Roger · Sue · Bob · Lynn · al · Rory

BLOOMING MANNERS

EXCUSE ME · I'M SORRY · YES MÀAM · LET'S SHARE · PARDON ME · HOW DO YOU DO · PLEASE · THANK YOU

Start your year with a review of proper manners; then use this display to remind your kids of the polite expressions they should use more often. Cut a background from dark-colored construction paper and letters from a contrasting color. Make flower petals from yellow poster board and print a different expression on each one. *BRENDA H. MCGEE*

Thorough & Efficient

$$3 \times 3 = 9 \quad 5 + 7 = 12 \quad 8 - 2 = 6$$

TESTS

TEACHERS

For this kid-made bulletin board, divide the class into small groups and assign each a different letter of the phrase "thorough and efficient." The kids are to think of words beginning with their letters that are related to responsibility for learning. Have them print the words next to each letter and illustrate them with construction paper cutouts. *SADIE CURCI*

Your children can learn to recognize basic colors with this bulletin board matching game. Cut eight clown faces and hats from oaktag and detail each in a different color. Now cut eight plain strips the same size as the hats and print the names of the eight colors you used across the front. Have students match the word with the appropriate color clown.   *KAREN STONE*

Children love to share their summer adventures; so why not let them do it with pictures on your bulletin board this year? Use a light blue background with the words "What Did You Do This Summer?" cut from yellow construction paper. Have the children draw pictures of their summer activities and tack them below bold-lettered captions such as "I went swimming!" or "I went camping!"   *ALICE S. HENNING*

Wind up your unit on foods and nutrition this year with the "Good Food Wagon" bulletin board. Start with a background of red burlap with green trim around the edges. Make letters out of yellow yarn to read "Hop on the good food wagon." Now cut the wagon from construction paper and felt, and fill it with pictures of foods from the four basic food groups. Pictures may be cut from magazines or drawn by you and your students.   *CLARA ROGERS*

Here's a clever bulletin board idea to welcome your students back to school. Cover the board with black construction paper and trim the top and bottom edges with newspaper strips. Using colored construction paper, cut a modern-day school house, trees, and any other scenery you desire. Now cut paper-doll figures from newspaper to represent the children in your class and glue them in groups across the board.
          MERIBETH PECK

SEPTEMBER: Bulletin Boards

MAKE your bulletin board a "Welcome to Our Room" poster. Cover board with white paper. Attach cutout colored-paper border, title, and bright 8" x 11" picture frames. As the kids enter, ask them to sign their names. Then invite each to take a sheet of paper and draw or write about himself (family, vacation, hobby), placing his contribution within a frame. Use finished poster as a get-acquainted device.   **Carolyn M. Wilhelm**

OVERCOME shyness and uneasiness as new faces meet with an icebreaker bulletin board. On a board covered with paper, have each child letter in his name with a felt pen. Then he crayon decorates it with cross-hatching, flowers, strips, and so on. Color area between to complete your first "class" activity.   **Joan Macey**

WELCOME your new students to sail with you aboard their classroom ship—the U.S.S. (your name). Cut out a black paper hull and white sails. Print their names on sails with colored felt pens. Secure ship to bulletin board covered with blue paper. Use cutout letters for title and ship's name. Later, read a sea story or poem and invite the children to create individual ships to carry them through the year. Save and display at open house.   **Claire Setterfield**

MR. OWL greets his first-grade family with individual name tags. To create your bulletin board, cover it with orange paper, white cutout-lettered title, and Mr. Owl cut from brown paper and decorated with crayon. Children's owl name tags are smaller versions of Mr. Owl with the names printed on them. Attach yarn loops to the tags for board display and also for easy wearing.   **Vivian Lynn**

WELCOME your newcomers with "yummy" individual name-tag cones. Big Scoop invites each to find his own name on his own cone. Background, cones, and title are cut from colored construction paper. Big Scoop's ice-cream head is cotton decorated with cutout colored-paper features. **Vivian Lynn**

Displays unlimited A sandwich pegboard covered wth burlap stretches Constance B. Shaw's, Lakewood, Colorado, classroom display space. This movable space-stretcher is an excellent spot for all kinds of materials. Or use it as a room divider, a learning station, or for anything the imagination can devise.

HANG ON THE LINE TO BE

CLEAN AND FINE

NUTRITION

A "clean experience" Lynn Bryant's students in Mullins, South Carolina, actively participated in a "down-to-earth" cleanliness unit. Each child hand washed some article of clothing, using buckets and cold water powder, and then hung them up to dry. As a result their display correlated the efforts and values shared.

OCTOBER

Say the word *October* and what do your kids conjure up? Flickering orange jack-o'-lanterns, howling black cats, groaning green goblins, and witches on broomsticks, we'll bet. Yes, Halloween holds special magic for children, but what about the many other special October days?

There's Fire Prevention Week and the World Series. And let's not forget Picasso's birthday, Columbus Day, International Letter-Writing Week, National Poetry Day, Universal Children's Day—the list runs on and on. To help you and your kids make the most of this glorious month, treat yourself to the ideas and activities in this chapter. They include a play for Fire Prevention Week, a miniunit on fall's free resource—leaves—and an explorer's kit to Columbus Day, not to mention bright ideas and bulletin boards. And don't worry. You didn't really think we'd forget Halloween, did you? There are also spooky songs, perilous plays, and bewitching stories. Now on with the fun and festivities!

Red letter days

ANNUAL OCTOBER EVENTS

These special events usually occur in October, but the exact dates may vary from year to year.

Universal Children's Day (first Monday)
Child Health Day (first Monday)
Fire Prevention Week (the week of October 8, the anniversary of the Great Chicago Fire of 1871)
Columbus Day (observed on the second Monday)
Discoverers' Day (second Monday)
World Series
International Letter-Writing Week
National School Lunch Week (beginning with the second Sunday)
National Handicapped Awareness Week (beginning with the second Sunday)
Rosh Hashana (usually in September or October)
Yom Kippur (usually in September or October)

1 The **first postcard** was issued in Austria in 1869.

2 Two freedom fighters were born on this date: **Mohandas Gandhi,** leader of the Indian independence movement, in 1869; and **Nat Turner,** leader of a black slave uprising, in 1800.

4 On the anniversary of the launching of **Sputnik I,** have your students compare our perceptions of outer space now to those before 1957.

6 The **first talking feature film** opened in New York City in 1927. Al Jolson spoke in *The Jazz Singer.*

8 Civil rights leader **Jesse Jackson** was born in 1941.

9 Norse explorer **Leif Ericson** discovered North America in A.D. 1000, almost 500 years before Columbus.

11 **Anna Eleanor Roosevelt,** U.S. diplomat, humanitarian, and first lady, was born in 1884.

12 **Columbus Day** is now observed on the second Monday in October, but today is the anniversary of the date Christopher Columbus first sighted the New World (San Salvador).

14 **Martin Luther King, Jr.,** won the Nobel Peace Prize in 1964 for his work in civil rights.

15 **National Poetry Day** commemorates the birthday of the ancient poet, Virgil, born in 70 B.C.

18 Russia sold **Alaska** to the United States in 1867.

19 By George, we won! In 1781, Lord Cornwallis surrendered to George Washington in Yorktown, Virginia, ending the fighting between Britain and its American colonies in the **American Revolution.**

20 Go ahead and clown around! "The Greatest Show on Earth" got off the ground when the **Ringling Bros. and Barnum & Bailey Circus** opened the big top in 1919.

21 **Thomas Edison** saw the light in 1879 when he invented incandescent electric light.

23 The **first National Women's Rights Convention** was held in Worcester, Massachusetts, in 1850.

24 It's **United Nations Day**—the founding of the UN and the establishment of the UN charter in 1945.

25 Spanish artist **Pablo Picasso,** the most prolific artist ever, was born in Barcelona in 1881.

28 "Give me your tired, your poor, your huddled masses yearning to be free. . . ." was first read this day in 1886 when the **Statue of Liberty** was dedicated.

29 The **stock market collapse** of 1929 began the Great Depression. More than 16 million shares of stock were dumped and billions of dollars lost.

30 The **ball-point pen** was patented in 1888. Also, Americans got the scare of the century in 1938 when the famous **"War of the Worlds"** radio show was broadcast and convinced them that a Martian invasion of Earth was really happening.

31 **National Magic Day** observed in honor of the great magician Harry Houdini who died in 1926. It's also **National UNICEF Day** and, of course, **Halloween!**

October facts

Use these fabulous facts for story starters, bulletin-board ideas, or just a little fiendish fun!

—In parts of Japan, a black cat crossing your path is considered good luck!

—The Halloween custom of bobbing for apples was used to predict the future in ancient England. Anyone who could fish the apples out of the tub without using his or her hands was guaranteed a prosperous year.

—More than 2,000 years ago, Halloween was New Year's Eve! The new year for the ancient Druids started on November 1.

—The Druids believed that on the last day of the year, October 31st, the ghosts of the dead were allowed to return to earth and visit their homes. People used to leave their doors and windows open to welcome them.

—According to Irish legend, jack-o'-lanterns were named for a man called Jack, who could not enter heaven because he was a miser. The devil didn't want him because Jack liked to play tricks on the devil. So Jack ended up walking the earth, carrying a lantern wherever he went. People called him Jack of the lantern or Jack O'Lantern.

—In Scotland, people carve turnips instead of pumpkins for their Halloween lanterns.

—The Celtics believed that if you dressed up on Halloween to look like a witch or a ghost, the evil spirits would mistake you for one of their own and not bother you with their tricks. Hence, our custom of wearing Halloween costumes.

OCTOBER: Bright Ideas

PATCHWORK PUMPKIN PEOPLE

Our classroom is populated with pumpkin people. Here's how to make these colorful, lifelike characters. You'll need butcher paper, tempera paints, fabric pieces, colored yarn, crayons, pencils, and newspapers.

First, have kids make large, stuffed pumpkin heads by cutting two identical heads from a sheet of butcher paper. Paint them bright orange. Draw a face on one head only and staple the two together, painted sides facing out, leaving a large enough opening so heads can be stuffed with newspaper. When heads are assembled, have kids add their own creative touches, such as yarn hair, mustaches, or paper hats.

Now have children take turns lying on sheets of butcher paper as partners trace around them. Make sure they keep hands flat with fingers spread, legs apart, and feet turned to the side.

When tracing is done, use colored markers or paints to fill in details such as collars, buttons, belts, jewelry, and pockets. Finally, glue fabric pieces to body outlines, creating patchwork shirts, dresses, or overalls. Attach bodies to pumpkin heads and display. Hang from your ceiling for a special, spooky effect!
LINDA MIX

NUTTY WITCHES

Use painted peanut shells to add a third dimension to witch portraits. Paint two half shells green and four or five halves white. Then draw or paint a witch's face on construction paper, cut a large mouth from

red paper and cut two white circles with black dots for eyes. Glue eyes onto green peanut shells and add to face. Attach a crooked white nose. Glue mouth in place and fill with white shell teeth. Strips of gray or black paper can be used for hair, with a black paper hat for a finishing touch.
LYDIA CUTLER

HALLOWEEN CROSSWORD
Duplicate this crossword puzzle for little trick-or-treaters.
Across
1. You cover your face with it. (mask)
2. The month Halloween comes in. (October)
3. What a witch rides on. (broom)
4. The dark part of the day. (night)
5. Frighten. (scare)
6. A scary black..... (rhymes with bat). (cat)
Down
3. A flying black animal. (bat)
7. The holiday on Oct.

31. (Halloween)
8. A mean, ugly old woman. (witch)
9. Casper, the friendly ..... (ghost)
10. A night bird--lives on small creatures. (owl)
11. What you do when you see something scary. (run)
CLAUDIA WILCOX

BODY CONSTRUCTION
Each year after studying the systems of the human body, my class does the following activity.

Each student lies on a piece of white butcher paper and a partner traces his outline. Then using books and models, kids cut out shapes of vital organs from scrap paper, make adjustments for size, trace them on colored construction paper, cut, and glue into place. Size and location of organs are effectively taught this way. Hang finished bodies around the classroom--if your unit falls around Halloween, they create a spooky effect!
DIANE WENGER

OCTOBER PLANNING COMMITTEE
After forming committees to plan various classroom projects, my second grade class constructed a Halloween planning committee for our bulletin board. Members were spooks, witches, goblins, demons, black cats, skeletons, and other Halloween types. A nasty witch chaired our committee, which suggested things like, "Let's make Halloween dark and spooky and full of spiders."

Each child made his committee member from crayons and construction paper, and we printed suitable blurbs in overhead "balloons."
MADELINE PECORA

JACK'S TREAT
Let your jack-o'-lantern give you a treat this year. After carving your pumpkin, separate seeds from the pulp, wash them, and mix with equal parts butter and Worcestershire sauce. Salt lightly and spread on cookie sheet. Bake at 350 for 20 minutes or until seeds look toasty. GLORIA CETRON

PEEKABOO SCREEN
Make an eight-panel screen with portholes, keyhole cutouts, and painted shapes, and let students create their own secret world. Cut each panel from 1/8" hardboard, 1' wide and 3' high. Hinge panels on both sides with 3" heating duct tape. Use saber or keyhole saw to make cutouts. Kids can use cutouts to poke their heads through; simulate occupational conditions such as banks, ticket offices, and food stands; have puppet shows; or invent their own games.
SHIRLEY SHRATTER

SEED BULLETIN BOARD
Motivate science interest with this seed bulletin board. Most flowers, trees, and vegetables now have mature seeds. Have students collect and dry seeds, then place each kind on index cards labeled with plant names.

OCTOBER: Bright Ideas

Tack on bulletin board. You can discuss shapes, sizes, colors, and weights of seeds. RICHARD LATTA

A HEADY IDEA
Make a scary two-faced Halloween decoration from any plastic sandwich bag. Use marking pen to draw a ghostly face on each side of the bag, and gummed reinforcements for spooky eyes. Gather top of bag and blow it up like a balloon; tie with string or rubber band. Then hang floating head from your ceiling or in the doorway of your classroom!
IDA M. PARDUE

THE BIG APPLE
Set aside an "apple week" in your class to discover the benefits of apples while using math, language, science, and thinking skills as well.

Get a selection of red, yellow, and green apples, and use them in counting exercises: How many apples are there? How many green ones? Which is the smallest? Choose a medium-sized apple. How many are larger? and so on.

Talk about how apples look and feel. Give each child a half and talk about the smell and taste.

Have an apple treat each day, such as applesauce,

cider, or apple pie. Discuss "an apple a day keeps the doctor away!"

What are the meanings of "the apple of my eye," "polishing the apple," "as American as apple pie" and other expressions?

Weigh and measure apples. If you can get to a local orchard, measure bushels, pecks, and so on.

Finally, let students play apple games like "Bobbing for Apples" and "Eating Apples on a String." You can even create your own apple games. BETTY WHITE

MY HALLOWEEN PIE
To set up a Halloween Pie Center you need: plastic sandwich bags, foil muffin cups, plastic bowls, egg beaters, measuring bowls, rolling pins, graham crackers, milk, cans of pumpkin, instant pudding, sugar, soft margarine, and candied orange slices.

In one area, assemble ingredients for graham cracker pie cup. Print instructions: Put 2 graham crackers in plastic bag. Seal bag and crush crackers into fine crumbs with rolling pin. Add 1 tsp. sugar and 1 Tb. margarine right in your bag. Press mixture into foil cup. Pass to "filling stations" and pick filling for your pie.

Instructions for

Halloween Pumpkin Pie: Measure 2 Tbs. vanilla pudding into bowl, add ½ c. cold milk and mix with beater until it thickens. Add 1 or 2 tsps. pumpkin, stir, and pour into crust. Use knife to cut orange slice to decorate your pie. Recipe for Halloween Chocolate Pie: Measure 2 Tbs. chocolate pudding into bowl and follow directions for Halloween Pumpkin Pie. JEAN STANGL

WHAT'S COOKING?
For a unique Halloween bulletin board, have your students write their scariest menus for witches and illustrate them. Such a menu might include rat-tail soup, pig's-eye salad, snake hamburgers on spider buns, frog-leg french fries, grasshopper turnovers. Let kids use crayons, construction paper, and any other "found" materials they can handle for drawings, then attach them all to your bulletin board.
FLORENCE RIVES

LET IT SNOW
If your climate cooperates, the first snowfall can be a learning experience for your students. When cold weather begins, make a Snow Prediction Chart. List students' names and the dates they think the first snow will fall. In the next month have them read weather reports in the paper and watch the weather news on TV. Teach the meaning of "precipitation" and talk about high and low daily temperatures.

Proclaim your best guessers "official weatherpersons" and print their names on big paper snowflakes. JULIANN D. HICKERSON

MYSTERY GHOSTS

Here's a Halloween bulletin board perfect for Parents' Night. Give each child a white construction-paper ghost. Have them write brief paragraphs about themselves, leaving out their names, and paste them to ghosts. Display ghosts against a black background under the heading "Mystery Ghosts in Room." See who can identify the most--can parents find their kids' mystery ghosts? LISA LITTLEWOOD

FIRE PREVENTION WEEK

Here are some activities to try during Fire Prevention Week to familiarize students with fire extinguishers and alarm boxes.
1. Take kids for a walk around the school, pointing out the location of alarms and extinguishers.
2. Ask a member of local fire department to visit and explain how to use these devices.
3. Visit the local fire station for a brief demonstration of how extinguishers work.
4. Make a list of dos and don'ts for fire extinguishers and alarm boxes and post it on your bulletin board. Have students contribute, too. MARILYN KARNS

FIVE PUMPKINS

Here's a simple flannel-board story that teaches size comparisons and delights kids. Five felt pumpkins have faces on one side and are plain on the other. As they become jack-o'-lanterns, they're turned over to show faces.

It was nearly Halloween. Five pumpkins, all different sizes, were growing in a field. The largest said, "I'm the biggest and best." He was big and orange and beautiful. The second one said, "I'm next. That's pretty good." The third one said, "I'm in the middle but I'm growing every day." The fourth one said, "I'm growing too. I'll catch up." They all told the littlest pumpkin, "You're the smallest. You'll never be big." He was very sad. He thought, "No one will want me."

Then along came a horse, donkey, dog, squirrel, and mouse, looking for pumpkins to make jack-o'-lanterns for Halloween. The horse found the largest pumpkin and said, "Here's a big one, just right for my barn." He took it and made his jack-o'-lantern. The donkey said, "Here's one just right for my shed," and took the second largest. The dog took the middle-sized one for his doghouse, and the squirrel said, "Here's one just right for my tree home," and took the fourth pumpkin. The little mouse was last. He saw the smallest pumpkin. "Here is the perfect one for me, just right for my doorstep!" he squeaked. Now all the pumpkins and animals were happy! WINIFRED COOPER

OCTOBER: Bright Ideas

TWO HALLOWEEN GAMES
These seasonal games, exercises in listening and number order, make learning more fun.

Who Is the Noisy Ghost?
All children but one sit in a circle with heads bent over; they are the ghosts. The remaining child is the "Ghost Robber" and walks around inside the circle. One of the ghosts, picked previously, says, "Boo!" The ghost robber tries to guess which ghost booed. If he guesses wrong, the ghost who booed becomes the ghost robber. If he guesses right, he may remain the ghost robber. The game continues until all have a chance to be ghost robber.

Find the Missing Goblin
Make two sets of cards with the numbers 1-10 printed on them. Each should also have a picture of a Halloween goblin. Place one set along the bulletin board with one or two numbers missing. Let the child find the missing goblins from the extra stack and put it in correct sequence with those on the board. These games will get kids in a spooky mood!
JANIE HALL

ROAD MAP BULLETIN BOARD
Here's an attractive bulletin board that can be a back-to-school geography lesson. Tack a large road map of the United States and Canada on your bulletin board before September. Then during the first week of school, have students use felt-tipped pens to mark places they visited over the summer, color-coding their routes from one spot to another. Use the marked map for geography exercises comparing distances traveled, routes taken, and proximity of different vacation spots.
JOAN MARY MACEY

SILKY WITCH TRESSES
Kids will take a closer look at corn with this Halloween project. Get some ears from your market and let children examine them. Have them draw a witch, make her as ugly as they can, but omit her hair. When pictures are done, squeeze glue on where hair should be and then press corn silk onto glue. The witches take on an eerie look with "corny" hairdos.
LYDIA CUTLER

ASK THEM
Kids love to fill out questionnaires, and in the first few weeks of school this can be an effective way to learn things about your students testing won't reveal. Devise a questionnaire asking about home and school life, opinions on certain academic areas, and so on. For instance:
1. What did you like most about school last year?
2. If you had one wish, what would it be?
3. What are you afraid of?
4. What subject do you like best?
5. Is there someone you can talk to if you have a problem?

Explain that answers will be kept confidential and encourage kids to be honest in their responses.
JIM DERBY

NATURE WALKS
Instead of collecting things on nature walks, try these kinds of nature activities.
1. Imitate bird flight patterns. Turkey vultures fly with their wings slanted, while hawks keep theirs level. What other distinctive patterns are there?
2. Identify wildflowers. Play a game of sounds suggested by flower names, such as mooing at cow parsnips or chattering for monkey flowers.
3. Go on a checklist scavenger hunt. Look for three birds, four insects, a pine tree with needles in bundles of three, and so on. Check off items on list, but make sure you don't touch anything!
WENDY DRESKIN

YUCKY-BOOK SWAP
To encourage kids to read and share, ask them to bring in books they DIDN'T like! Have them sit in a circle, put the "Yucky-Books" in a pile, and tell

why the book was awful. Then each child gets to pick a book from the pile. They'll quickly learn the meaning of "one man's meat is another man's poison." Keep a special shelf in the classroom for Yucky-Books, and give each child a bookmark to use to "reserve" books until they are finished. You may end with permanent trades between kids or "White Elephant" book sales.
CAROL GOLD

A BOUNCING MATH LESSON
To help kids with the idea of skip-counting (two, four, six, and so on), take a trip to the gym and give each child a tennis ball. Bounce the balls by twos, next by threes, then fives, and finally tens. Somehow, the physical act of bouncing seems to reinforce the concept.
BELLE BLUEFIELD

SLOGANS FOR READING
My 38 reluctant readers were encouraged to think of short, eye-catching slogans to promote reading. In no time we had 250 different slogans, and students were so enthusiastic they decided to share the project and posted the slogans around the school building.

We then decided to hold a schoolwide Reading Slogan Contest. Slogans had to sell reading and couldn't duplicate ones already posted. My kids were judges and took the job very seriously.
Some winning slogans:
1. Read your way around.
2. If you want to succeed, learn to read.
3. Reading lasts a lifetime.
4. Read...indeed!
  All contest winners were rewarded with, what else? Books!
MIRIAM GOLDBAUM

DON'T CARVE THAT PUMPKIN!
To use pumpkins without carving them, tape on paper eyes, ears, nose, and anything else, with pieces of rolled tape. Pumpkins with ski caps and scarves remind kids to wear winter clothes again. Students might write stories about the adventures pumpkins have after school. Uncarved pumpkins last a long time in a cool spot, so you can use them to make Pilgrims or even turkeys when Thanksgiving time rolls around.
CAROLYN WILHELM

KILL THE COSTUME WOES
Costume problems for your school plays can be solved with the simple jerkin made from a short length of material with a hole in the middle to go over a child's head. The jerkin can be made from oilcloth, unbleached muslin, or any firm fabric, and can hang straight, be fastened by snaps on each side, or held in at the waist with a belt. Use one or many colors, then add names or symbols to suit your theme. For a nutrition play, add construction paper or fabric vegetables; for a safety play, stick on Stop or Slow signs; for a community play, paint on a stethoscope for doctor, badge for police, and so on. For designs, use iron-on tape or draw them on directly. Real objects such as fringe or feathers may be fastened right on the jerkin. For fabric jerkins, attach appliques with loose sewing stitch that will pull out easily. These decorations are easily removable without damaging base material-- a basic set of jerkins can last several years.
JEAN GATCH

OCTOBER: Fun and festivities

October is a scary month, a discovery month, a fun-to-be-around month. On the next few pages, you'll find stories, songs, plays, and activities to help you promote laughs and learning in your classroom all month long!

Activities for Columbus Day

Discovery Ho!

In Hawaii October 12 isn't just Columbus Day. It is also *Discovery Day,* saluting all great discoverers from the Phoenicians to the astronauts. Each state in the country has had its own explorers and it is a good time to look at their many accomplishments.

Discuss the concepts *discovery* and *explorer.* Most sections of the world were inhabited at the time of their *discovery.* So, why do we say they were *discovered?* Then try these activities.

1. Name explorers of your state or region. For example, Oregon has Lewis and Clark; Alaska—Vitus Bering; Florida—Ponce de Leon; Wisconsin—Jean Nicolet; California—Drake, Coronado, and Fremont; the northeastern states—Leif Ericson or the Cabots; Hawaiians—Captain Cook. Research information about them. Do plays, special reports, and biographies.

2. Read about the heritage in your own area. In Hawaii students study the work of the Polynesians. Look at what native peoples did in your region of the world.

3. Kids are interested in the polar regions and the explorations of space and the oceans. Research information about current explorers. Have kids imagine what is left to explore. (Answers might include

the galaxies, jungle areas on earth, and so on.) Let students speculate as to what they might do as modern-day explorers.

4. Look at discoveries of the past. For example, find information about Sir Edmund Hillary's first climb to the summit of Mt. Everest.

5. Read about discoveries in medicine, physics, and biology.

6. Research important archaeological findings.

7. Study the lives of famous explorers. What kind of training did they have? Experience? Write a comparison and contrast study of two or more of them.

8. Look at the various kinds of transportation different explorers used—from the foot travel of Marco Polo to the space capsule of astronauts Alan Shepard and John Glenn. How were ships different in size and style?

9. What geographic knowledge did explorers have at the time they made their discoveries? Can students find pictures of old maps?

10. Have students trace on a map the routes various explorers took.

11. What was the reaction of native people in the areas at the time of the explorers' arrivals? Pick one (Columbus, for example) and try to find stories about the

inhabitants at the time.

12. What was the impact of the explorers on the land? What were the results of the expeditions?

13. Become familiar with such terms as navigation, quadrant, sextants, chronometer, dead reckoning, scurvy, anchorage, longitude, latitude, cartographer, landfall, crows nest, log, bark, circumnavigate, orbit, oceanography, geologist, geodetic, solar system, satellite.

14. Develop motor control activities for your children. Simulate the climb to the masthead of an old square rigger or portage of a canoe through the wilderness.

15. Teach a folk dance popular at the time of Columbus—the sailor's hornpipe. (Information about other folk dances is available in many books.)

16. Develop a bulletin board about the different personalities kids discover.

17. Challenge children to discover things in their own neighborhoods—an ant hill they hadn't noticed, for example.

18. Women are conspicuously absent from most historical expeditions. Sacajawea is a noted exception. But look at the achievements of other female explorers—Amelia Earhart, for one.

Barbara Wessinger

Look Out!

d min.

Look out for wit-ches, Look out for bats, Look

A7
out, look out for gob-lins, Look out, look out for

A7
cats. If you should see them, it's time to shout out

[open]
BOO! And say, and say, I'm not a-fraid of you!

Words by Tom LaHaie
Music by Elva S. Daniels

A playlet

What Will You See?

Your primary kids will love this Halloween playlet, and so will you! It doesn't require full costumes, only simple masks and props to give personality to each character. For example, in verse one, the witch needs no more than a black, pointed hat and maybe a crooked, crepe-paper nose just for fun. "The Halloween Scene" may be performed two or three times at one recital to give everyone a chance to participate. While the chorus reads the verses, have other children pantomime the various characters in the playlet. You could even give neighboring rooms a Halloween treat by sharing your production with them.

What will you see come this Halloween?
A wicked witch stirring some stew.
With tall, pointed hat and long, crooked nose,
She'll grin as she says, "Howdy BOO!"

What will creep out when the sun goes down
From under those rustling shocks?
Just two tiny goblins with mischievous ways
Giving windows and doors scary knocks.

Who will greet all from porches and steps
With snaggle-tooth grins of delight?
Why, three jack-o'-lanterns who flicker and glow
In the darkness of Halloween night.

And up in the air, with their dark wings spread wide,
Four hideous bats dive and hover.
When they plunge toward the ground, you'll look all around
For a place to find shelter and cover.

I see yellow eyes staring down from that tree!
They look awfully spooky and mean.
Don't worry—it's only an old hootie owl
Who is part of the Halloween scene!

So keep your eyes open and maybe tonight
You'll see all of these creatures appear.
Greet each with a smile and a wave of your hand.
Halloween only comes once a year!

Jane K. Priewe

OCTOBER: Fun and festivities

The Littlest Pumpkin

Fingerplays are usually popular with early primary children. And this activity, using paper dolls in a similar way, can really liven up Halloween. Here's how.

Cut out paper, fold accordian style in the shape of a particular image: owl, pumpkin, ghost, cat, broom, witch, hat, skeleton, and so on. Make sure the paper remains essentially one piece. Then, unfold the paper as you recite a nonsense verse. Do one about five pumpkins sitting on a gate, for example.

Fold an eight-inch paper in thirds and then again in half, to get six folds. Cut off one fold and hold the five remaining folds while cutting on the dashed lines. It is important that the pumpkin and gate outline reach the sides so they are still attached after cutting.

After folding the cutout make up a simple rhyme. Here is one a student came up with. It is about five little pumpkins and as it is recited the student unfolds the paper cutout.

Five little pumpkins sitting on a gate
One fell down and broke his plate.
Four little pumpkins sitting on a gate
One fell down on top of Kate.
Three little pumpkins sitting on a gate
One fell down and lost his skate.
Two little pumpkins sitting on a gate
One fell down and lost some weight.
The littlest pumpkin sitting on a gate
fell down and said, "No more
pumpkins are up on that gate!"

Deborah Miller

Poetry day. On October 15 salute Poetry Day. Read poems, recite favorites from your anthologies, and of course create your own. Try an *acrostic* poem. There are so many fantastic words with great images in October—falling leaves, explorers, goblins, ghosts. Create poems about one of these images. Take one word. Write the letters down on a sheet of paper. Then write a phrase about the word beginning with the letter. Then rewrite your verse and share poems in class.

Monster words. October is monster season. People read about monsters, watch scary monster movies, dress up as monsters. But few people build their monster vocabulary! Here is a snappy quiz developed by elementary teacher Robert E. Rubstein of Eugene, Oregon, who gives it to students and faculty alike. Answer the six questions on a separate sheet of paper.

Do you know...
1. What does *monster* mean?
2. Where does the word *lullaby* come from?
3. When someone has a bad dream at night we say they have a *nightmare*. Where does the word *nightmare* come from?
4. The word *werewolf* is a two part word. Extra points if you guess where this word comes from.
5. Now, for the ten dollar prize—what does *Lycanthrope* mean?
6. *Dracula* was a real person. Do you know who he was and where he lived? Answers are on page 78. (No cheating!)

I Ain't Afraid

We are big boys. We are big girls. We are not a-fraid of Al-ley cats or big black bats that live in big dark caves. We are big boys. We are big girls. No-thing makes us shake! Not e-ven spi-ders who drink up our cider; not e-ven ghosts on wie-nie roasts. We're too big to be scared___ so there!

Words and lyrics by David Hunt

This song will ease any Halloween fears young children may have! Create new lyrics for measures 13 through 16. For example, "Not even witches who hide in dark ditches" or "not even a skeleton who jiggles like gelatin." Words can be as silly as the mood of your students, and they need not rhyme. Alter the rhythm of the melody to fit the lyrics. You can also turn the song into a choral reading between boys and girls, with everyone joining in on the last two stanzas. **Elva S. Daniels,** INSTRUCTOR'S music consultant.

The Halloween Scene

PRIMARY children can become Halloween cats, bats, jack-o'-lanterns, skeletons, ghosts, owls, and witches in this action-packed playlet. Perform it in the classroom or auditorium with all characters "onstage" or entering from the wings on cue. Costumes may be adult- or child-made. (Children's drawings representing characters can be used as props or serve in lieu of costumes.) To make scenery, have students draw Halloween figures, paste them on a large strip of brown butcher paper, and use as a backdrop. Note: Alternate dialogue in parentheses is suggested for preprimary players.

Announcer—
Goblins and ghosts
And monsters are seen,
But it's all right
'Cause it's Halloween!
(Scary things are seen
'Cause it's Halloween!)
(*Action: Blows horn.*)

Black cats—
Black cats prowl
Throughout the night,
Howling and hissing;
They give you a fright!
(Black cats howl at night,
Giving you a terrible fright!)
(*Action: Cats crawl around howling and hissing.*)

Jack-o'-lanterns—
Big orange pumpkins,
So fat and round,
Soon parade
Jack-o'-lantern frowns!
(Pumpkins fat and round
With jack-o'-lantern frowns!)
(*Action: Carry pumpkin faces or make weird faces.*)

Ghosts—
Spooky ghost shapes
Quietly float by.
You can see them
If you try!
(Spooky ghosts come floating by.
I'm scared, but I won't cry!)
(*Action: Ghosts in white sheets float onstage.*)

Owls—
Mean-eyed owls
Stare at you.
Come close and see
If you dare to! Whooo!
(Big-eyed owls stare at you.
Now come close. Whooo!")
(*Action: Look through large paper eyes and say, "Whooo!"*)

Skeletons—
Skeleton bones
Rattle and quiver.
They make everyone
Shake and shiver!
(Skeletons rattle and quiver,
Making you shake and shiver!)
(*Action: Dance like skeletons on strings.*)

Bats—
Huge black bats swoop
Round your head,
Filling you
With an awful dread!
(Big bats fly round your head,
Chasing you off to bed!)
(*Action: Make swooping and flying motions.*)

Witches—
Green-faced old witches
On their brooms
Fly around
In the foggy gloom!
(Witches on brooms
Fly in the gloom!)
(*Action: Skip around stage straddling old brooms or rolled lengths of brown paper.*)

Announcer—
Children from all over town:
Trick or treat on doors they pound!
(Children all about.
"Trick or treat!" they shout.)

All—
We're all dressed up
To holler, "Boo!"
Bet you can't guess
Who is who. BOOO!
(*Action: Gather around announcer before speaking.*)   Helen Taulbee

OCTOBER: Fun and festivities

A play for Fire Prevention Week

Fire!

Characters: Jack Larkin, Peggy Larkin, children (as many as you have representing ideas for fire prevention), announcer.
Scene: Living room. **Jack** and **Peggy** are studying at small table on one side of room, leaving space for action to take place on center stage. Books and papers are on table.

Jack: Ho-hum! (Gives tremendous sigh, blowing papers on the floor).
Peggy: You'll blow us away if you do that again. What's the matter?
Jack: I have to write a paper for school tomorrow. (Sighs again.)
Peggy: What is it to be about?
Jack: Fire prevention week. (With big yawn.) How to prevent fires (yawns), what to do if one starts (yawn), stuff like that. (Sighs again, blowing more papers to the floor.)
Peggy: You're a menace, Jack Larkin! Look, here's a book with some ideas to start your paper. (She finds book on table and opens it to show her brother. She then exits.)
(Jack leans head on hand, muttering to himself.)
Jack: (Reading) Fire Prevention Week. Boy, do I need some bright ideas! (He looks sleepy, nods, and puts head down on desk.) (Enter child wearing or carrying large cardboard likeness of a lighted bulb with the words BRIGHT IDEAS printed on the bulb.)
Bright idea: (Going to center.)
> The time is Fire Prevention Week,
> And so without ado,
> Here are a few suggestions
> Of *Dos* and *Don'ts* for you! (Exit)

(Enter announcer)
Announcer: Never let old rags and rubbish pile up around the house.
(Enter children, any number, covered with large gray and brown rags. Hidden underneath these are bright strips of red cloth or paper for "flames." They come to center and stand close together to represent a pile of oily rags.)
Rags:
> We're oily rags and rubbish,
> Our danger you might miss,
> But if you leave us piled up here,
> Look out! We might do this! (POOF!)

(They suddenly wave their arms, showing the red strips of paper underneath the rags as they ignite.)
Announcer: Keep oily rags in a closed container.
Rags: (arms down again)
> Just pop us in a tight tin can;
> It takes you just a minute
> We'll never worry you one bit
> If you will keep us in it.

(Enters child wearing a tall cardboard likeness of large container. Child puts the "rags" inside by pushing them back of the cardboard, then shoves the whole thing off the stage.)
Announcer: Safety matches are best to use.
(Children enter dressed as safety matches. They wear trip caps. They stand in a very straight row.)
Safety matches:
> Though mice could chew on us all night,
> We'd never flame or flare,
> We have a special safety top,
> (pointing to caps)
> Just take us anywhere!

(The mice run over and nibble on the safety matches. Nothing happens. The mice get excited and jump up and down, look at each other puzzled, scratch their heads, then go off the stage in despair.)
Safety matches:
> You'll find us in most any store
> In brightly colored packets.
> We come in neat and tidy rows
> With little cardboard jackets.

(Safety matches bow, then march out in a straight line.)
Announcer: Do not go away leaving an iron or other heating appliance plugged in.
(Enter children carrying real appliances or wearing cardboard likenesses of them, such as an iron, frying pan, mixer, and so on. There is a long cord attached to each.)
Appliances:
> Don't plug us in and go away
> To answer door or phone,
> You never know how long you'll be,
> We might burn up your home.

(Enter child who acts as if plugging each appliance into an outlet. Sound of telephone or doorbell off stage. Child hurries off to answer. Appliances begin to groan, acting as if they are getting hot. They then explode, showing strips of red paper attached to back of appliances. Child reenters, stops, acts horrified, and shouts for help. Two or three others rush in. All stare at the flaming appliances.)
Announcer: Know how to call your fire department quickly and give the information clearly.
(Enter child wearing or carrying very large telephone book.)
Telephone book:
> Your firemen come day or night,
> Don't tear your hair to shreds;
> (pulls at hair)
> They'll pull their boots and jackets on
> And jump right from their beds!

Telephone book (continuing):

Don't run around in dizzy rings,
Or feel you've turned to stone!
Just have their number in the book
And call them on the phone!

(One of the children runs around in dizzy rings and another stands as if turned to stone.)

(Sound of siren is heard from off stage. Children dressed in red paper hats represent fire fighters and rush in with extinguishers to put out the fire. The flames disappear from the back of the appliances. Everyone exits. Peggy enters stage again.)

Peggy: (waking up Jack) How is your paper going?

Jack: What paper? Oh, I guess I fell asleep. But boy, did I have a weird dream! You know, I think I have the ideas for my paper. (He starts to write frantically.)

Peggy: Good! Why don't you have a fireman come and visit your class with you tomorrow to talk about more ideas for fire prevention week.

Jack: Good idea, Peggy. Thanks. (both exit)

The end

A story for Halloween

The Witch's Brew That Wouldn't Do

The night before Halloween, Wendy the witch landed in an old country cemetery. She unhooked a big iron pot from her broomstick. "What a trip!" she said to herself. But she sighed happily. She knew at last she was going to get her big chance.

On Halloween Wendy was to serve refreshments for the annual convention of the Honorary Society of Witches. She was going to make a special drink or brew. If the members liked it, Wendy knew she'd be admitted. If they didn't, she'd never have another chance.

Wendy opened her batwing bag and counted her supplies: 85 lizard tails, 53 hoptoad toes, 72 woolly worms, 29 pheasant feathers. "Surely the society would like this brew!" she thought.

The next day the cemetery was alive with the rustling, bustling, cackling, chattering witches. Wendy filled her pot with water, danced a jig, added the ingredients, and chanted:

"Hoptoad toe, in you go
let that brew, fizz and stew
lizard tail, do not fail
it is up to you to make good brew!"

Wendy stirred the mixture with her broomstick. All afternoon she stirred and muttered chants until the brew was ready.

Silently, the witches lined up—each holding a snakeskin container. Esmeralda, the president, was the first to taste the brew. Esmeralda wrinkled her long crooked nose. "My dear," she said slowly, "something is missing."

Wendy's heart sank to the bottom of her pointed boots. As she poured more brew, Fenella uttered, "Yuk!" And so it went with the other witches.

Wendy asked them to wait. She frantically searched the cemetery for more tidbits. She finally added 45 toadstools, 56 tarantulas, 13 poison ivy leaves. Wendy chanted even harder.

"Brew, brew, bubble and pop
otherwise you'll be a flop!"

The witches lined up again. Esmeralda tasted the brew. "My dear, this is much better. But it is too bitter. All good brew must have zing, but it must taste good too."

Wendy asked them to give her a few more hours, and hopped aboard her broomstick. She had until midnight when the witches would expect the ceremonial brew after an evening of witching.

Wendy sped over the countryside, hoping to find the right ingredient. She spotted a small town below her and swept low through the dark empty streets. All she saw were faces on great orange balls grinning at her from doorsteps.

Just as she was about to give up, she saw a light from a house window and peaked in. A group of children dressed in funny costumes were singing and laughing.

One boy was drinking a sparkling light brown liquid, smacking his lips and smiling. "Delicious," he said. "Give me some more of that brew."

"Brew!" Wendy shouted. Perhaps *now* she had what she needed. She waited until the group left the room. It was very dark then; so she crept inside, grabbed the bottle containing the brew, tied it to her broom, and sped back.

When Wendy arrived the line was forming. Esmeralda held the bottle. Quick as the blink of a bat's eye, Wendy poured her new concoction.

"My dear, this is simply marvelous," Esmeralda crooned, clasping her hands together. "What is it called?"

"Apple cider," said Wendy, sighing with happiness. She knew at last she would be admitted to the society! (And that is how we have come to have apple cider on Halloween night!)   **Joann Crawford**

OCTOBER: Mini-teaching unit

Mini-teaching unit on fall's free resource:

Leaves!

WHAT has three points, a stem, veins, is green in summer, and changes color in autumn? A maple leaf, of course. This is only one of the many leaves primary children can study—so bring colorful autumn into the classroom today. The following suggested activities will start you off and motivate interested "leafers" toward further studies.

Talk about leaves When do the leaves appear? How long do they stay on the trees? How does a tree use its leaves? (for making food, to carry seeds) How do we use leaves? (for shade, compost) Do animals use leaves? How and when? Can you think of other ways people and animals use leaves?
Study a leaf. Draw a large leaf on the chalkboard and talk about its three parts, labeling them as you go—the *blade* (broad part of leaf in which are found the leaf's veins and food-making cells), the *petiole* (stem), and the *stipule* (stem end which is attached to tree).

Collect and examine Many leaf samples will be found on the ground but some will need to be picked. Before collecting, establish the following rules:
1. Pick only as many as needed.
2. Always get the complete leaf. To do this, pull the stem gently between thumb and forefinger, being careful not to break the branch to which it's attached.
3. Do not tear off branches.
Place collection on display and hold a hands-on study. Talk about which

leaves are short or long; ribbed, rough, or smooth; stiff or soft. Compare shapes and colors.

Using the encyclopedia or *A First Look at Leaves,* by Selsam and Hunt (Scholastic Book Services, 1976), identify the leaves by shape, texture, and color.
Make a tree chart. Choose a tree that can be seen from the classroom. Visit it in autumn, winter, and spring, noting the changes during each season (draw pictures or take photos).

Leaf activities *Make rubbings* of different kinds of leaves. Place a leaf under a smooth piece of paper. Gently rub with the side of a crayon in the same direction across the leaf and around its outline. Do several leaves, overlapping them. Use finished rubbings to decorate covers of individual science notebooks.
Preserve leaves by placing firm ones between pieces of waxed paper. Lay waxed paper on several thicknesses of newspaper, cover with more newspaper, press with warm iron (help children do this), and remove newspaper. Hang in sunny windows, around bulletin board, or send to a friend or relative.
Try leaf printing with dried leaves. Using a brayer or homemade block printing dabber (rolled paper toweling), coat one side of leaf with thick one-color tempera. Gently lay leaf, paint side down, on a piece of heavy paper; lift carefully and repeat process. For different effects, use the same color paint and paper, paint and paper in different shades

of the same color, or two colors, one for paint and one for paper.
Color leaves which have been traced. (Because this might be difficult for kindergartners, use cardboard shapes instead of original leaves.) When leaves are colored, use a watercolor wash of bright yellow over them. When dry, repeat on opposite sides.
Make a leaf alphabet from leaves cut out of colored paper. Print letters on individual leaves in crayon, and attach to wall. Use for practice when learning the alphabet; as a game, "Who can find the letter _____?"; or to point to when learning to sing the alphabet song.
Pantomime a leaf's life to music—coming out on a tree, growing, rustling in the wind, changing color, falling in autumn, being raked up.
Read a poem aloud about leaves. For example, "The Last Leaf," by Harry Behn from *The Reading of Poetry* (Allyn and Bacon, 1963). Make up a class poem.
Write stories about leaves. Some suggested titles: "The Maple Leaf Who Wanted to Play Baseball," "Johnny Leaf Lost at Sea," and "The Mysterious Leaf Family of Black Stump Forest."
Start a classroom "leafers" club. Collect as many different kinds of leaves as possible and build a club scrapbook. As a club project, study leaves of other plants—vegetables, flowers, shrubs. Add their leaf samples to scrapbook. □

Mary E. Matthews, a retired teacher, taught kindergarten and children's crafts for many years in Dallas, Texas.

OCTOBER: A language unit for UN Day

October 24 is United Nations Day. Use the language and culture activities on these pages to celebrate the UN and promote global awareness in your students this month and all year long.

Janice Green

If you feel at all uncomfortable teaching a foreign language—start small, but think big. First, introduce your class to the "idea" of foreign languages through social studies. Cultural materials and realia are available in infinite variety. Call the cultural attaché of the nearest consulate. You will receive an official assortment of materials and suggestions plus a place on the consulate mailing list.

Foreign airlines (Air France, Alitalia, Lufthansa, Iberia, and so on) offer posters and ethnic restaurants will supply menus and perhaps recipes. Foreign magazines are available at public and college libraries, in particular the large pictorial magazines with full-page ads representing the dream, if not always the reality, of daily life abroad. And not to be overlooked are the foreign periodicals designed for use in the elementary classroom. The public relations departments of foreign corporations and importers will often prove generous, although you will need to sort the wheat from the chaff. Picture postcards (the stamps alone are fascinating) and travel snapshots, to be discovered by students in attics and bureau drawers at home, will feed your overhead projector and bulletin board indefinitely.

The next step—if you feel adventurous—might be to call on a most valuable, and often underestimated, resource: the foreign-born members of your community, many of whom would welcome an invitation to share their heritage and native language.

You may choose not to venture beyond steps one and two—and that's fine. You will have succeeded in opening windows on the world for your students. But if your background and talents include some college-level foreign language (FL) courses, an acceptable pronunciation, a belief that learning how other people live and speak is a rewarding kind of fun, and a willingness to experiment and innovate—then step three is for you.

Although the program described here is in French, it is a model for teaching any modern language. If your background is in Spanish, Italian, German, Russian, Portuguese, or whatever, you will have no difficulty making linguistic and cultural substitutions. The focus is on speaking and listening, not on reading and writing. Daily 15-minute periods are more productive than longer spans two or three times a week. If this arrangement is impossible, reduce learning objectives accordingly. Remember, you are not preparing your pupils for college boards, but rather for enthusiastic response in an unpressured climate and for mastery of a limited and structured body of material.

K-3 Curriculum

To facilitate presentation, the following material has been arbitrarily broken down into three areas: vocabulary and contextual, language, and cultural. Actually, these are inseparable parts of a whole and must be treated as such.

Vocabulary and contextual activities—

1. *La Politesse* (greetings, names, and polite expressions).

Bonjour, au revoir, madame/mademoiselle/monsieur

Comment vas-tu? Comment allez-vous? Très bien, merci. Pas mal.

Comment t'appelles-tu? Je m'appelle . . . . (Use the foreign version or pronunciation of a child's name or suggest some reasonable facsimile.)

S'il te plaît/s'il vous plaît. (The familiar form of address, tu, will be used except when a child addresses either the teacher or another adult. This important cultural point, a signal of social relationships, should be briefly explained, then simply viewed as a fact of life.)

2. *La salle de classe* (classroom objects and people).

L'élève, le garçon, la petite fille, l'ami

Le papier, le livre, le tableau noir, la craie, le crayon, le stylo, le cahier

La table, la chaise, la porte, la fenêtre

3. *Impératives* (classroom directions).

Assieds-toi, lève-toi, montre-moi, montre-lui, dis-moi, dis-lui, répète, écoute, regarde, ferme, ouvre, prends. (If you are addressing the group as a whole, or more than one student, use the plural or formal mode of address: regardez, répétez.)

4. *La famille* (the family).

Les parents: la mère (Maman) et le père (Papa); ma soeur, mon frère, l'enfant, le bébé. (Add other relatives at will.)

La maison, l'appartement, le jardin, chez moi, chez lui, chez nous

Les pièces; la chambre, la salle de bain, le salon, la cuisine, la salle à manger

5. *Nombres, jours, et mois* (numbers, days, months).

Un, deux, trois, quatre, cinq, six, sept, huit, neuf, dix

Deux et deux font quatre.

Quel jour est-ce aujourd'hui? C'est aujourd'hui lundi, mardi, jeudi, . . .

Quel mois est-ce? C'est le mois de janvier, février, . . .

6. *Le corps* (the body).

La main, la tête, la bouche, la jambe, . . .

7. *Les animaux* (animals).

Les animaux domestiques: le chien, le chat, le coq, le cheval, le mouton

Les animaux de la jungle: le tigre, le lion, l'éléphant, le singe

Le coq français dit cocorico.

Le chien français dit oua-oua.

8. *Les adjectifs de couleur, de dimension, d'émotion* (the adjectives of color, size, and emotion).

9. *Les adverbes* (adverbs).

Très, beaucoup, bien, mal, peu, aussi, encore, toujours

10. *Les prépositions*. Prepositions are always introduced in context, as part of a pattern or expression: à, de, dans, sur, chez, sous, devant, derrière.

11. *Les verbes et les expressions verbales* (verbs and verb expressions). Verb forms are

OCTOBER: A language unit for UN Day

to be learned in context, not as paradigms to be memorized. Avoid explanation and analysis of number and gender. The relationship of the feminine/masculine pronouns, adjective endings, articles, and so on will become evident through use. Plural verb endings are distinguished by sound changes. As verb patterns are learned, also use the question and negative patterns.

Language activities—These language activities have three key factors in common. They simulate meaningful communication; they create a situational need to respond either through word or action, as in normal communication; the speech patterns that are elicited, although seemingly free responses, are in reality highly controlled as to syntax and lexical range. This example illustrates these points.

Teacher (pointing to picture of dog): Qu'est-ce que c'est, Jeanne?

Jeanne: C'est un chien, madame.

Teacher (pointing again): Dis-moi, Paul, est-ce un chien ou un crocodile? (Here the child has the option of fact or humor, but not of syntax.)

Paul: C'est un crocodile!

Teacher (dramatically): Oh, quel crocodile! C'est vrai? C'est un crocodile? (Again, several possibilities, but all correct as to structure. Incidentally, that "oh" is a French "oh," à la Maurice Chevalier. Children will pick up on such sounds and enjoy them.)

The drills and repetition necessary for language facility can be in the form of games, minidialogues, question/rejoinder techniques, and even songs. Choral practice, particularly of new items, is fun and productive. Be dramatic, energetic, and enthusiastic as you model the utterances and lead the chorus of repeating children.

1. To teach the adjectives *grand/petit,* use pictures, broad gestures, and repetition.

Teacher: Voici un éléphant. Il est grand, très, très grand. Répétez, s'il vous plaît. Grand. Grand. Très grand. Il est grand, très grand. (Call for several choral repetitions of each word and phrase; then ask smaller groups and individuals to perform. Model the utterance frequently.)

Teacher: Voici un chat. Il est petit, très, très petit. (This practice could lead naturally to subsequent drill based on the pattern: C'est un grand/petit animal, livre, garçon, etc. Vary also with practice on color adjectives and so on.)

2. *Où Est?* (Where is?) Hide or relocate classroom objects, pictures, and so on.

Teacher: Où est la craie?

Responses: Voici/voilà la craie. La craie est sur la table, derrière le livre, and so on.

3. *Object identification and description.* Use pictures, flannelboard cutouts, actual objects. Each child chooses or finds an object, shows it, names it, describes it, asks a question about it, and so on.

4. *Devinettes.* (Riddles are fun and excellent for listening and comprehension.)

Je pense à deux nombres qui font cinq. Quels nombres?

Je pense à un animal pas très grand. Il est noir et blanc et il dit oua-oua.

5. *Counting games.* One child taps a ruler, the others count. Someone tells the leader how many. Team scores inspire competition.

6. *Simon Dit.* (Simon Says is a great favorite, good for positive and negative commands. Children and teacher take turns giving commands. Verbs are added as learned.) Levez-vous, touchez le nez, ne touchez pas la bouche, regardez la fenêtre.

7. *Imite-moi.* Teacher begins; each child imitates his predecessor and adds an action, remembering the sequence and verbalizing the actions.

8. *Racontons une histoire.* Use one or more color pictures, preferably but not necessarily representative of the foreign culture. Each person contributes a sentence or rejoinder or even just a word to the story in a progressive and joint effort. After some practice, tape the story and use it as a basis for a play or skit. Read this example.

Voici une petite fille. Elle est française. Elle a les cheveux bruns. Elle s'appelle Françoise. Aujourd'hui elle va chez son amie, Marie-Hélène. Maman va aussi. Marie-Hélène joue avec son chat Minou . . . .

9. *Dialogues.* These should be memorized through repetition and use, then acted out. Dialogues should be carefully constructed so as to utilize familiar material and also supply one or more new items. For example:

On frappe à la porte.

Jean: Qui est là?

Monique: C'est moi, Monique.

Jean: Entre, Monique.

Monique: Bonjour, Jean, Comment vas-tu?

Jean: Bien, merci, et toi? . . .

Such a dialogue can easily be reduced or expanded and other nouns, verbs, and adjectives substituted. Never try to teach more than a few lines in any one session, and use repetition, drill, and role-playing techniques.

10. *Chansons et petit poèmes.* Songs and short poems are excellent for pronunciation and intonation. Besides "Frère Jacques" and "Alouette," pupils will enjoy counting and alphabet songs, traditional children's songs, holiday songs, nursery rhymes, animal poems, and so on.

Cultural activities—In discussing the teaching of a foreign culture to younger children, we are concerned primarily with the daily life, activities, customs, values, and priorities of a people. The language-learning experience in itself will provide important insights (the appropriate uses of tu and vous, the formulas of politesse that are part of everyday speech and behavior such as "Bonjour, madame" instead of "hi," and "Oui, monsieur" rather than "yeah"). In this sense language is indeed culture. But much remains to be dealt with explicitly and objectively in the classroom. The following suggestions will be generally useful.

Culture instruction and activities are to be offered in the native language. It will be quite a while before your pupils (and possibly you) will be able to handle free discussion in the foreign language. Avoid, if at all possible, mixing or alternating the two during a given instructional period.

Do use colorful and authentic realia and opt for quality over quantity. Change your bulletin board often, even if the display is limited to one poster or a small exhibit of foreign coins. A painless method of introducing a little culture with a capital *C* is by a one-at-a-time posting of art reproductions, which can trigger a variety of valuable language activities.

Aim for simplicity of presentation and appropriateness. Munching on a tartine, a favorite casse-croûte among French children, or listening to a story about Père Noël will leave a lasting impression. Here are some suggestions.

1. *Les enfants français* (French children). Role play a typical French elementary school day, games indoors and out, food and table manners, family fun, summer vacations.

2. *Les fêtes* (holidays and celebrations).

3. *Les contes.* Many stories and books enjoyed by French children can be found in translation. Favorites include the endless adventures of Babar the Elephant and Perrault's fairy tales. Try reading aloud in French "Le Petit Chaperon Rouge" (Little Red Riding Hood) or "Le Petit Poucet" (Tom Thumb) to the accompaniment of pictures and your brand of mime, and see how much smaller the world appears. Consider also French picture books, alphabet books, and so on from

your college resource library.

4. *Le monde francophone* (The French-speaking world). Not all French-speaking people live in France. Quebec, parts of the Caribbean, Africa, Louisiana, even parts of New England offer distinctive views of francophone culture. Whether for specific geographic or ethnic reasons, or simply because you think it important, consider including at least a brief realization that people the world over speak some form of the French language and have inherited aspects of French culture.

4-6 Curriculum

This program will include all the vocabulary, structures, and expressions detailed earlier. The material that follows builds upon the foundation already established and provides activities suitable for older or more proficient children.

Vocabulary and contextual activities—
1. *Les vêtements* (clothing).

Le pantalon, le blue-jean, le pull-over, le chandail, le manteau, la chemise, la jupe, la robe, la veste, les chaussures, les snow-boots, les souliers.

Qu'est-ce que tu portes aujourd'hui? Je porte un pantalon bleu et une chemise blanche.

Qu'est-ce que tu fais le matin? Je m'habille.

2. *L'heure, les saisons, le temps* (time, seasons, weather).

Le matin, l'après-midi, le soir, la nuit
Bonsoir, bonne nuit
En été, en automne, en hiver, au printemps
Il fait beau/du soleil/mauvais/froid/chaud.
Il pleut. Il neige. La neige est blanche.

Aujord'hui, demain, la semaine prochaine. (Note: This program involves only the present tense and the immediate future as in ''je vais manger. Il va neiger.'')

3. *La nourriture et les repas* (food and meals).

Le pain, la baguette, le petit pain, le poulet, le biftek, la poisson

Les légumes: les carottes, les petits pois, les haricots, les tomates, la salade

Les fruits: la pomme, la pêche, l'orange, la banane, le pamplemousse, (grapefruit), les raisins

Qu'est-ce que tu prends comme dessert, Simone? Je prends une pomme et de fromage, merci.

J'aime bien le lait au chocolat. Moi, je préfère la limonade.

4. *Les magasins* (shopping).

La boucherie, l'épicerie, la boulangerie, la

Speaking of Foreign Languages . . .
A survey at the University of Michigan for the President's Commission on Foreign Languages and International Studies revealed the following:

● A large number of those surveyed felt foreign-language study is important.

● Of those respondents who were parents, an overwhelming number wanted their children to study a foreign language.

● More than three-fourths felt strongly that foreign languages should be taught in elementary schools.

---

laiterie

Où vas-tu? Chez le fruitier, le pastissier . .

5. *Les sports et les divertissements* (sports and recreation).

Jouer au football.

Aller au cinéma. Ecouter la musique/les disques. Regarder la télévision (la télé)

Est-ce un bon film? Oui, très bon, très amusant.

6. *Adjectifs*.

7. *Adverbes et conjonctions* (to be learned as needed).

8. *Verbes et expressions verbales*. Continue to introduce verbs and verb expressions as needed and with discretion.

Language activities—(in addition to those described earlier)—*Montrer et raconter* (show and tell). Follow the familiar procedure, but in the foreign language. If the subject of discussion bears on the foreign culture, so much the better. For results, go over the previous day's presentation with the child. The rest of the class is expected to listen actively, ask and answer questions, perhaps work on a related dialogue or story. For example:

Voici un pain français. C'est une baguette. La baguette est très longue. Elle est délicieuse. J'achète la baguette chez le boulanger. Je porte la baguette chez moi comme ça sans un sac de papier. Les francais mangeant beaucoup de pain. Ils aiment beaucoup le pain. Moi, j'aime le pain aussi.

1. *Vingt-et-une questions* (twenty questions). Play it as usual, but choose subjects carefully.

2. *Number Bingo* (easy number practice). The winner reads the numbers aloud.

3. *Faire ou ne pas faire*. (Students may mime affirmative but not negative statements and are eliminated when in error.) Good for listening comprehension. Example:

Le matin je me lève. Je ne ferme pas la

---

fenêtre. Je me brosse les dents. Mais je ne me brosse pas les cheveux. Je prends mon petit déjeuner. Et je mange beaucoup . . . .

Cultural activities—In addition to the topics already described, consider sports, recreation, transportation, and family relationships. The unit on food suggests a little basic French cuisine, maybe a cafe luncheon complete with garçon and serveuse. According to your facilities and talents, how about a sandwich du fromage or a croque-monsieur (grilled ham and cheese) or even an omelette and a mousse au chocolat?

Expand your literary adventures to include legends of the past. Aesop's fables are part of every French child's heritage, as are the stories of Renard the Fox and his animal friends. Tales of Roland and Oliver, Joan of Arc, Madame Curie, Louis Pasteur, and the little juggler of Notre Dame will leave lasting impressions of dedication and courage in the French tradition. And on the lighter side, try French comic books: the Asterix series (available in translation), the adventures of Tin Tin, even Peanuts and his friends, published in many languages.

As a more ambitious project, plan a French Day and invite another class or two to join yours for music, games, storytelling, food, maybe a play or some original skits. You may find your FL program taking hold in all directions.

Concluding Thoughts
The curriculum guide presented in these pages is limited by intent. It is limited as to objectives, requisite training, and cost. No mention is made of the excellent electronic teaching aids, filmstrips, prepared audiovisual series, and the like that are for sale. If your budget can take the strain, fine, but you don't need them for a successful, limited program.

No mention is made of techniques for introducing reading and writing skills, nor of the means of achieving good articulation with secondary school programs. We are only concerned here with the initiation of a small-scale, well-defined, feasible FL program for your students. The returns on a relatively small investment of time and effort may be altogether gratifying. So, bonne chance and bon travail!

Janice Green is a senior academic officer for the Massachusetts Board of Higher Education. Dr. Green will be happy to answer questions you might have about foreign-language programs in the elementary school. Send your questions to INSTRUCTOR, Department FL, 757 Third Avenue, New York, New York 10017.

OCTOBER: Bulletin Boards

SURPRISE your pupils on October 1. Let them decorate the entire classroom for Halloween. Explain that each is to choose a bulletin board and make something for it. To get ready, have all your boards empty except for backing paper, border, and caption. In the bottom right-hand corner of each, place directions.

Lighted Jack-o'-lanterns—Draw, color, and cut out a jack-o'-lantern. Light it by taping yellow paper to the underside.

What Did the Mother Goblin Say to the Little Goblin?—Answer with an illustrated riddle.

Great Pumpkins—Make a great pumpkin from construction paper.

Scary Salad—Think up a tasty salad. Draw and label a picture of it.

Our Halloween Forest—Make a tree, a moon, a goblin, a ghost, or an owl. **Carolyn Wilhelm**

Wish your kids a happy Halloween with this lighthearted bulletin board display that can even be constructed on a blank wall. Make ghosts from white poster board, then outline and fill in details with black markers. Cut scarecrow, phones, and letters from colored construction paper. Use two real telephone cords if possible. *SARAH B. TOPKINS*

Use this Halloween display to motivate your kids to complete special assignments. Have each child make a plain orange pumpkin with his or her name attached and pin it to the bulletin board. As assignments are completed, the kids may add eyes, noses, and mouths to their pumpkins until they've all become jack-ó-lanterns. *GAIL MADDEN*

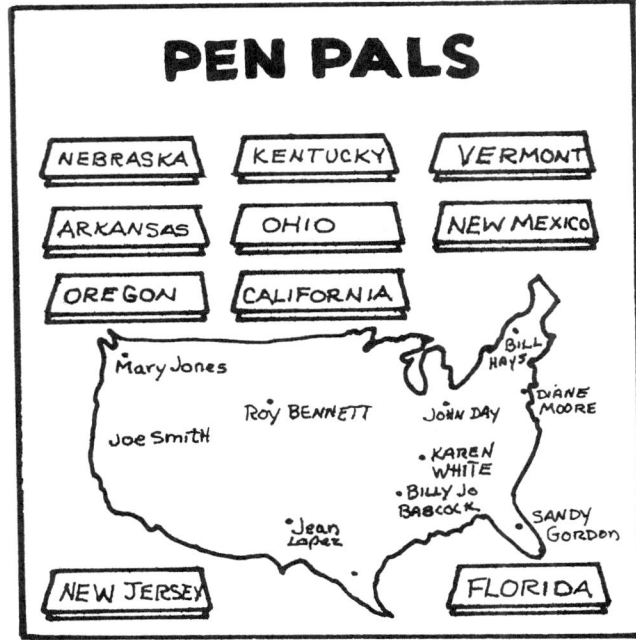

MOTIVATE YOUR PRIMARY CHILDREN with "Build a Good Foundation" when you begin the study of addition skills. Or adapt Mr. Brick Mason to your class needs. For example, he can build an alphabet wall, a color-recognition tower, a spelling-word house. Use him large on the bulletin board or small on a duplicating master. **Robert E. Ward**

MAKE ONE CORNER of your bulletin board a permanent pen-pal display. Keep track of your pals on a map silhouette and on state lists. Exhibit letters, pictures, and other exchanged materials at the side. Doing so makes display changes easy and keeps it current. **T. H. Mathre**

OCTOBER: Bulletin Boards

Using black construction paper, design a haunted house like the one pictured above with dozens of open windows. Starting a few weeks before Halloween, let the kids make construction-paper ghosts, goblins, witches, and ghouls to hang in the windows and on tree branches. Use the finished product for a Halloween story starter.   *SHARON LAMERS*

If you make tagboard patterns for the scarecrows, trees, fences, and other figures in this autumn display, your kids can take it from there. Provide them with colored tissue paper for leaves, real fabric pieces for the scarecrows' clothes, tempera paints, and so on, and watch your basic design develop into an effective fall scene.   *SISTER DOLORES CROSBY*

PRIMARY CHILDREN can create their own learning-to-tell-time ghost-clock bulletin board with a little help from you. The board's title and the clock with its ghost numbers and movable broomstick hands can be your contribution. The kids cut out the other ghosts, and all are displayed on and around the board.   **Kevin B. Herdman**

HANG an old lampshade for an unusual display area. Cover it with cloth or Con-Tact—presto! You've a **new** writing center (as illustrated) where students pin up written work. Hang from ceiling with heavy twine or braided yarn. Change display idea often—a leaf collection, lost and found station, trading post board. Create a shade mobile, enlarging display space. **Dennis Adams**

SECOND graders can celebrate birthdays with a life-sized clown. Cut from heavy cardboard and decorate with poster paint; then attach to the bulletin board. Each child makes his own poster-board candle with name, age, and birth date on it. Birthday candles for the month are tacked to top of cake. At the end of the month, birthday kids and a parent helper bake a cake which everyone shares at lunchtime. Summer birthdays are celebrated in the last month of school. **Janice Livengood**

MATH is in the swim with this bulletin board for individual study. Cover board with blue paper. Cut green tissue seaweed; paste in place. Cut out fish, draw features, crease top fins; paste to board. Glue paper-punched numbered circles in place. Mark answers underneath fish. (Add hook and shark as decorations.) Cut out jelly fish, print directions, and attach. Now for that first fisherman! **Peg Alexander**

MAKE a mural for Halloween. Cover bulletin board with white butcher paper. One group of kids sketch and paint a Halloween scene. Another group chalk-illustrates favorite Halloween characters on black or orange paper. Display at top and bottom of mural in alternating colors. **Alice S. Henning**

NOVEMBER

It's November and there's a lot to be thankful for! Teachers can be thankful Halloween is finally over. Students can be thankful that another favorite holiday, Thanksgiving, is just a few short weeks away.

Thanksgiving wasn't always in November. The first Thanksgiving Day service was held by a small group of colonists on August 9, 1607, in Maine. The Pilgrims celebrated their first Thanksgiving with a three-day feast sometime during the autumn of 1621.

It was on November 26, 1789, that President George Washington issued a proclamation of a nationwide day of thanksgiving, but credit is given to editor Sarah J. Hale for establishing the day as a national holiday. It was her editorials and letters to President Lincoln that resulted in his proclamation in 1863.

In class, try some of the many November activities that follow. You'll agree—there are more ideas than you can shake a drumstick at for Thanksgiving and all the November days ahead!

Red letter days

NIFTY NOVEMBER EVENTS

These special events usually occur in November, but the exact dates vary from year to year.

Election Day (first Tuesday after the 1st Monday in November)

Sadie Hawkins Day (usually on the first Saturday)

National Children's Book Week

American Education Week (first full week before Thanksgiving)

Thanksgiving (fourth Thursday)

Hanukkah (movable Jewish Feast of Lights usually in November or December)

2 Put a candle in a cookie to say happy birthday to the world's most lovable monster—**Cookie Monster!**

3 **Sandwich Day** is celebrated in honor of every kid's favorite lunch, the sandwich, and the man who invented it—John Montagu, the Fourth Earl of Sandwich. He was born on this date in 1718. The story goes that Montagu was too busy to eat a full meal so he grabbed a piece of meat, put it between two slices of bread, and the sandwich made its debut!

5 **Vivien Leigh,** the actress who played the part of Scarlett in *Gone with the Wind,* was born in 1913.

6 Using a soccer ball and some peach baskets, James Naismith, born on this date in 1861, invented the game of **basketball** in 1891. Basketball became an Olympic sport in 1936.

7 Two famous women were born on this date: chemist and physicist **Marie Curie** in 1867; and opera singer **Joan Sutherland** in 1926.

8 **Dunce Day** is celebrated in remembrance of Duns Scotus, a medieval scholar whose concern with picayune technicalities brought the word "dunce" into the language. Duns Scotus died on this date in 1308.

9 **Benjamin Banneker,** mathematician, astronomer, inventor, and writer, was born in 1731. He is best known for his work surveying our nation's capital, Washington D.C.

Also today, the first **Smokey the Bear** died in 1976, but you and your students can keep his memory alive by helping to prevent forest fires.

11 **Veterans Day** was formerly called Armistice Day. It's the anniversary of the Armistice signed between the Allied and Central Powers of World War I in 1918.

12 **Nadia Comaneci,** the first gymnast ever to score a perfect 10 in competition, was born in 1961.

Also, women's rights leader **Elizabeth Cady Stanton** was born in 1815.

13 All the PB & J fans in your classroom will want to know that this is the day **peanut butter** was invented. A St. Louis doctor invented it as a high protein food to build up his patients.

Also today, **Robert Louis Stevenson,** author of such classics as *Treasure Island, Kidnapped,* and *Dr. Jekyll and Mr. Hyde,* was born in 1850.

14 Newspaper reporter **Nellie Bly** set out from New York City in 1889 to go around the world in less time than the fictional record set in Jules Verne's *Around the World in Eighty Days.* Traveling by ship, train, rickshaw, and burro, she made it in 72 days, 6 hours, 10 minutes, and 11 seconds! How's that for precision?

18 **Sojourner Truth,** abolitionist, was born a slave in 1787.

Also, on this date in 1928, **Mickey Mouse** made its screen debut in the first animated cartoon talking picture, Walt Disney's "Steamboat Willie," and a star was born!

19 In 1863, Abraham Lincoln gave what was quickly recognized as one of the most eloquent speeches in the English language, the **Gettysburg Address.** And here's a surprise! His speech lasted less than two minutes.

20 In 1620, **Peregrine White** became the first child born to a Pilgrim family in the New England colonies.

21 Say happy birthday to actress and feminist **Marlo Thomas.**

Also today, Thomas Edison invented the **phonograph** in 1877.

22 In 1963, **John F. Kennedy,** the 35th president of the United States, was assassinated by sniper fire in Dallas, Texas.

Boris Karloff, the actor behind all your students' favorite movie monsters—Dr. Fu Manchu, the Mummy, and more, was born in 1887.

24 Read *The Adventures of Pinocchio* in class today. The author of the story, **Carlo Lorenzini** (better known as Carlo Collodi), was born in 1826.

25 Batters up to celebrate baseball great **Joe DiMaggio's** birthday. He was born in 1914.

26 Good Grief! Today's the day **Charles Schulz,** creator of that lovable Peanuts gang, celebrates his birthday.

Also, in 1864, Charles Dodgson sent a 12-year-old friend named Alice Liddell a story he had created for her called *Alice's Adventures Underground.* Today we know that story as *The Adventures of Alice in Wonderland,* and Dodgson by his pen name, **Lewis Carroll.**

28 "Hello, U.S.A.!" That's what Captain Cyril Turner wrote when he flew over New York City and treated Manhattanites to America's **first skywriting** in 1922.

29 Lord Carnarvon of England and his American assistant, Howard Carter, discovered the tomb of **King Tutankhamen** in Egypt in 1922.

Also, **Louisa May Alcott,** author of *Little Women,* was born in 1832.

30 Samuel Clemens, better known as **Mark Twain,** was born in 1835 in Florida, Missouri. Read *The Adventures of Tom Sawyer* or *Huckleberry Finn* in class.

Also born on this date in 1924 was **Shirley Chisholm,** U.S. Congresswoman.

NOVEMBER: Bright Ideas

MEDALS OF HONOR

To express our thanks to the volunteers who give their time and talents to our school, we made ceramic medallions for them. First we removed both ends from a tomato paste can and used it to cut a circle of nonhardening clay for a model medallion. We raised some areas by adding bits of clay and pushed in other areas. Then we added a 3-inch wall of the same clay around design. Next we added plaster of Paris up to the top; after plaster set, we removed nonhardening clay and had our "stamp."

We rolled out ceramic clay ¼" thick, cut circles with the can, and stamped each one with our design. A nail was pushed through clay as hole for stringing. Medallions were bisque-fired once, then glazed on one side. Macrame twine was put through hole and knotted to slip over head.   DOROTHY JOHNSON

CAPTURING GOOD WORK

To stress the importance of learning basic concepts, my primary group set up a display using a poster of Spiderman. Each child made a pin and string web on the bulletin board with his or her name on it. A paper spider was added every time a particular skill was mastered.
MELISSA WYLIE

NOVEMBER BIRTHDAY

The Sesame Street star, Cookie Monster, was born November 10, 1969. To celebrate his birthday in our media center, we sent an invitation to primary rooms which read:
Dear Pupils:

You are invited to the media center to celebrate Cookie Monster's birthday on Tuesday at 12:30 p.m. To R.S.V.P., please do one of the following:
1. Design a birthday card for Cookie Monster.
2. Make a birthday poster.
3. Create a recipe for a Great Monster Cookie.
4. Draw a portrait of Cookie Monster.

Please bring your responses to the center

by Friday. I hope you can come.

Your pal in the M.C.,
Mrs. White

Responses were fantastic and were hung to create a party atmosphere. Recipe books and magazines with cooking articles were put on tables. Also, special recipes for HAPPINESS, SUCCESS, LONG LIFE, and so on, were displayed on posters. The Monster Corner was filled with books on monsters-kids read about such creatures as Nessie and Big Foot. We also had Cookie Monster puppets with directions on how to make them. For food, we served a great variety of cookies and juice. What a party!
BETTY WHITE

HERE'S JOHNNY APPLESEED

Take advantage of fall's healthy supply of apples and organize a unit on the man who made this tasty fruit so popular.

First set up a large bulletin board display with apple theme. Start with a brown construction-paper tree trunk with several branches, then tack apple name tags for each child to branches. Cut letters from green construction paper to spell "The Good Apples" and tack across top.

Distribute apples to each student and as they munch away, start a class discussion on apples. How are they grown? How nutritious are they? What foods are made with them? Are there stories or songs about apples?

Next day, discuss the story of Johnny Appleseed. Check your local library for information on Johnny and record it on cassette tape for kids to listen to during free time. A good source for posters, books, stories, records, and free catalog of teaching aids is: International Apple Institute, Pennsylvania Ave. NW, Washington, DC 20037.

You might also assemble an apple cookbook and try recipes in class. Kids love applesauce and baked apples, and they're easy to make. End unit with a visit to an orchard if possible, or have kids write original stories about Johnny Appleseed and illustrate them.
MARILYN KARNS

PARENTS' NIGHT PREMIERE

To add pizzazz to parents' night at my school, I present a slide show for parents, showing their kids on a typical day at school and narrated by the kids themselves.

Three weeks before the big night, the kids decide what subjects they want to include; then I photograph them, taking shots of materials we use in class and kids using them. I combine candid and posed photos. After slides have been processed, we choose the best ones, organize them, and write info for each one. We tape the information, with each child reading a part, then we show slides together with recorded narrative--excitement builds as kids see what their parents will view. And this format provides children with valuable experience in language arts, organizational skills, and cooperation. Watch parents' faces as they see their children on the screen!
RONNA JACOBSON

HANG IT ALL

Save plastic handles from plastic shopping bags and use them to hang charts, posters, and pictures. Attach chart or poster with clothespin to handle and slip handle over a nail or hook in the wall. This causes no wear on visuals and does not hurt appearance. What a great device!
NANCY DICKINSON

NOVEMBER: Bright Ideas

EASY-MAKE COSTUMES

As the holidays draw near, so do school dramatic productions. Here are ideas for costumes kids make during art class--simple, inexpensive, and because they only hint at characters protrayed, allowing for lots of imagination, too!

Head dressing Devise a head covering that relates to a particular character. Kids can use construction paper, felt, crepe paper, yarn, and so on to make hats, crowns, hair, flower petals to identify their characters and make them more believable.

Hand-drawn masks On thin sheets of cardboard, have kids draw faces resembling characters, then color them. Cut around head

outlines, cut two holes as eyes, then draw on hair or make it from yarn or crepe paper and paste in place. Paste ruler-sized stick behind mouth of mask for the child to hold in front of face, or tie mask in place with string.

Head-to-foot cover-ups

Have your actors lie on pieces of cardboard while partners draw outlines around them, leaving 3-4 inch margin all around and leaving out arms and feet. Cut around outline, make face-shaped holes at the top and two arm holes. Actors will place arms through holes, keeping cardboard in place and allowing for gestures. Try these ideas, and put an end to costume woes!
JANE K. PRIEWE

PENNY CANDY

If your students are chewing gum or eating candy, have them find out how much it costs, with the help of simple math. If a candy bar that weighs one ounce costs 15¢, how much does it cost per pound? Multiply 16 (number of ounces in a pound) by 15. That candy costs $2.40 a pound--a lot of money! When children figure out how much their candy is costing them, they begin to see apples, oranges, and other fruit as real nutritional bargains. RICHARD LATTA

JUST FOR THE RECORD

Have you wanted to keep anecdotal records on your students but couldn't remember all the things that had happened by the end of the day?

Set up a 3" x 5" file box with index tabs for each student. Every morning put stacks of cards and a felt-tipped marker in different places around the room.

During the day, if a child shows growth in a certain area or a need for improvement, jot down the student's name and a quick note. At the end of the day, date cards and file them. Records help a lot at report card time and in parent conferences.
ROSEMARY DIEHL

samantha

WHAT'S IN A NAME?

A baby name book was the source of one of my most successful projects. As my kids learned the literal translations of their names, there was no holding them down! First, students helped me alphabetize their names on large chart paper, then we looked up all the definitions and discussed whether the names fit the kids. We laughed to discover that Brian meant "strong"--Brian had been opening thermos bottles for me all week! To end our study, each child drew a picture illustrating the meaning of his or her name. Jason, "the healer," drew a doctor and Samantha, "the listener," drew a girl with big ears.
KATHLEEN RICHKO

BOOKS TO GOBBLE ABOUT

Here's a reading motivator to carry you through the Thanksgiving holiday. Use brown construction paper to make turkey head and body and tack it to your bulletin board with the caption "Books to gobble about." Then cut construction paper tail feathers of different colors and leave them on a nearby table. After kids have read a library book and given a report on it, they may select a feather, print their names and tack it to the turkey on your bulletin board.
CAROLYN PUTNAM

BATTER BUDDIES

At Thanksgiving, when everyone's thoughts turn to food, cross-age cooking can be an effective way to improve relations across grade levels. Primary children will enjoy interacting with older kids, and the older ones will gain a sense of importance as they use their reading skills in this simple recipe for cranberry muffins. You may need to double or triple the recipe as needed.
2 cups sifted flour
1 cup sugar
1½ tsp. baking powder
1 tsp. salt
½ tsp. baking soda
¼ cup butter or margarine
1 egg, beaten
1 tsp. grated orange peel
3/4 cup orange juice
1½ cup raisins
1½ cup chopped cranberries
Sift all dry ingredients into large bowl. Cut in butter until mixture is crumbly. Add egg, orange juice and peel, and stir until mixture is moist. Fold in raisins and cranberries. Spoon the mixture into muffin tins and bake at 350 degrees for about 20 minutes.

Pair older kids with younger ones and assign pairs different tasks such as measuring, sifting, and stirring. Make sure all get a chance to help. After the batter is in the pans, let everyone go to the cafeteria to see the muffins put in the oven. When muffins have cooled, hold a party and use placemats and decorations kids have made in art class.
J.E. ROCKWELL

BOOK JACKET PUZZLES

Book jackets, brand new or worn, can be of great value in the classroom. Cut off the front section and paste onto a piece of cardboard. Laminate or cover with clear plastic. Cut into uneven pieces to create a jigsaw puzzle. Write a number on the back of each, for easy re-sorting in case pieces get mixed up during use. Place pieces in envelope or box with title on it. Such puzzles develop manipulative skills and act as reading motivators for reluctant readers as well.
JUDITH TRAUB

REMEMBER WHEN?

To strengthen memory skills and develop time awareness, try a memory game. Ask kids such questions as these.
1. When was the last time you had chocolate ice cream?
2. What was the first present you opened at Christmas?
3. What do you remember about your first day in kindergarten?
4. What were you doing last Saturday at 2 p.m.?
5. What was the first book you read all by yourself?
6. When did you learn to write your name?
7. What was your favorite toy when you were four?
8. What was the first sound you heard this morning?
GENEVIEVE BYLINOWSKI

TURKEY PLUCKIN' CONTEST

Here's a contest that will reinforce student library skills while providing info about Thanksgiving. Work with your school's media specialist to set up half-hour periods in the center for six kids at a time. Then make six paper turkeys with detachable tail feathers. On each feather, print a question about Thanksgiving that kids must answer using reference material. Each turkey should have a different set of questions with each one followed by a clue to the appropriate reference book. Then give kids answer sheets, and when signal is given, they are to pluck their first feather and find the answer. When they have the answer, they write it down and move on to the next feather. First to find all six answers wins.
BETTY WHITE

NOVEMBER: Bright Ideas

CRUMBY CANDIDATES

I use the following election activity with my kindergartners to give them a clearer idea of what free elections are. My voting booth is a screen borrowed from the school nurse. Inside is a table with three boxes of cookies on top. Kids are given a ballot (slip of paper) as they line up outside booth. They enter one at a time and vote for their favorite cookie by sliding paper under the box of their choice. Then, ballots are counted and winning cookie is served as a snack for that day.
FAITH SOLOMON

LETTER FROM A FRIEND

For a Thanksgiving lesson in punctuation, have kids insert the six missing commas in the following letter.

> Trail 4
> Burlington North
> Carolina
> November 17 1981

Dear students

It has come to my attention that the day of giving thanks will soon be here. I know most of you like to eat turkey on this special day. I'm writing to warn you of its danger. Yes it can be dangerous! Sometimes not all the feathers are plucked off the unlucky bird before roasting. This carelessness has been known to tickle people to death!

Children I am asking you to eat peanut butter sandwiches for your own good this Thanksgiving. Then we'll all give thanks!

> Sincerely yours
> Tom Turkey

Now have kids write replies to Tom Turkey.
BRENDA McGEE

THE BOOK CONNECTION

Try some of these unusual ways to bring children and books together as you celebrate National Children's Book Week this month.

Book commercials Have kids write scripts for TV commercials promoting books they've read and enjoyed. Commercials shouldn't be over one minute "air time." Let kids read aloud to the class, using illustrations.

Newspaper ads Have kids use white construction paper and black felt-tipped pens to design newspaper ads for their favorite books, with title, author, and one-sentence description. Use movie ads for inspiration.

Critics' corner Bring in book reviews from newspapers or magazines, have kids read some, then write their own reviews. Display them on bulletin board labeled "Critics' Corner." Children should choose one reviewed book to read themselves.

Book Olympics Let kids earn bronze, silver, and gold medals by reading a predetermined number of books. Use metallic wrapping paper to cover cardboard discs for medals. Tack medals on bulletin board--as kids earn their medals, they can take them off and pin them to their clothes.
ALBERT A. BERTANI

OUR "MOST WANTED" POSTER

Next time parents visit your classroom, display a large sheet of paper with the heading "Careers In Our Room." Tell parents they should sign and illustrate their career on the poster. If they would be willing to come back and share their careers with the class, have them draw stars after their names. This poster provided me with valuable resource people all year long!
DIANE GETZ

TABLE TRIMMINGS

For a useful Thanksgiving art idea, let your kids make table decorations they can take home.
Place cards Give each kid oaktag rectangles the size of index cards, and fold them in half so they stand up on desks. Next make "thumbprint turkeys" on each card by dipping thumbs in black tempera paint, and use paints or felt-tipped pens to make turkey legs, necks, heads, and feathers. Finally, print names of family members across bottom.
Centerpiece A pretty centerpiece can be made with dried flowers and weeds gathered from

school grounds or kids' backyards. You might also buy straw flowers from a local florist. Unique bases can be made by sawing logs into one-inch slices. Have kids place flattened balls of clay on top of log pieces to hold the arrangement in place. Decorative napkins Give kids paper dinner napkins, fold them as for the table, and place one autumn leaf or several smaller ones in lower right-hand corner. Cover with clear, self-adhesive paper. These decorations will add to any Thanksgiving table. BARBARA HEISEY

THANKSGIVING, TURKEY STYLE
Here's a simple art idea to put all your kids in the mood for Thanksgiving. Draw the front view of a turkey on manila paper and substitute the word "Thanksgiving" for his tail feathers. Color firmly with bright crayons, then go over whole picture with a wash of watercolor. You'll have one crayon-resist turkey who says Thanksgiving in a big way! IREENE ROBBINS

THE QUESTION IS
To take the boredom out of review in any subject, I

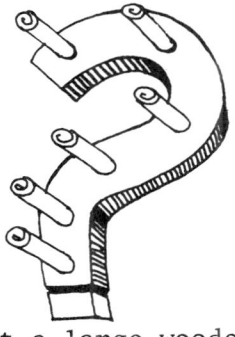

cut out a large wooden question mark and drill holes in it. I write questions on pieces of paper, roll them up, and place in holes. Kids choose any paper, pull it out, and read the question and answer it for the class. Or they can read a question and call on classmates for the answer. Kids enjoy this game-type review and don't feel they've been deliberately called on to answer a question with which they have had difficulty. JOYCE ANNE MUNN

A CORNY PARTY
This November, celebrate the corn harvest with a classroom party. Some ideas to get you started: Decorations Tie together a few dried ears of corn, loose corn husks, and dried flowers in autumn colors. Use a red or an orange bandanna to secure and attach to your door. To make a scarecrow for the front of your room, turn a broom upside down and tape a yardstick across the middle of the broom for arms. Drape a shirt over frame and put a straw hat on top. Cut eyes, nose, and mouth from black paper and tape to broom's bristles.

Entertainment Before the party, record "corny" sounds such as corn popping, corn stalks rustling, or songs with lines like "The corn is as high as an elephant's eye," from Oklahoma's "Oh, What a Beautiful Morning." Play tape and have kids identify the sounds.
Games Fill large jar with unpopped corn and let kids guess how many kernels are in the jar. Make ten "bowling pins" by gluing corncobs to cardboard bases and have kids use plastic balls to knock them down. Place colored ribbon, fabric pieces, nut cups, construction paper, glue, scissors, and popped or unpopped corn on table and let kids make corny party favors. Give prizes for these games and favors.
Refreshments If you have a kitchen, make corn fritters and popcorn. Or serve cornbread instead. MARTHA J. BECKMAN

TURKEY TAIL SUPREME
Save odds and ends of braid, lace, rickrack, and ribbon for your students to cut up and glue on crayoned turkey for feathers. JO FREDELL HIGGINS

NOVEMBER: Book Week activities

Books are the most important part of any reading program. Celebrate them during National Children's Book Week and all year long with the activities that follow.

Open books

Step right up! It's time to try some of the greatest book-opening ideas on earth! They're fun! They're unusual! And they're guaranteed to make your kids glide through reading with the greatest of ease. Use these activities to start off your celebration of National Children's Book Week, but don't forget about them when the carnival leaves town. Most can be used year round to get your kids into the habit of reading.

Design-a-bookmark contest Choose a theme for your Book Week celebration such as, ''Books Light Up Your Life'' or ''Books Can Be Real Eye Openers.'' Now hold a class or schoolwide contest to illustrate the theme on bookmarks. Cut sheets of oaktag or drawing paper to an appropriate size and give one to each participant. This will keep all the designs uniform in their dimensions. After the contestants have completed their designs, they are to leave them in a designated spot in the front of your classroom or in the school lobby. Choose a panel of teachers and parents to decide on the grand-prize winner. If your entire school participates in the activity, have individual classroom winners chosen as well. Use the grand-prize choice for your official Book Week bookmark and make enough copies of it for every child in your class or school. You might want to keep the grand-prize winner a secret until you're ready to distribute the copied bookmarks. And don't forget that every student's work is worthy of display. Mount all the entries on large sheets of poster board labeled with your Book Week theme and hang them in a prominent spot for all to see. What about prizes for the winners? Give them books, of course!

Book advertisements Here's a creative exercise that will really ''draw'' your kids into books their classmates have read. Ask each child to choose a recently read book and illustrate its theme on a sheet of poster paper, billboard-style. The illustrations should be labeled with the book's title and author, plus an appropriate slogan. For instance, if a student chose *Jaws,* by Peter Benchley, the slogan might read, ''This book will really grab you!'' To add to the fun, have your kids hold a mock auction in class and try to ''sell'' their books via the advertisements. Of course, anyone who buys a book must read it, too!

Comic strip stories Here's an idea that will motivate your students to read short stories and reinforce their sequencing skills at the same time. Have each child choose a short story from your basal reading series or a popular story anthology. The children are to read the stories, then list the major events in order of occurrence. Now instruct them to illustrate the events, a la comic strips, and mount them on poster board, making sure to include the story's title and author. Display the finished products on your classroom walls.

Book mobiles This idea combines reading and art in a classroom decorating project. After your kids have read short stories or entire books of their choice, give them each a wire coat hanger, several tagboard discs, and some colored yarn. The children are to use the discs to draw pictures of the major characters in the books or stories they've read with the characters' names and brief descriptive paragraphs on the other side of each illustration. Have them use the yarn to attach these illustrated discs to the coat hangers. Now hang the finished mobiles from your classroom ceiling. As your kids view their classmates' creations, they'll be motivated to read some of the stories themselves.

Sequence wheels This idea will provide your kids with unusual props for use when giving oral book reports. Give each child a large paper plate, a construction paper arrow, and one paper fastener. Instruct each student to draw lines on his or her plate, dividing it into sections (like pie wedges), each representing a different part of the chosen book. Now have the kids draw appropriate illustrations in each section and attach the paper arrows when finished. The children are to hold their plates in front of them as they give their reports, moving the arrows from drawing to drawing as the corresponding story parts are discussed.

Read-a-thon Start a month-long read-a-thon during Book Week to encourage all the students in your school to read more books. Give each child who wishes to participate an individual student record sheet on which to record the titles of every book read during the month. Schedule a time at the end of each week for participants to share information about the books they've read with classmates and teachers. This can be done through oral reports, summary cards, illustrations, dioramas, role playing, and so on. After these weekly activities, give each contestant one tally slip for every book read. Each slip should contain the student's name, grade, and room number, along with the title of the book. Place these slips in a large jar or box in the lobby of your school. To keep the contestants motivated all month long, hold weekly drawings and give small prizes to the students whose tally slips are picked. At the end of the month, ask volunteers to tally the results, and award a grand prize to the student who has read the most books during the month.

Character sketches Have kids choose their favorite characters from recently read books or stories and illustrate them on large sheets of construction paper. The children should then write detailed character descriptions on the backs of their drawings and use them to introduce the characters orally.

Paperback book drive Does your classroom paperback book library sometimes get that tired, faded look of a book collection in need of a pick-me-up? If so, start a paperback book drive during Book Week to encourage students, teachers, and other staff members to contribute books from home that are still in good condition. A good motivation technique for the kids might be a credit slip in the form of a 10¢ or 20¢ ticket for every child who participates in the drive, regardless of the number of books contributed. These tickets could be applied toward the purchase of a new book at your school's next bookmobile or book fair. Or ask a student volunteer to design a certificate of contribution, duplicate the design, and give one to each participant. Once the drive is over, ask for one or two volunteers from each classroom to help sort the books according to subjects and age levels, putting them in boxes in a large, open area like your school cafeteria. Individual classes can then be scheduled to come to the cafeteria and select some new titles to add to their paperback libraries.

Reading center ideas The thought of finishing an entire book is overwhelming to some kids. These children need to ease into reading slowly with shorter, less intimidating materials. You can provide these kinds of materials in reading centers that make use of some unusual subjects and sources. Following are some topics and activity ideas to get you started.

Automobiles: You'll need to provide several brochures from car dealers in your area. Have kids read the brochures, then write brief paragraphs describing which cars they'd most like to buy and why. Or have them choose two different cars, then compare prices and available features.

CB jargon: Posters and booklets on CB operation and jargon should be available from local dealers. After students have read the material, have them choose two "handles" (CB operators' code names) and write a brief dialogue using CB jargon.

Make sure to provide the kids with sample situations such as, "You're stranded with a flat tire and must radio for help."

Sports: Supply several copies of *Sports Illustrated, Inside Sports,* and a few clippings from the sports section of your local newspaper. Instruct the children to read at least one article and capsulize the events as a radio or television sportscaster would. These may be read aloud to classmates if desired.

Mary Nied is assistant principal at the Margaret A. Neary School in Southborough, Massachusetts.
Pat Widdowson is a language arts teacher at Copeland Elementary School in Dobson, North Carolina.

Kooky book clubs

The Get-a-Yoda Reading Club Remember that lovable, lumpy creature from the movie, *The Empire Strikes Back?* Make him the star of a book club sure to capture the attention of all the sci-fi buffs in your classroom. In addition to membership certificates illustrated with a picture or drawing of Yoda, you might want to make miniature Yodas out of green modeling clay for every member of the club.

The All-Star Book Club For the sports fans among you, a book club with an athletic theme. Encourage the kids to read biographies of prominent sports figures and make membership certificates in the shape of baseballs, footballs, rackets, and so on. If you're really feeling creative, you might want to create small reading trophies out of papier maché.

The Thoroughbred Reading Club There's no horsing around in this club! When kids can choose from books they're interested in, they'll actually race to read them! Print a list of books on horses or other animals available in your school library and make certificates in the shape of horseshoes.

The Big Top Book Club If you've got circus lovers in your class, this club is for them. Make certificates in the shape of clowns, balloons, circus animals, and so on.

Inspector Reado's Mystery Book Club All kids love mysteries, so it won't be hard to get them to join this club. Membership certificates? Print them on paper magnifying glasses, of course!

The Check-it-out Book Club What kid wouldn't want to earn a big, flashy button that reads, "Check it out!" Use these buttons (made from laminated tagboard discs) to get your children into the habit of checking out library books—and reading them, too! Require a short oral report for every checked-out book.

Book nooks

Book bath If you're lucky enough to find one of those old-fashioned bathtubs that stand on four legs, you can turn it into a reading oasis no child will be able to resist. Just find a relatively quiet spot for it in your classroom, fill it with pillows instead of water, and watch your kids literally bathe themselves in books! This idea will be so popular, you'll probably have to set up a schedule so every child will have a chance to take a "book bath."

Hollow tree For some kids, there's nothing better than curling up under a tree with a favorite book. Of course, that's not possible in the classroom, but you can create a structure resembling a hollow tree trunk for your kids to read in. You'll need a large wire spool and some green pile carpet.

Simply cut away the spool's central panel to create a hollow tree effect and cover the remaining wood with carpet pieces. If you've got access to several of these spools, you might want to make a miniforest in a corner of your classroom. Kids will love the cozy atmosphere.

Personalized reading pillows Let your kids make their own pillows to snuggle up against when reading. Give the children one large square of white sheeting each and have them use paints or felt-tipped pens to personalize their squares. They might want to draw pictures of themselves, their homes, favorite foods, and so on. Anything goes as long as it represents the artist in some way. Now give each student a fabric piece the same size as the illustrated

square and help them stitch three edges together, right sides facing. Turn the squares right side out, stuff, and stitch together the remaining edges. Let the kids take their pillows home at the end of the year.

Peachy seats What's less enticing for reading than straight-backed wooden chairs? Why not have your kids design their own reading chairs from discarded peach crates? These are readily available at most grocery stores and fruit stands and once decorated, they have a special appeal for young children. Just give the kids tempera or latex paints and let them go to work on turning their crates into personalized reading stools. They may want to paint stripes, polka dots, flowers, stars, or any other design on them.

NOVEMBER: A play for Thanksgiving

The case of the gone gobbler

Frances B. Watts

BRING MYSTERY AND SUSPENSE into your middle- or upper-grade classroom with "The Case of the Gone Gobbler." Though the play handles Thanksgiving with a light touch it offers advice on values of family and community life.

Use it as a big stage production with scenery, costumes, props, and all the trimmings. Or, produce it as a radio sketch and give it over the school communication system.

Scene One

(Curtain rises on the Thompson living room. Dad is sitting in his chair. Scottie enters and sails a paper airplane across the room, stumbling over Dad's feet.)

Dad—For heaven's sake, Scottie! Why don't you take that plane outside and sail it?

Scottie—Sorry, Dad. But it's raining out. I'll be more careful.

Mom—What a miserable Thanksgiving Day! The rain is beginning to turn to snow. Wouldn't it be awful if the folks couldn't drive in from the farm?

Scottie—Both Grandpa and Uncle Ed are good drivers. They'll make it.

Mom *(to Dad)*—You'll help put the table leaves in soon, won't you, Chet?

Dad—Of course. Just give me a minute to finish the paper, Jennie.

Mom—All right. But there's so much to do! I'm going to stuff the turkey now. Scottie, be careful where you sail that plane! You might break a lamp.

Scottie—OK, Mom.

Mom—If you want to be useful, go upstairs and call your sisters out of bed. I need their help.

Scottie—OK, Mom.

(Scottie and Mom exit. Dad keeps reading. Soon Mom rushes back.)

Mom—Chet, you'll never believe what I'm going to tell you!

Dad *(still reading)*—I'll believe it.

Mom *(paces floor)*—The turkey is gone! It's not in the refrig, or anywhere in the kitchen. I think it's been stolen!

Dad *(drops paper)*—I don't believe it! Who in the neighborhood could possibly be a thief?

Mom—Nobody. This is the most respectable area in Westbury.

(Diane, Lisa, and Scottie enter. Scottie sails plane.)

Diane—Surprise, Mom! We were already up.

Lisa—Stop it, Scottie! You almost hit me in the eye with that plane!

Mom—Do be careful, Scottie. We already have a family emergency, and we don't need another.

Diane—What emergency?

Dad—Our Thanksgiving turkey seems to have been stolen.

Scottie—What! That's not only an emergency, it's a tragedy!

Diane—Who could be mean enough to steal a Thanksgiving turkey?

Scottie—Maybe some cat or dog sneaked in and swiped it.

Lisa—A cat or dog couldn't open the refrig, silly. Mom, what are we going to feed Grandma, Grandpa, Uncle Ed, and Aunt Doris?

Mom *(worriedly)*—That's what I've been wondering. All I have is hamburg

Scottie—Who filched that turkey?

Mom—We'll find out, but right now we have dinner to worry about. I simply can't serve hamburg on Thanksgiving!

Diane—I agree, Mom. All those years we went to Grandma's, she always had a twenty-pound turkey.

Lisa—Say, why don't we call Stokey's store. It's the one store in town that stays open on Sundays. They might be open today, and have an extra turkey.

Mom—Good idea, Lisa! I'll call them this minute. *(Mom dials phone. Scottie sails plane and trips over a chair.)*

Diane—Quiet, Scottie!

Mom *(puts down receiver)*—No answer. If Stokey's not open, no store will be.

Dad—Out on the farm the folks are sure to have something to eat. Should we call and suggest they stay home?

Mom—Indeed not! Thanksgiving is a family day. We'll get together here, even if I do have to serve hamburg.

Scottie *(sighs)*—Hamburgers are good!

Lisa—I hope we can nab that thief!

Mom—We will! Tomorrow I'm going to report the theft to the police. Now girls, let's start on the pumpkin pies.

(Mom and girls exit. Scottie keeps flying plane.)

Dad *(shakes head)*—Turkey thieves in Westbury! What's this world coming to?

Scene Two

(Curtain opens on same set. Everyone's on stage.)

Mom—Well, dinner's about ready, such as it is. Any sign of the folks yet?

Dad—No, but they'll make it. The snow has slackened a little.

Scottie—I'm so hungry I'm even going to be thankful for hamburgers.

Lisa—I'd be thankful if Scottie would stop buzzing that silly plane around.

Scottie—Aw, I'm not hurting anybody.

Dad—Here they come!

Scottie—Boy, wait 'til they find out about the stolen turkey!

(Dad opens door. Grandma, Grandpa, and Aunt Doris enter. Greetings are exchanged and wraps removed.)

Mom—We're so glad you're here! The snow had us worried. Where's Ed?

Doris—He's getting the turkey out of the trunk.

The Thompsons *(stunned)*—Turkey?

(Uncle Ed enters with a turkey roaster, puts it on a chair, and removes wraps.)

Ed—Hi, folk‿. Better warm up that turkey, Jennie. It's sure to have cooled off on the drive over here.

Scottie—Jeepers, Uncle Ed. How did you know we needed a turkey?

Ed—What do you mean?

Mom—Why this a perfect example of ESP. Our turkey was stolen and something told you folks to bring one along!

Grandma—ESP, fiddlesticks! That's your turkey, Jennie. It wasn't stolen. Grandpa and I stopped by last night. You weren't home, so we just took the turkey and left.

Mom—You took the turkey! Why?

Grandpa—Grandma got it into her head that she wanted to help out by stuffing and roasting the turkey.

Mom—But why didn't you tell me?

Grandma—Glory be, Jennie, are you losing your eyesight? I left you a note on the kitchen table.

Mom—I didn't see any note. *(To Dad and children.)* Did any of you find a piece of paper on the kitchen table?

Scottie *(sheepishly)*—Was it on a large white piece of unlined paper? *(Holds up plane.)* Like this?

Grandma—That's the one! Land sakes, my note's an airplane!

Scottie—Sorry, Grandma. But I didn't notice any writing on it.

Grandma *(takes paper and unfolds it)*— That's my note all right. It says, "Have taken your turkey home to stuff and roast. Thought you might be thankful for some help with dinner. What's more, everybody is crazy about my oyster stuffing."

(All laugh.)

Mom *(hugs Grandma)*—I am thankful, Mother. But we were upset for awhile.

Diane—It's Scottie's fault! He and his childish paper airplanes!

Dad *(chuckles)*—But it is pretty funny that the one clue to the mystery was whizzing around our heads all morning, and we never knew it.

Scottie—I really am sorry. Will everyone forgive me?

Grandma—Of course, we will. You didn't mean to do it. And on Thanksgiving Day no one wants to hold a grudge.

Scottie—Now the mystery of the stolen turkey has been solved, the whole family's together, and we're going to have turkey with hamburgers as a side dish. Happy Thanksgiving, everybody! ☐

NOVEMBER: Exploring a sticky subject

Activities for National Stamp-Collecting Month

THE postage stamp offers an excellent opportunity to bring into the classroom, at every grade level, a variety of learning experiences.

An effective way to initiate your unit on stamps is to mail each of your students a letter. Tell them that the class will soon start to study stamps and the post office, and ask them to bring the canceled stamp from the envelope back to class. When all the stamps are returned and supplemented by a large assortment you provide (inexpensive bags of stamps from stationery or hobby stores), a host of stamp-related activities can begin.

The following sample ideas are starters to stir your imagination and to act as a guide in developing some of your own. Note the ideas are divided into two groups: **Things to Do**—appropriate for the younger children—and **Things to Find Out**—for older children.

Things to do

1. Make a stamp collage. Glue loose stamps to sheets of plain paper. Have children make individual arrangements of colors, sizes, and designs, or construct a class collage.

2. Make a paperweight. Glue overlapping stamps to a rock or other heavy object and varnish it.

3. Make a vase or gift box. Decorate a cigar box, a coffee can, or a plastic bottle with stamps.

4. Start a stamp book. After gluing loose stamps to sheets of paper, bind several sheets together to make a booklet.

5. Take a field trip to the local post office. Ask the postmaster to talk to the class about the mail system, explaining the important part stamps play.

6. Play "Who Sent My Letter." Using the traditional grab-bag idea, have each student draw out a name, and mail a letter to that person through a classroom post office. When the letters are delivered the recipients have to guess the sender from clues given in the letters.

7. Use a microscope to study in detail the design of a favorite stamp.

8. Do math with postage stamps, adding and subtracting the denominations. For example, a student might have a 13¢ and a 9¢ stamp; another a 17¢ stamp. What stamp would the second child need to get the total value of the first one's stamps?

9. Hold a math bee. Using an overhead projector, flash stamps on the wall. Students then multiply, divide, subtract.

10. As a culminating activity, conduct a Design-Your-Own-Stamp contest. Display all entries, highlighting winners.

Things to find out

1. Have each student select a small research project on the subject of postage rates and classifications. What are bulk rates, book rates, package rates? How much faster is foreign air mail than surface mail, special delivery than first class, and so on?

2. Invite, if possible, a philatelist to show and explain his collection to the class.

3. Collect 15 foreign stamps. Locate the country for each, using maps and globes.

4. Research nonpostage kinds of stamps and their uses: Christmas or Easter seals, trading stamps, stamps attached to commercial products to show taxes have been paid (cigarettes, playing cards, alcohol).

5. Organize a research unit on the history of the postal service in the United States and the world. Divide the class into three groups. Group one selects and reports on common methods of mail transport. Group two researches more unusual modes like the Pony Express and messenger services. Group three discusses rural free delivery and today's transportation of mail.

6. Find out how and where postage stamps are made. What materials are used in making stamps? What is made in the Bureau of Printing and Engraving in Washington, D.C.?

7. See how well zip codes work. Mail two letters to a distant place. Leave the zip code off one. Does it arrive any later than the letter with the zip?

8. Discuss the etymology of the word *stamp*. Note how it works in words of phrases like *stampede* and *stamp out*.

9. As a culminating activity, ask each student to choose a commemorative United States stamp, research its history, and write a one- or two-paragraph composition about it. ☐

Jean Beam teaches kindergarten in Clemmons Elementary School, North Carolina; **Peggy Rhodes** substitutes at the R. J. Reynolds School, Winston-Salem, North Carolina.

NOVEMBER: Diane Crane's gift ideas

From teacher with love

Something edible

Students will always enjoy an edible gift. Two favorite recipes of mine are:

Peanut Butter Balls

1 lb. or 2 c. crunchy peanut butter
1 lb. confectionary sugar
6 tbsp. margarine
1 tbsp. vanilla
¼ c. evaporated milk

Mix together with a processor or hand mixer. Form into balls and dip, on the end of a fork, into chocolate coating made by melting a large bag of chocolate chips in top of double boiler. Put on waxed paper to harden. Makes 80 balls.

Snap, Crackle, Pop-Its

Cook together, stirring constantly for 6 minutes:

1 stick margarine
1 egg
1 lb. (2½ c.) cut-up dates
1 c. sugar

Add 2 cups of Rice Krispies. Form into balls and roll in coconut. Makes 50.

Package balls by placing a square of waxed paper on the back of a small decorative paper napkin, putting balls in center and tying edges up and together with bright rug yarn.

Personalized presents

Buy a small child's printing set. Discard the printing pad included with the set and use regular stamp pads to make small sets of personalized stationery bearing each child's initials, or stamp first name in a repeat pattern on brown lunch bags. For a handy over-the-arm carrier for any bags, fasten two spring clips together with a length of braided yarn. Paint child's initials on clips with nail polish or model paint. Fold top of bag over twice before clipping.

Decorate purchased Christmas ornaments by painting child's name, grade level, and year on them. Even a plain colored ball is treasured when it is decorated like this. Stickers can provide additional decoration.

Use permanent markers to decorate inexpensive plastic glasses with children's names and a simple design like the old favorite happy face. Or add names to attractive paper place mats or cut large, simple animal shapes from colored paper. Laminate mats to make them more permanent.

Keep your eyes open for novelty items in drugstores or variety stores. Plain leather-disc key chains can be tooled with children's initials and used for identification on instruments, lunch pails, or zippered clothing. Flat wooden discs and squares sold in hobby and craft shops can be deco-

rated by woodburning initials and then drilled with holes for key chains.

If you are a virtuoso at the sewing machine, whip up pencil cases, small totes, or two-piece hand puppets out of felt. Glue on children's initials and a design using scrap material.

Be whimsical

Attach bits of artificial fur or bulky yarn with rubber cement to pencils and erasers to create small wigs or beards and glue on a pair of wiggly eyes above a painted smile. Erasers can even have a set of arms or legs cut from pipe cleaner and embedded in end or sides with a bit of glue.

Staple-its are hits

All kids love little books. Staple blank pages and covers made of plastic upholstery material or scrubbable wallpaper samples. Use titles written in permanent marker to indicate "Autograph Book," "Memory Book 1981," "My Diary in 5th Grade," and so on. To make such a gift especially welcome, add an informal picture of the child to the first page or cover. Use colored tape to mount photo and frame it at the same time. The same tape can conceal staples to make book more elegant.

NOVEMBER: Bulletin Boards

ARE you reading or studying about fish? Then culminate your unit with a bulletin-board aquarium made from colored paper and individual student-drawn cutouts. **Gail Einerson**

LET the keys, illustrated below, become the hub of your reading activities during Children's Book Week. Pieces are cut from colored construction paper. **Ruth Byers**

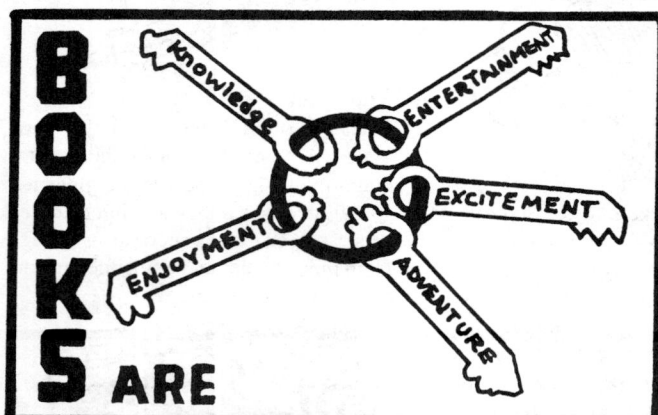

EXCITEMENT runs high as kids strive to fill their gum-ball machine. "Chews" are added when each improves, from test to test. Store "chews" in envelope at bottom. **Sandra Frey**

TELL the story of Thanksgiving with a class-made felt banner. Then share it with parents and friends at your Thanksgiving program. Banner is yellow, approximately 30 by 62 inches. Three simple yarn tassels decorate bottom edge. Story squares in contrasting color are illustrated with figures glued on, then buttonhole-stitched in place.

Divide class into groups which will cut out and prepare banner, design and make picture squares, and sew squares to banner. Hang by a wooden dowel slipped through hem at top or tack to bulletin board. **Gail Einerson**

LOOKING FOR A GOOD MYSTERY?

Use these bulletin boards to spark students' interest in reading different types of books. The castle scene above is great for a fantasy theme, and book jackets from actual fairy tales complete the picture. The silhouette, left, is especially striking on a yellow background and will lure your children into mystery stories when surrounded by appropriate book covers. Grab your students' attention with this bulletin board, right, that introduces books about the old west. The pick, shovel head, and panning dish are made from aluminum foil for real eye-catching potential. A clever play on words introduces the display below that focuses on animal stories. Cut figures from construction paper, cut in half, and join with red yarn. *CAROL FREELAND*

NOVEMBER: Bulletin Boards

AN UNUSUAL clockface signals children about the new and exciting reading material to be found on the library shelves. Cut out a large poster-board alarm clock. In place of numbers, use book jackets on face, add hands, and attach to bulletin board covered with bright paper. Print title on background. Mix and match subject areas and reading levels. **T. H. Mathre**

FIRST graders like to rap with their addition magician giraffe, reviewing number facts from 1 to 10. Individually, in pairs, or in a group, kids can change his number name and pick out correct matching number sentences from envelope. This math center is easily made from colored poster board and housed in a large piece of heavy cardboard which folds for easy storage. Adaptable for use with other studies. **Mary Dempsey**

CHILDREN express proud thoughts about parents for display at open house. Each writes a paragraph describing his or her parents, mounts it on an index card, decorates card with an animal and a descriptive sentence—"A parent is like a lion because he needs to be able to roar." **Darby Anderson**

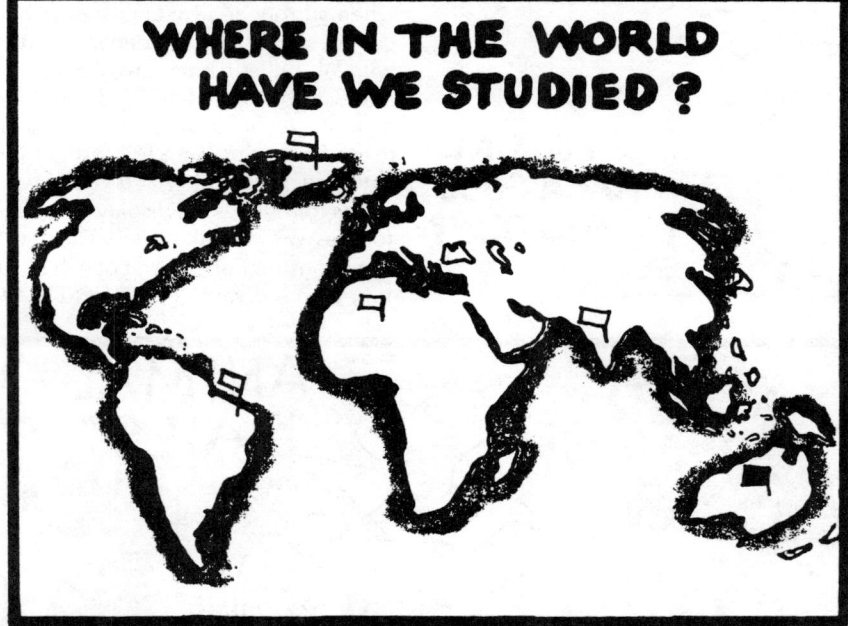

HELP to orient children to location, size, and distance between countries studied and the United States with a large bulletin-board map of the world. Cover board with white paper. Trace map on it using an opaque projector; label countries. As countries are studied, attach a paper replica of each country's flag. (When constructing your map board, use a bulletin board which can be left as is all year.) For related activities, have students draw small pictures of each country's leading products and/or industries and place beside flag. **Mary Lue Summerlin**

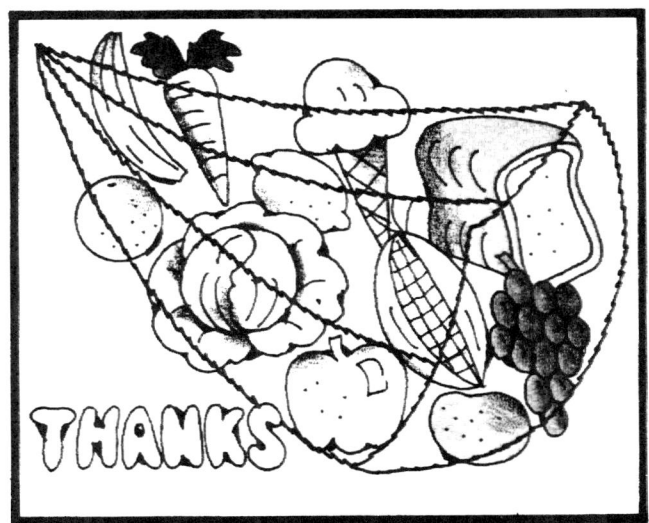

Here's a Thanksgiving bulletin board your kids can have a hand in. Start with a light-colored background; then use heavy, black yarn to make the outline of a large cornucopia or "horn of plenty." Where do the kids come in? Have them make construction-paper cutouts of fruits, nuts, vegetables, and so on to be tacked inside the horn. LYNN BRYANT

This sunny bulletin board can be made in a snap and will really motivate your kids to do their best work. Start with a black background, then cut a large sunflower from yellow and green construction paper. Fill in details with watercolors or felt-tipped pens, and cut the words "Shining Papers" from yellow construction paper. JACQUELINE ARMIN

For this autumn bulletin board, have your kids make construction-paper flower pots and staple them to 12'' × 18'' sheets of orange tissue paper. Now let them collect dried flowers, weeds, leaves, and so on from the school grounds and arrange them inside their pots. Tack them to your bulletin board under the heading, "Nature's Garden." T.H. MATHRE

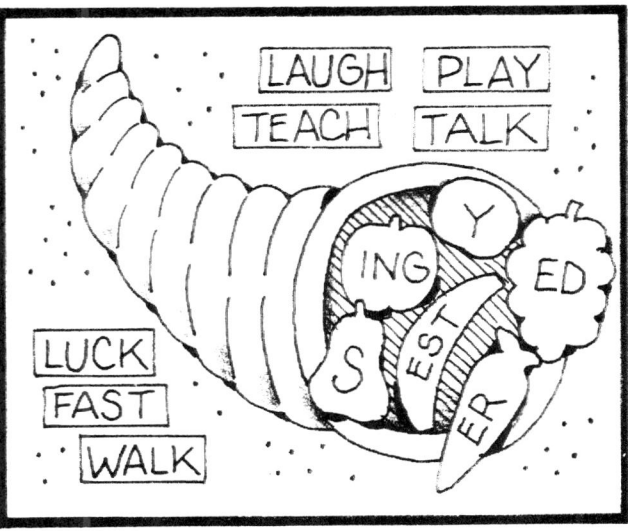

Here's a Thanksgiving bulletin board and learning center rolled into one. Have kids match root words you've printed on index cards with word endings printed on construction-paper fruit. Let them take turns placing the new words inside a large construction-paper cornucopia and attempting to pronounce them correctly. MARY ANN PECCI

DECEMBER

Ah, December. This is the month your children have been waiting for. For some, it's a time when visions of romping reindeer, jingling bells, and jolly old St. Nick dance in their heads. For others, it's a time for spinning tops, scrumptious latkes, and candlelit get-togethers. How do you squeeze learning in? Easy. This chapter helps you make the most of this joyous time in the classroom with quick holiday activities, Hanukkah games, stories about Santa and Mrs. Claus, Christmas plays, seasonal songs, and bright ideas by the bushel. And that's not all. We'll show you how to give the month an international flair with background on 12 holidays from around the globe. There are more ideas, more activities, and more ways to celebrate this month because—you know what they say—"the more, the merrier!" Enjoy!

Red letter days

ANNUAL DECEMBER EVENTS

These special events usually occur in December, but the exact dates vary from year to year.

Hanukkah (movable Jewish Festival of Lights in November or December)

First day of winter

1 Say happy birthday to Allen Konigsberg, better known as comedian and filmmaker **Woody Allen.** He was born in 1935.

Also today, the **first gas station** opened in Pittsburgh, Pennsylvania, in 1913. Before this, gas was purchased in stables and garages.

2 Discuss the pros and cons of nuclear energy. In 1942, the **first self-sustaining nuclear reaction** was achieved in Chicago.

Also, George Washington nicknamed New York the **Empire State** in 1784.

3 **Illinois** was admitted to the union in 1818 as our 21st state.

4 **Manila paper** was patented in 1843.

5 **Walt Disney,** best known for his animated films starring Mickey Mouse, Donald Duck, and a host of other cartoon characters, was born in 1901.

6 Who could top this? The 3,300-pound capstone was placed on top of the **Washington monument** in 1884.

7 **Pearl Harbor Day** commemorates the day in 1941 when the Japanese bombed Pearl Harbor in Hawaii.

Also, **Willa Cather,** who wrote about American prairie life, was born in 1873.

8 The **first New Year's greeting card** was printed in Germany in 1840. It said, "Glückliches Neues Jahr" (Happy New Year)!

9 The **first roller skate** was patented in 1884.

10 It's **Human Rights Day** and the start of Human Rights Week. It's also the day poet **Emily Dickinson** was born in 1830.

11 **Indiana** became our 19th state in 1816.

12 The first U.S. woman ever to win a medal in international gymnastic competition, **Cathy Rigby Mason,** was born in 1952.

13 **Phillips Brooks,** composer of "O Little Town of Bethlehem," was born in 1835.

14 **DNA,** the molecular basis of heredity, was first created in a test tube in 1967.

Also, **Alabama** joined the Union in 1819 to become our 22nd state.

15 **Sitting Bull,** leader of the Sioux nation and commander of the Indian nations that defeated Custer, died in 1890.

16 The American Revolution began to brew in 1773 when colonists dumped boxes of British tea into the Boston harbor to protest the high tax on tea. The event went down in history books as the **Boston Tea Party.**

Also, American anthropologist **Margaret Mead** was born in 1901.

17 Ebenezer Scrooge and Tiny Tim made their debut when *A Christmas Carol,* by Charles Dickens, was published in 1843.

Also, two bicycle repairers named Wright got their idea for the **first airplane** off the ground in 1903.

18 The **13th Amendment** was ratified in 1865, bringing an end to slavery in America.

Tchaikovsky's famous Christmas ballet, *The Nutcracker,* based on a story by E.T.A. Hoffmann, was first performed in St. Petersburg (now Leningrad), Russia in 1892.

19 The first issue of Benjamin Franklin's *Poor Richard's Almanac* was published in 1732.

21 Tennis ace **Chris Evert Lloyd** was born in 1954.

Also, for the puzzle lovers in your class, the **first crossword puzzle** was published in the *New York World* in 1913.

22 **International Arbor Day**

23 In 1968, U.S. astronauts Frank Borman, James A. Lovell, Jr., and William A. Anders, traveling in Apollo VIII, became the **first men to orbit the moon.**

24 **Christmas Eve** Also, "Silent Night" was first composed and sung in 1818.

25 It's **Christmas.** Have a merry! It's also the day **Clara Barton,** founder of the American Red Cross, was born in 1821.

26 **Boxing Day** is celebrated today in Canada, England, Ireland, and Australia, in honor of all those who serve the public, such as mail carriers, newspaper deliverers, and so on.

Also today, **Mao Tse-tung** was born in 1893.

27 Kick up your heels! Today's the day the curtain went up in **Radio City Music Hall** in New York City in 1932.

28 **Chewing gum** was patented in 1869 by W. F. Semple.

Also, **Iowa** was made our 29th state when it was admitted to the Union in 1846.

29 **Texas** became our 28th state in 1845.

It's also the anniversary of the **Wounded Knee Massacre** when soldiers killed more than 200 native American men, women, and children in 1890.

30 **Rudyard Kipling,** author of *The Jungle Book,* was born in 1865. Read the book in class to celebrate!

31 Get out the streamers! It's **New Year's Eve!**

Also in 1892, Ellis Island in New York Harbor became the receiving station of all immigrants entering the United States on the Atlantic Coast. From this date until 1954, 16,000,000 immigrants passed through here.

DECEMBER: Bright Ideas

MAGIC RECIPES

Giving recipe books for Christmas is hardly a new idea, but when the recipes list ingredients for such concoctions as "Love," "Happiness," and "Caring," they're very unusual gifts. These recipes can even help solve problems between students. For example, after a bout of poor sportsmanship on the playground, your kids might want to write an original recipe for good sportsmanship. A sample recipe follows:

Sportsmanship
1 cup controlled temper
1 pint fair play
3 gallons of no fighting
2 cups of shaking hands after a game, win or lose.

Mix well. Serve to every person you meet.
BARBY BAFARO

A TREE FROM THE SEA

If you're lucky enough to spend spring or summer vacation at the beach, try gathering a quantity of small shells with holes in the top, sand dollars, and starfish. Keep them until Christmas, then give each of your kids one to decorate with tempera paints. Then hang them on your class tree with thick red yarn. On the day of of your class party, let each child take his or her ornament home to enjoy in years to come. What a great Christmas gift!
PHYLLIS SCARCELL MARCUS

LUSCIOUS LATKES

Latkes are the most traditional of all foods for Hanukkah. Some say that the oil in which latkes are fried was a symbol to the Maccabees of the oil that burned for eight days and nights. Try this simple recipe in your class this year and watch the kids eat 'em up!
3 large potatoes
1 small onion
3 eggs
1 teaspoon salt
2 tablespoons flour
vegetable oil
Wash, pare, and grate the raw potatoes. Grate and add the onion. Beat eggs well; add to potatoes. Add salt and flour. Mix

well. Fry mixture in pan of hot oil. When the underside is golden brown, turn and fry the second side. Drain on absorbent paper. Makes 18 pancakes. Serve with sour cream or apple sauce. Kids will eat them up!
SANDRA WYNN

HANUKKAH MOBILE
Here's a quick idea for an attractive decoration to display in your classroom during Hanukkah. On a piece of paper, draw a menorah, Star of David, and dreidel. Cover the paper with plastic wrap. Squeeze glue on outlines. Press yarn into glue. After glue sets, coat yarn with glue and dry. Peel away plastic. Suspend motifs from dowel.
ELLEN COHEN

SPACE ALPHABET
If your kids enjoy reading about space exploration and discovery, but find some vocabulary words too difficult, try launching a space alphabet book project. Have each child staple construction paper together to make a booklet with one page for each letter of the alphabet. Then let kids print space vocabulary words on their appropriate letter pages. Now have the students carefully illustrate each word. When the booklets are completed, let the authors share them with classmates. This project with help your class better visualize and understand space words, which are becoming more important every day.
MARY COBB

WORD FROLIC
Try a class contest to give kids practice in the technique of alliteration. Choose a student to pick one letter of the alphabet. He or she must then make up a sentence using only words beginning with that letter. The child who makes the longest sentence wins the contest.
JOAN KNUTH

NEW LOOK FOR AN OLD POEM
"A Visit from St. Nick," a poem that's a real favorite with kids, happens to be a great source of instruction as well. Here are some ideas for teaching grammar through this well-known poem.
Nouns   Kids work in small groups to make lists of all nouns in the poem. Then, they place the words into categories of people, places, and things.
Verbs   Ask children to list words in the poem that express movement. Let them incorporate these words into their own holiday stories.
Adjectives   Students team up to make lists of adjectives and then separate them into categories like, "Which one?" "What kind?" and "How many?"
Similes   Introduce your class to similes by pointing them out in the description of St. Nick. Have kids find others in the poem. You might want kids to illustrate them, too.
MARILYNN R. HALL

FOOTBALL SPELLING FUN
Now that football season has been with us for a few months, try this game with your kids to spark interest in spelling review. Draw a football field on a large sheet of poster board. Laminate it, then make a small football out of brown construction paper. Now divide the class into two teams and have each team choose a captain. Give the two captains a spelling word and have them print it on the chalkboard. The first to spell it correctly may move the ball to his or

DECEMBER: Bright Ideas

her team's 20 yard line. Then two other team members must go to the board and spell a word. Players may "run" for five yards by spelling the word correctly, or "pass" for ten by defining it, too. Any incorrect answer is a "fumble," and the other team gets the ball.
ULA JEAN METZLER

CHRISTMAS GAME

Here's a game kids can make themselves and take home to reinforce math skills, vocabulary words, and so on over the long Christmas vacation. Some time before the last day of school, give each child a sheet of poster board, with 2" squares marked off along the perimeter. Now instruct the children to print their names on the inside square and draw a picture of their family celebrating Christmas

below it. Then on your chalkboard, print some instructions for the kids to fill in random squares. Some possibilities are:
1. Go ahead one space for making some of the gifts you gave.
2. Go back one space for peeking into presents.
3. Go ahead one space; you're on Santa's "good list."
4. Go back two spaces; you opened someone else's present by mistake.

Have kids mark the first square "start," and the last square "win." They should leave several free squares, then fill them in with pictures of tree ornaments or decorations like holly sprigs.

After the game board is completed, let the kids work in groups to make their own flash cards. The cards should contain math problems, vocabulary words, or questions for review. Players are to draw a flash card from the deck, answer the question, then roll dice to advance his or her game marker. If a player cannot answer a question, he or she may not advance and must wait a turn to draw another card. First person to move around the entire board wins.
CAROLYN WILHELM

QUICKIE SPACE MAKERS

Here's a speedy way to make heavy-duty shelf space in your classroom from grocery store throw-aways. Ask your grocer for several of the boxes that grapes are shipped

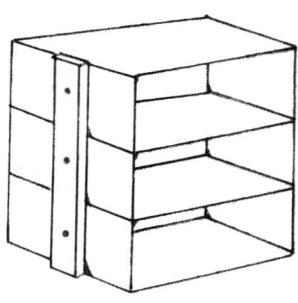

in. Pull the nails out of the front or back panel of each box. Remove the remaining flap by cutting along the edge with a sharp knife, small saw, or heavy scissors. The boxes may be painted at this point, or you may wish to do the painting after the shelves have been put together. To do this, stack the boxes on top of each other and fasten them together with a strip of board running down the right and left sides and nailed to each box.
ANITA KLEIN

YUMMY HORNBOOKS

Gingerbread hornbooks are fun to make. Teachers in the 1700s often baked them and let pupils eat the portions of the alphabet they had learned. This recipe is sufficient for eight hornbooks.
3/4 cup shortening
3/4 cups sugar
3/4 cups light molasses
3/4 tablespoon vinegar
1 egg, beaten
4½ cups flour
3/4 teaspoon salt
3/4 teaspoon soda
3/4 teaspoon cinnamon
1/2 teaspoon ginger

Cream shortening. Add molasses, egg, vinegar, and mix well. Combine all dry ingredients and add to shortening mixture. Mix into a large ball.

Dough will be "claylike" in consistency and easy to shape. Divide into eight portions. Use one portion for each hornbook. With your hands, form a rectangle about 4" by 6" and ¼" thick. Add a handle. Use a clean rubber stamp with letters about ½" to 3/4" tall to

print the alphabet. Bake at 375 degrees for 12 to 15 minutes. The letters will be very visible. ESTHER M. MEISEY

HOLIDAY THANKS
Over the Christmas vacation, cut out a large snowman for every student in your class, and write a personal message on each one. Make sure to include your thanks to those kids who might have given you a holiday card or gift. Leave these snowmen on the children's desks the day after vacation. Your kids

will all be elated to discover these personal notes from you!
PHYLLIS SCARCELL MARCUS

SANTA'S NEW SUIT
Third and fourth graders are usually tired of the traditional Santa figure. So try displaying a drawing of Santa dressed only in his winter underwear! Your kids will welcome the chance to design the old fellow a brand-new, modern-styled suit, hat, coat, and boots.   BRENDA MCGEE

JOB PLATES
Here's a way to assign classroom jobs that can be used as a bulletin board all year long. Start with enough plain, white paper plates for each of your students. Cut the plates in half and print each child's name on the bottom half, using a red felt-tipped pen. Now use the top halves to print classroom jobs and duties with a blue felt-tipped pen. Tack the children's names under the specific jobs to complete each "pie." This way, you can easily move the name plates around to assign new jobs from time to time.   LYDIA FERGUSON

SURPRISE FROM SANTA
Make a colorful border for your board by first outlining a sock on white paper for each pupil. Have them cut out and color the socks and write their names across the top. Using red or green

paper, outline another sock for cutting. The top should be narrower than the first sock and triangular in shape. Place the crayoned sock on top of the colored one using staples to "sew" them together. Tack them around the board. On the day before vacation, fill the socks with holiday candy, nuts, and raisins. JO GERSBACH

CHRISTMAS TOY PARTY
This is the season when kids can discover for themselves the joys of giving and receiving. Arrange a used-toy drive for needy children. Set up "Santa's Toy Shop" in the room where students can deposit their donations. Before you pass on the toys, use them for a Yuletide celebration. Here are some suggestions for party activities:
Find the toy Hide some toys around the room, making sure a portion of each is visible. Kids try to spot the toys from their seats. Once discovered, children can collect them. Continue until all toys have been found.
What am I? Print names of all toys donated on slips of paper and pin them to students' backs. Let kids take turns asking classmates "yes" or "no" questions about their identities. Give a small prize to the student who guesses the toy in the shortest amount of time.

DECEMBER: Bright Ideas

What's Missing? Place toys on the floor. Have kids cover their eyes as you remove a toy from the group. The first child to identify the missing toy wins a prize.
ERMA REYNOLDS

CHRISTMAS CALENDARS
A month before Christmas, have kids bring in last year's greeting cards. Children can cut around the pictures on the cards and paste them to the inside of folded paper. Assign each student a date in the month, from the 1st through the 25th, and have them print it on the outside of the folded papers. The pictures and dates can then be decorated with glitter, sequins, yarn, and so on. Arrange them on the bulletin board so that only the date appears. Kids turn over cards when their date arrives to display the holiday decoration inside.
ALICIA KAZIMIR

SANTA'S MAILBAG
Use this "Santa's Mailbag" learning center display to stimulate creative writing at holiday time. Tack eight envelopes to a cutout of Santa's pack. One envelope contains writing paper, the others are labeled to hold students' imaginary letters. Kids write to Santa from the viewpoint of a mother, Mrs. Claus, an elf, one of the reindeer, a four-year-old, their teacher, or themselves.

Read the letters at your parent program.
CAROLYN WILHELM

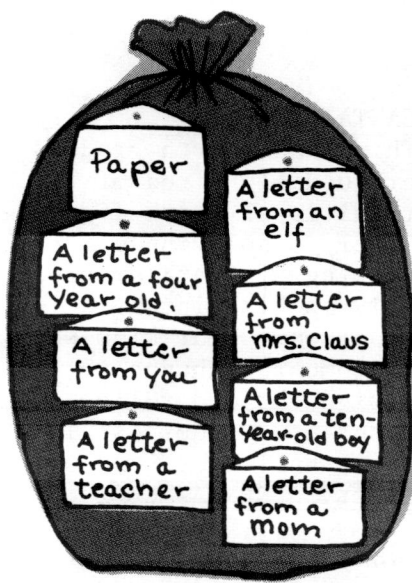

SYLLABLE GAME CARDS
Make self-checking syllable cards to help students who might have problems dividing words. Cut cardboard into 6" x 3" cards. Print one word on each card, each letter a pencil's width apart. Then, slip rubber bands around the cards, positioned so that the words are divided correctly. Draw lines over the rubber bands on the back of the cards. Slide the bands out of their correct positions and distribute cards to the class. Students must attempt to divide the words and then flip the cards over to see if your markings and the bands line up. ANNE M. TINKEL

CHRISTMAS POSTCARDS
Use the holidays to help teach your kids about our postal system.

Christmas postcards are easy to make by first cutting out standard sized postcards from oaktag. Let kids use crayons, markers, or paints to decorate them on one side. On the other, they draw vertical lines to divide the cards in half. Show students how to address the cards, making sure to leave room for stamps. Holiday messages to parents can then be written. If there's a post office nearby, have kids mail their own card together as a class. Try to arrange for them to watch the initial processing.
PHYLLIS SCARCELL MARCUS

CLIP-ON ORNAMENTS
Decorate trees and packages with these easy-to-make ornaments. You'll need wooden clothespins; paper; glue; scissors; and traceable Christmas shapes. (Use cutouts from greeting cards and plastic cookie

cutters as the shapes.)
Outline a shape on white
paper and then cut it
out. Cut details like
hair, clothing, holly,
and so on, from colored
paper and glue them to
the white outline. Glue
the finished cutout to
a clothespin, making sure
the bottom is close to
the clip part. The
ornaments can then be
easily clipped to tree
branches or package
ribbons. JANE K. PRIEWE

RIBBON MOSAICS
Recycle leftover gift
ribbon to make colorful
mosaic designs. Kids
outline a simple picture
on cardboard or plywood,
filling in enough detail
to guide them later.
Then, they cut ribbons
into all shapes and sizes
and glue the pieces to
the design they've
sketched, making sure to
leave spaces between
pieces as in a tile
mosaic. Students may not
be familiar with mosaics,
so show them examples
before starting the
project. FLORENCE RIVES

FILING IN SHOE ORGANIZERS
Organize all the loose
ends that accumulate in
your room by using shoe
organizers. You can find
them in most dime stores
at a reasonable price.
They generally contain
nine sections that are
just right for holding
standard-size paper. Use
the compartments for
extra duplicating sheets,
art supplies, papers to

be returned or graded,
science equipment, and so
on. CAROLYN ROBERTS

HANUKKAH WORD SCRAMBLE
In the left-hand column
are scrambled words all
related to the holiday
of Hanukkah. Write them
on the board and have
kids see who can be the
first to unscramble the
entire list.
RANHOEM ....Menorah
TAIATASHMT ...Mattathias
NAMOHNEAS .....Hasmonean
LANDSEC ....Candles
CEBMACSEA .....Maccabees
HAAKKUNH ....Hanukkah
DDELRI ....Dreidl
KESLAT ....Latkes
SUCHOINAT .....Antiochus
YNAIRS ....Syrian
GABRIELLA LEVENTHAL

ADDRESS: NORTH POLE
Here's a behavior
modification technique
in Christmas wrap--a
letter to Santa from
you. Request a special
gift for each class
member. It should be
tailor-made with a touch
of humor to suit each
child. For example,
give an alarm clock to
the late arriver or an
automatic handraiser for
the child who always
blurts out answers. Read
the letter aloud--none
will take offense since
all the kids are included.
This can really help to
improve students' less
desirable actions.
CHRIS CALDWELL

QUICK GIFT
Have kids make booklets
in which parents can

record the serial numbers
of items such as TV sets,
tape decks, stereos, CB
radios, and so on, in
case of theft. Pictures
of similar objects can
be drawn or cut from
magazines and pasted into
the book. FLORENCE RIVES

A SPECIAL BOARD
The "We would like to
say Merry Christmas,
too!" bulletin board can
be created by your kids.
Using holiday characters,
storybook people, or
characters from students'
current readers, kids
cut figures from large
paper and tack them to
the board.
CAROLYN WILHELM

71

DECEMBER: Celebrate! Celebrate!

Where is Santa?

Svea and Ronald Allgeier

THIS simple all-class production allows primaries an opportunity to creatively express their expectations about Santa's visit. Keep costuming to a minimum, and coordinate stage movements with dialogue.

(Children are decorating tree, singing "Jingle Bells." Mother and Father stand near tree, helping. Grandmother and Grandfather sit near children. After song, children sit in speaking order before tree.)

Todd—Where is Santa Claus?

Glen—I told you there's no Santa. See! He isn't coming.

Mother—Off to bed. Santa won't bring presents if you aren't asleep!

Todd—We aren't sleepy, Mom.

Father—Go to bed and he will come.

Nancy—Oh, I don't believe there really is a Santa Claus.

Eric—I hope there is a Santa! Or all my letters I wrote to the North Pole will be wasted.

Grandpa—What? Don't believe in Santa Claus?

Grandma—Grandpa, the children want to see Santa tonight.

Denise—Let's hide. Santa might come if he doesn't see us.

All—Can we, Mom, can we?

Mother—Oh, all right.

(All children hide onstage.)

Jeff—*Still* no Santa!

All—Shhhh!

(Bells ring, offstage.)

Melissa—I think I hear someone.

Tommy—I hear bells.

(Two Christmas elves enter.)

Elves—We are Christmas elves. Santa's on his way! We help him fill the stockings.

(Elves fill stockings on fireplace. Bells jingle loudly. Santa and reindeer enter.)

Santa—Ho! Ho! Ho! Merry Christmas! Merry Christmas!

All *(come out from hiding)*—Surprise, Santa, Surprise!

Santa–-Ho! Ho! Ho! Hello, boys and girls. Here are my reindeer.

Dasher—I'm Dasher,

Dancer—I'm Dancer,

Prancer—I'm Prancer,

Vixen—I'm Vixen,

Comet—I'm Comet,

Cupid—I'm Cupid,

Donner—I'm Donner,

Blitzen—I'm Blitzen,

Rudolph—And I'm Rudolph!

(Children gather round Rudolph and sing, "Rudolph the Red-Nosed Reindeer." Then everyone faces audience and sings, "Santa Claus Is Coming to Town," "Up on a Housetop," "We Wish You a Merry Christmas." □

Holiday Square Dance

Words and music by **Elva S. Daniels**

Hol-i-day square dance, hol-i-day square dance, Loos-en up and vol-un-teer.

Hol-i-day square dance, hol-i-day square dance, Hol-i-day sea-son's fi-n'ly here. *Fine*

Dance to cel-e-brate the hol-i-day, Hol-i-day, hol-i-day.

Dance to send a lit-tle cheer this way, Lis-ten to the fid-dle play. *D.S. al Fine*

"CLAP your hands and stamp your feet"—this simple square dance can be an effective part of your holiday celebrations.

Hol - i - day (clap three times)
square dance (stamp right foot twice),
hol - i - day (clap three times)
square dance (stamp left foot twice),
Loos - en up and (right hand on hip, then left hand on hip)
vol - un - teer (jump in place three times). Repeat the above movements for next two measures.

Dance to cel - e - brate the (face partner and clap partner's hands against yours twice)
hol - i - day (brush your hands against your shoulders),
Hol - i - day (brush your hands against your thighs),
hol - i - day (brush your hands against knees three times).

Dance to send a little (clap partner's hands against yours twice)
cheer this way (brush your hands against your shoulders),
Lis - ten to the fid - dle play (boys stand still, clap three times, while girls walk forward to find new partners. On last beat of this measure, new partners snap fingers while turning toward the center of the square, so the dance can begin again).

Repeat entire dance until each girl is back with original partner. The dance can also be done with the boys advancing to new partners. **ESD**

DECEMBER: Celebrate! Celebrate!

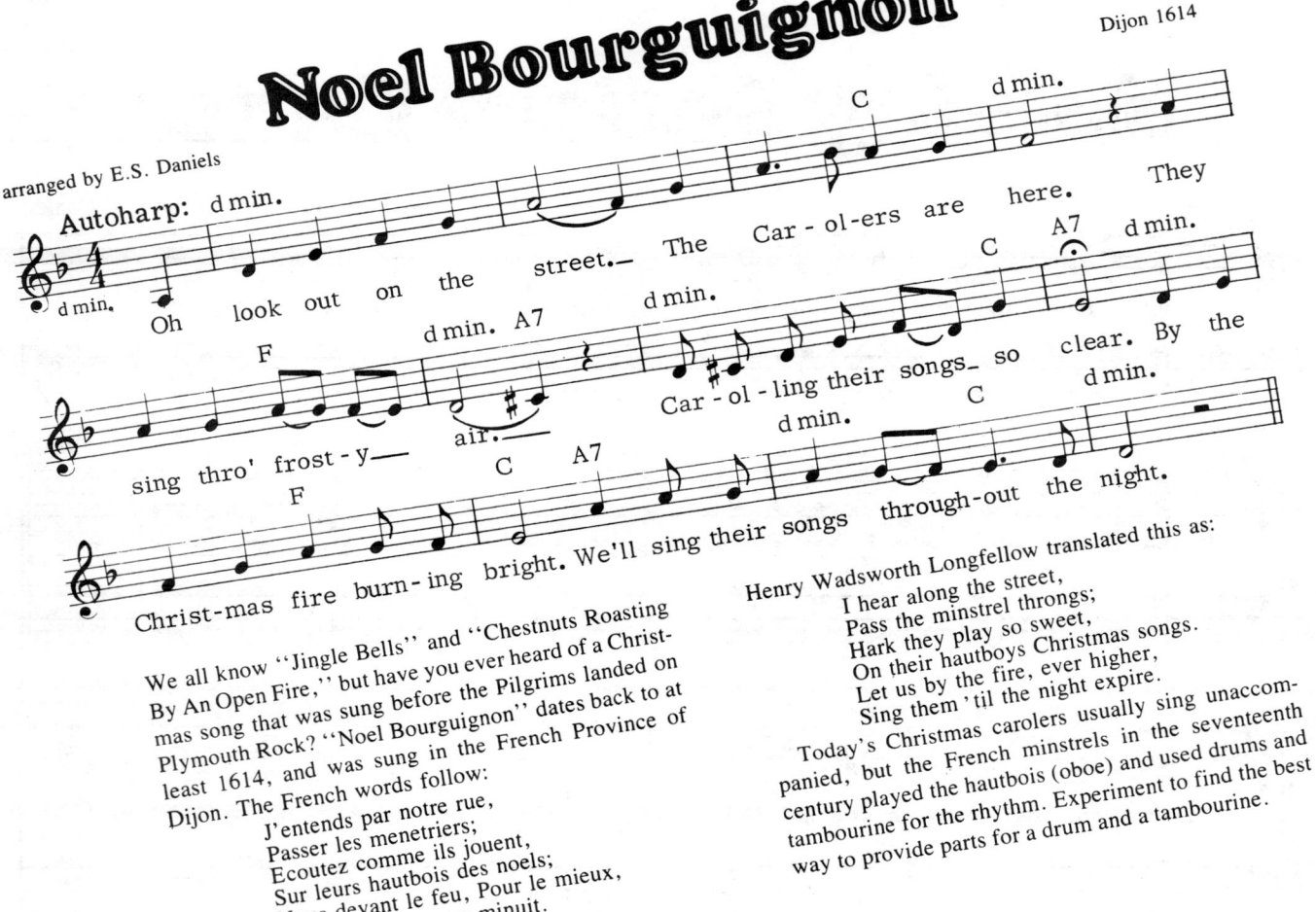

Noel Bourguignon

Dijon 1614

arranged by E.S. Daniels

Autoharp: d min.

Oh look out on the street.— The Car - ol-ers are here. They sing thro' frost - y— air.— Car - ol - ing their songs_ so clear. By the Christ-mas fire burn - ing bright. We'll sing their songs through-out the night.

We all know "Jingle Bells" and "Chestnuts Roasting By An Open Fire," but have you ever heard of a Christmas song that was sung before the Pilgrims landed on Plymouth Rock? "Noel Bourguignon" dates back to at least 1614, and was sung in the French Province of Dijon. The French words follow:

J'entends par notre rue,
Passer les menetriers;
Ecoutez comme ils jouent,
Sur leurs hautbois des noels;
Nous devant le feu, Pour le mieux,
Chantons en jusqua minuit.

Henry Wadsworth Longfellow translated this as:

I hear along the street,
Pass the minstrel throngs;
Hark they play so sweet,
On their hautboys Christmas songs.
Let us by the fire, ever higher,
Sing them 'til the night expire.

Today's Christmas carolers usually sing unaccompanied, but the French minstrels in the seventeenth century played the hautbois (oboe) and used drums and tambourine for the rhythm. Experiment to find the best way to provide parts for a drum and a tambourine.

Hanukkah Games

Judith Newman

Hanukkah is a happy holiday, and children love to celebrate it. Its story is exciting, and the many festive observances connected with it make it a very special time for children. You can help your kids celebrate by playing some of these Hanukkah games. (For the kids who don't know it, and to please the ones who do, tell the story of Hanukkah first. It will make the games more fun as well as more significant.)

Hanukkah is partly the celebration of the Jews' victory in their fight for freedom from the Syrian Greeks in the 160s B.C. The fight was led by a man named Mattathias and his sons, the Maccabees. *Maccabee* is a word which means "to hit hard like a hammer." As the fight progressed, more and more of the Jews went up to the hills to join the Maccabees. "Maccabee Cross Over" is a game for the playground or gym. One child is chosen to be Mattathias. The rest of the children stand in a line, one next to the other, facing Mattathias. Mattathias says "Who will be a Maccabee?" then "Maccabee cross over!" and calls out the name of a student in the line while throwing a soccer ball to that student, fast. If the student whose name was called catches the ball, he or she becomes a Maccabee and joins Mattathias. On the next turn, Mattathias calls "Who will be a Maccabee?" and then throws the ball to the new teammate, who says "Maccabee cross over!" and throws the ball to a student in the line as Mattathias did.

As more players join the Maccabees, Mattathias continues to start each round by calling "Who will be a Maccabee?" and throwing the ball to the second player, who throws it to the third and so on until it reaches the newest member, who says "Maccabee cross over!" and recruits a new teammate as the others have done. If a player opposite the Maccabees misses the ball, he

Quick Holiday Activities

1. Scandinavians celebrate the superseason by putting out food for hungry birds. On a tree, hang popcorn and cranberry chains; pinecones stuffed with a paste of suet, birdseed, and raisins; and orange rinds filled with peanut butter and cornmeal.

2. Research, plan, and perform short skits depicting origins of seasonal traditions. Lighting the Menorah in the Hanukkah celebration began twenty-one centuries ago in Judea when a single day's supply of oil miraculously kept the holy lamps lit for eight days. Santa Claus is based on a real-life fourth-century bishop in Asia Minor—Nicholas, patron saint of children.

3. Take your class caroling, with a twist. Sing your favorite carols in a new way: as a round ("Jingle Bells" sounds beautiful); in two-part harmony; or as partner songs, in which two carols are sung at the same time ("Up on the Housetop" and "Rudolph the Red-Nosed Reindeer" fit nicely together). Take your carolers to unexpecting but appreciative audiences—principal, cooks, custodians, bus drivers, and parents.

4. Preserve memorable events of the superseason in student-made scrapbooks. Whether titled "Twelve Days of Christmas" or "A Gift to Myself in 1997: Recollections of a Christmas 20 Years Past," these journals will be treasured possessions for the creators.

5. Decorate your room tree a new way. Put short math problems on strips of paper, spelling words on construction-paper stars, and reading assignments on work sheets that can be folded into paper cubes. Each completed decoration goes on the tree.

6. Before Christmas cards came to be (in England in 1843), children used to send holiday greetings on elaborate scrolls. Compose scroll messages, pen them in very best handwriting, and add watercolor embellishments. With a touch of macrame or beadwork, these cards can be gifts too.

7. Read a classic story of the season. Such works as O. Henry's "Gift of the Magi," Dickens's "A Christmas Carol," Thomas's "A Child's Christmas in Wales," and Davies's "Miracle on 34th Street" introduce kids to some enduring themes of the season.

8. Evergreen is a symbol of the continuity of life. A giant California redwood, growing when Christ was born, has been designated as our national Christmas tree. Ceremonies are held at its base each season. Decorate a live tree on school property and hold a ceremony around it celebrating life.

9. Help your community celebrate! Create classroom window decorations that can be seen from the street. Decorate a window in a store, community center, or police station.

10. Make up a short skit to put on for other classes. Try these ideas: a class present to Santa; how metrics helped Santa find his way; Mario and his skateboard bring Christmas to the hospital; our bionic reindeer; the present you couldn't buy; snowed in at school for the holidays; the girl who found herself under the tree; grandmother's Christmas memories.

11. Make a giant butcher-paper mural with a superseason theme—Santa and elves, a caroling group, or traditions around the world. Cut holes for faces. (Photograph parts of it to make personalized greeting cards.)

12. Newspapers often carry personal interest stories during the holiday season. Challenge students to find articles they like and share them.

---

or she stays in the line until his or her name is called again. When the last player has caught the ball, he or she joins the others and says, "We are all brave Maccabees. *Hag Hanukkah Saméach!"* which means "Happy Hanukkah!" in Hebrew.

Probably the most well-known Hanukkah game is "Dreidl." Legend originates "Dreidl" back in the days of the Maccabees. The story goes that in the little villages of Judea, men would gather in the courtyards to make plans to help the Maccabees. They gathered outdoors to avert suspicion; and when Greek soldiers came by, they would pull out a dreidl and pretend to be playing this harmless gambling game.

The dreidl itself is a four-sided top that tapers to a point at the bottom. Each side of the top has a Hebrew letter on it. The letters are **נ** —*Nun,* **ג** —*Gimmel,* **ה** —*Hay,* and **ש** —*Shin,* the first letters in the Hebrew sentence *Nes gadol haya shom.* This means "A great miracle happened there," referring to the miracle of the light in the temple (newly reclaimed from the Greeks) that burned for eight days with only one day's worth of oil, and to the miracle as well of the Jewish victory that occurred.

To begin playing "Dreidl," get a great quantity of candies or peanuts and divide them equally among the players. Each child puts one peanut into the central pot (try to keep each group of players fairly small so turns can be frequent) and the playing begins. The first player spins the dreidl and watches until it falls. If *nun* lands uppermost, the player adds nothing to the pot and takes nothing out. If *gimmel* faces up, the player must give one peanut to the central pile. If *hay* lands on top, the player takes half the pot; and if *shin* is up, the player takes all. After each turn, everyone adds a peanut to the pot, and the game continues. "Dreidl" is over when everyone is bankrupt but the winner, or at the end of a specified period of time if you want to spread the winnings more evenly. At the end of the timed version, the remaining pot may be divided equally among the players.

Commercially produced dreidls are easy to find in many areas. Or you can make one using stiff paper and a dowel.

These games can help you bring the festivities of Hanukkah to your classroom. Have a good celebration—*Hag Hanukkah Saméach!* □

DECEMBER: Celebrate! Celebrate!

A read-aloud story for primaries

Mrs. Santa's secret

Elsie Kerbow

MRS. SANTA CLAUS was being very mysterious. Two days before Christmas she locked herself in her big, bright kitchen for the morning. The loveliest smells kept slipping out underneath the door and through the keyhole. But no matter what excuses the elves thought up to get into the kitchen and see what was cooking, Mrs. Claus would not open the door or tell them what she was doing.

"It's a surprise!" was all she would say.

Mrs. Claus's magnificent idea had come to her just a month before Christmas. As she watched the elves busily working, she thought how wonderful they were to help Santa make toys for all the children, year after year. That's when the wonderful idea began wiggling way back in her mind.

For weeks Mrs. Santa Claus shut herself up in her sewing room, scissors flying and needles flashing through bright red fabric. All this time the elves were busy as little beavers, working from early morning until suppertime every night to make sure every child had a present from Santa on Christmas morning.

Two days before Christmas Mrs. Claus finished her work in the sewing room and hid everything away very carefully. Then she locked herself in her big, warm kitchen and the wonderful smells of sugar and spice began, making the elves so curious.

The morning before Christmas, Mrs. Claus woke Santa very early and sent him out into the woods with Rudolph. She gave him strict instructions as to what she wanted.

Two hours later, when Santa returned bringing what she wanted on Rudolph's back, she hurried him quickly into the big kitchen before anybody could see.

"What is going on?" asked Santa.

"You'll find out soon enough," she said, a bright smile lighting up her face. Then she sent Santa off to get ready for his Christmas deliveries, while she locked herself back in the kitchen. Santa and the elves could hear her singing away inside, but whatever she was doing remained a mystery.

In the workshop, Santa and the elves loaded the sleigh as Donner and Blitzen and the other reindeer snorted softly and pawed the snow-covered ground outside. Soon everything was ready. The elves waved and shouted as Santa's sleigh rose into the clear night air, bells jingling merrily.

But when Santa was out of sight, gloom descended on the North Pole. The elves stood in silence, watching the sky where Santa had been. Their work was finished and suddenly there was nothing to do. Slowly, one by one, they turned and walked back to the empty workshop. As they shuffled into the shop, who should be standing there, beaming a big smile, but Mrs. Santa Claus herself.

"Come, come!" she said, "Don't look so glum! It's Christmas Eve! Now I will show you my big surprise!" She bustled off to her kitchen with the elves trailing behind.

Mrs. Santa Claus threw open the door to the kitchen, and the elves' eyes got big as saucers at what they saw—a big beautiful Christmas tree, all ready to be decorated. There were dozens and dozens of colorful cookie ornaments waiting to be attached to the tree with red ribbons.

"Merry Christmas!" cried Mrs. Santa Claus, "Merry Christmas!" The elves stood staring, their mouths open. Never had they seen such a sight. Mrs. Claus laughed. "It's for you," she said. "It's your very own tree for your very own Merry Christmas!" Then they danced with glee as she showed them how to decorate the tree with the frosted cookie ornaments and how to string the popcorn and cranberries into bright garlands to hang on the tree. Laughing and shouting, they trimmed their tree.

When they finished, Mrs. Claus served punch and Christmas cake, and they sat around smiling and admiring their beautiful tree.

But Mrs. Claus still had that mysterious smile!

Just then they heard the bells on Santa's sleigh as he returned from delivering toys to the children. Instead of putting the sleigh away in the reindeer barn, Santa landed on the roof of his own house and came down the chimney, his bag over his shoulder, shouting, "Ho! Ho! Ho! Merry Christmas!"

Mrs. Claus smiled merrily, for this was the best part of all! Santa reached into his big bag and brought out a present for each of his helpers. A beautiful new red suit just like Santa's for each of the elves, all trimmed with white fur just like his. And there were new boots, too.

It was the most wonderful Christmas ever at the North Pole! □

The Little Pine Tree

A Christmas play for all age groups

Dennis Andersen

Characters

PINE
REDBIRD
PEACH
CHILDREN

Scene 1: A hill outside of town. Spring.

REDBIRD: Good morning, Pine! How do you do?

PINE: Not very well, Redbird, and you?

REDBIRD: What's wrong, old friend? What can it be?

PINE: I feel so dull—just being me.

REDBIRD: Why, tell me more. I'd like to know
Why your branches droop so low.

PINE: The peach tree makes me feel so plain.
She's beautiful in sun and rain.
And all the children love to play
Around her branches now in May.
Oh, no! She sees us! Now she'll speak.
I feel my pinecones growing weak.

PEACH: Good morning, Redbird. Hello, Pine.
My, I'm feeling awfully fine.
I love the spring, I must confess.
My blossoms make a pretty dress.
In all the world, it's best to be
A peach tree on a hill—like me!
It's clear the children think so, too.
They never come to play by you.
Oh, here they are! Goodbye, goodbye.
We have such fun—my friends and I!

(The CHILDREN enter and dance around PEACH.)

PINE: You see now why I feel it's not
Good to have the things I've got!

REDBIRD: Pine, listen to me well and true.
You'll find a season just for you.
And then the peach tree and the rest
Will see you at your very best.

Scene 2: Summer.

PINE: Oh, woe is me! The summer's come.
And I'm still feeling sad and glum.

REDBIRD: You mean to say you feel the way
You did when we last talked in May?

PINE: Oh, much, much worse—from top to root.
The peach tree *now* is bearing fruit!

PEACH: How pretty I was three months ago.
Yet I've improved from head to toe.

PINE: All she does is make long speeches
About the joy of having peaches!

PEACH: It's true. I do. But I've been blessed.
I'm so much better than the rest.
The children think so, too, for they
Always come near me to play!

(The CHILDREN enter and dance around PEACH.)

PINE: It's just too much for me to bear.
I don't believe the world is fair.

REDBIRD: Pine, listen to me well and true.
You'll find the season just for you.
And then the peach tree and the rest
Will see you at your very best.

Scene 3: Christmas.

(The CHILDREN enter looking for a Christmas tree.)

CHILD ONE: It's Christmas day and I declare
There's not one good tree anywhere.

CHILD TWO: The trees have lost their leaves
and they
Aren't pretty as they were in May.

CHILD THREE (points to PINE):
Wait! This one's great!
The best we've seen.
Let's decorate this evergreen.

(The CHILDREN decorate PINE who beams
with pride. REDBIRD flies in.)

REDBIRD: Why, I must say, my dear friend Pine.
You're looking happy, fit, and fine.

PINE: At last I feel appreciated!
Just look at me: I'm decorated!
It's true that Peach in summer and spring
Was really quite a lovely thing.
But now it's Christmas and, you see,
She can't compare with handsome me.
There's a star upon my head.
My ornaments of gold and red
Cheer me so I've just forgotten
What it was like to feel so rotten.
Thank you friend, how right you were.
My time has come! And look at her!

(PINE points to PEACH who begins to cry.)

PEACH: No, please, don't turn to me and stare.
I feel unlovely, gray, and bare.

REDBIRD: Pine, I'll say one thing and then no more:
Remember how *you* felt before.

PINE (looks at PEACH with understanding):
Peach, listen to me well and true.
There is a time that's just for you.
Your seasons will return and then
You'll be your pretty self again.

PEACH: Thank you, Pine, I shall not grumble.
From this time on, I'll be more humble.
And from my heart, I'd like to say:
How fine you look this Christmas day.

REDBIRD: Friends, now you see it's best by far
To be exactly what you are.

(PINE and REDBIRD smile at PEACH as the
CHILDREN sing a carol and stand looking up at PINE
in all his Christmas splendor.)

CURTAIN

DECEMBER: Celebrate! Celebrate!

HOLIDAY DANCE

Ch Ch (like "CHA CHA" without the vowel sound)

Kl Kl (click tongue against roof of mouth)

St (stamp foot)

CL. (clap hands together)

SL. (brush palms against thighs)

Autoharp: C G7
When the dance that I'm danc-ing is live-ly, When the

C
step that I'm do-ing is fun, When my feet make a beat you can

F G7 C *Fine*
hear down the street, Then I know that the hol-i-day's come.

Am E7 Am
When my two hands are clap-ping to-geth-er, When the rhy-thm I'm

E7 Am Em
clap-ping is neat, When the slap and the clap make a

F C *D. C. al Fine*
(unaccompanied — — — — — — — — —) G7
sharp tri-ple tap, Well, it sounds like a hol-i-day beat.

Celebrate December the international way with 12 holidays from around the globe.

Delight your kids with these globe-trotting holidays to study and enjoy. Start with Christmas, but give it a twist. Discuss customs in other countries. Then celebrate with 11 other holidays from people and places around the world. Discuss themes and traditions these holidays share. Try the activities mentioned. Go international this holiday season!

The many faces of Christmas

American children arise early Christmas morning to open gifts under the Christmas tree. In many European countries, this ritual is held on Saint Nicholas Day. Named for a bishop noted for his kindness to children, St. Nicholas Day is celebrated December 6, his birth date. St. Nicholas Eve children leave shoes, instead of stockings, to be filled with candies, nuts, and cookies. No bright red suit and tummy that jiggles like "a bowl full of jelly" for St. Nick. He is most often pictured holding a golden staff; tall and thin in long robes and a high, pointed hat. Instead of elves, he is accompanied by a Moor leading a donkey, two large wicker baskets filled with toys and candy strapped to its back. Our Santa Claus derives his name from the Dutch *Sinterklaas*. In the land of canals, Sinterklaas arrives by boat, riding down the gangplank on a white horse.

Gift exchange, an important part of our celebration, varies from country to country. During an eight-day celebration in Ghana, children pay calls to neighboring homes, singing and playing trumpets made from pawpaw sticks and spiderwebs. The callers receive small gifts, much like our Halloween. The New Year is a popular time for gifts in Armenia. Gift ex-

change takes place after the New Year in certain parts of Italy, also. Traditionally held on Twelfth Night, January 5, the Befana, an old woman dressed in black and carrying a broom, distributes presents. Good children receive gifts; naughty ones, a piece of charcoal. In Taiwan, gifts are given only to the poor. In some countries, there is no gift exchange among family or friends.

Feasting, light, and song are traditionally parts of the Christmas celebration. Filipino children begin caroling weeks before Christmas. A favorite is "Maligayon Pasko" ("Merry Christmas") sung to the tune of "Happy Birthday." Children in Pakistan sing carols in four languages. Nigerians sing from darkness to dawn. Paper stars, lighted by candles, adorn homes in Burma. Lanterns decorate homes and courtyards and huge firework displays add a festive air to "Big Day," Christmas in India.

Juleaften (Christmas Eve) meal is a special tradition in Denmark. *Risengrod,* a rice pudding cooked with cinnamon and butter and hiding an almond, is served for dessert. A special prize is given to the feaster who finds the almond. Pudding is saved for *Julenisse,* the Christmas elf who brings toys to good children. Albanians have a similar custom. The Christmas table is lighted with as many candles as there are guests. A large cake studded with nuts, raisins, and a gold piece is served. Tradition says the holder of the gold piece will have good luck in the coming year.

Games are also a part of Christmas convention. Ethiopian children play *ko-lee,* a shepherd's game. Similar to ground hockey, it is played with a stick shaped like a golf club and an irregular-shaped ball carved from wood. Ethiopians believe it was played by the shepherds in Bethlehem the time Christ was born.

In the Southern Hemisphere, Christmas falls during the summer months. How would that affect your celebration?

Hanukkah, the Festival of Lights

Hanukkah is the eight-day Jewish holiday celebrating the victory of Judah Macabee and his followers. According to legend, upon regaining control of the Temple of Jerusalem, they found only enough oil in the sacred Menorah (candelabra) to last one day. Miraculously, the oil lasted eight. Hanukkah is celebrated by lighting candles in a menorah for eight successive nights.

Like other celebrations, Hanukkah is a time for feasting, songs, games, and gifts. Traditional foods like *latkes,* potato pancakes cooked in oil, ganished with sour cream and applesauce, are served. Children are given gifts of money. A four-sided top with Hebrew letters on each side, called a *dreidel,* is a traditional amusement. The letters—*Nun, Gimel, Hay,* and *Shin* translate "a great miracle happened here." Make dreidels for your Hanukkah celebration. Using a sharpened pencil, dot the center of a four-inch square of construction paper. Fold each corner in to meet the center dot. Draw the Hebrew letters: ש ה נ ג   Insert pencil to spin.

DECEMBER: Holidays around the globe

Saint Lucia's Day

Lucia means "light." St. Lucia's Day *(Luciadaggan)* is a celebration of the sun and light in Sweden. Before dawn on December 13, the oldest daughter (Lucia queen) dons a white robe and places a crown of lighted candles on her head. She goes from room to room waking her family with a special song, inviting them to a breakfast of coffee and *lussekatter* (Lucia's cats), a twisted saffron bun with raisin eyes. However, St. Lucia's Day is not just a home celebration. Every village chooses its special Lucia. Lighted candles illuminate the parades and parties marking the holiday.

Several legends explain the origin of the Lucia festival. The oldest tale, dating to pagan days, combines the goddess Freya, whose symbols were light and the household cat, and the winter solstice, which fell on December 13, according to the old Julian calendar. A maiden with a crown of burning candles who brought food to a starving village is the source of another version. Others say the festival stems from an Italian legend. A Sicilian Lucia, condemned to death for her religious beliefs, was later canonized. The Italian song "Santa Lucia" became the traditional song of the Swedish Lucias, still sung during the festival today.

Make Lucia cats for your international holiday festival. You will need: 2 cakes yeast; ¼ cup warm water; 1 cup evaporated milk; ⅔ cup sugar; 3 large eggs; 1 teaspoon salt; ½ cup butter, melted; 4½ cups flour; 1½ cups rolled oats; 1 teaspoon saffron or crushed cardamon seed.

Dissolve yeast in warm water. Blend evaporated milk, sugar, eggs, salt, and melted butter. Mix thoroughly. Add yeast mixture, rolled oats, saffron and half the flour. Beat well, then stir in enough flour to make a soft but workable dough. Turn onto floured breadboard and knead until smooth. Place in bowl, brush with butter, cover, and let rise until double. When doubled, punch down, turn out on board, cover, let rest for 10 minutes. Take small portion of dough at a time and roll into a rope. Cut ropes into 5-inch strips, each strip about ½-inch wide. Cross to form an X; turn each end out slightly. Place on buttered cookie sheets and let rise. Decorate with raisins or almonds and brush with butter. Bake at 350° for 15-20 minutes.

Posadas—the Mexican holiday

Posada, in Mexican meaning "inn" or "lodging house," commemorates the hardships of Mary and Joseph in their attempt to find shelter in Bethlehem. For nine consecutive nights, beginning on December 13, the search for lodging is reenacted in a festive ritual.

Houses are decorated with Spanish moss, flowers, and colored-paper lanterns. During the festival, children carry *faroles,* transparent-paper lanterns containing lighted candles attached to long poles. The procession is followed by a party with fireworks, *colaciónes* (small baskets of sweets), and the breaking of the *piñata.* A brightly colored earthenware or paper-mache object made in the shape of a bird, donkey, ship, and so on, is suspended from the ceiling. Blindfolded, each child tries to break the piñata with a stick while it is raised and lowered. When broken, children scramble for the candy and gifts that spill out.

Add a touch of the Posadas to your celebration by making Mexican lanterns. Use plain construction paper or decorate foil. Draw a rectangle. Cut out and fold in half lengthwise. On the wrong side, draw a margin the width desired for the top and bottom edge of lantern. Fold each side outward along line to make crease. Open out these folds but keep paper folded lengthwise. Starting at fold, cut slits about ¼ inch apart, only up to second fold lines. Make a handle from a long, narrow strip of paper and paste in place. Push outer edges of lantern toward center so top and bottom form two circles, then separate circles. Fasten edges together with paste. Hang around your room!

Divali, Indian Festival of Lights

Honoring Lakshmi, the goddess of good luck and prosperity, Divali is observed sometime in December each year. A popular holiday in India, the three-day celebration also honors King Rama, who according to ancient legend returned during this season after a 14-year exile. People bathed the city of Ayodhaya in light and rejoiced until dawn to welcome Rama, the symbol of goodness, virtue, and nobility.

To prepare for this holiday, every home is scrubbed spotless. Diya lamps are made by placing wicks in small earthenware bowls, then filling them with oil. On the third day, families dress in their best and eat an elaborate 14-dish breakfast served on a round tray called *thali.* The center is filled with rice or a flat bread called *chapaty.* Most celebrants eat with their fingers, using only the right hand and never allowing food to reach above the first joints of the thumb and two fingers. Friends and relatives exchange gifts. A colorful parade with bands, streamers, and firecrackers is held. At dusk, thousands of colored lamps are lit to attract the blessing of Lakshmi, who flies on the wings of the Heavenly Swan. Girls float their diya lamps across the river. If the light burns until the lamp is out of sight, it means good luck will visit the family in the coming year.

Loy Krathong—a Thai holiday

In Thai, *loy* means to float and *krathong,* leaf cups. Loy Krathong, celebrated during the month of December, is the festival of floating leaf cups in Thailand.

This holiday also has several meanings. Some believe it is to ask pardon from the goddess of the water for pollution of the rivers and canals. Others celebrate the worship of Buddha's footprint, which legend says was left on the shore of the Nammada River.

To make a krathong, the Thais cut two round pieces from banana leaf and place them one atop the other. Making a five-cornered cup, they fasten each seam with a sharp bamboo pin. Jasmine is put along the edges, and the center is stuffed with small pieces of leaf; a slim candle, incense sticks, and gardenias are placed in the middle. At nightfall, friends and relatives go to the river bank singing a special song. Wishes made, lighted krathongs are floated as fireworks explode in the sky. Thais believe if the light lasts until the krathong disappears, the wish will come true.

Kwanza, an Afro-American celebration

Kwanza is derived from African festivals celebrating the first fruits of the harvest. On each night, a candle is lit in the *kinara*, a seven-branched candelabra representing the seven principles of traditional African society: unity, self-determination, collective work and responsibility, cooperative economics, purpose, creativity, and faith. The kinara rests on the *mkeka*, the traditional straw mat, along with an ear of corn for each child in the family and fruits and vegetables—harvest symbols representing "food for life." On the last day of the holiday, New Year's Eve, a great community feast is held. There are red, black, and green decorations; gifts; and songs. Children give friends and relatives homemade necklaces and pot holders. Make Kwanza necklace by stringing macaroni shells painted red, green, and black.

Wren Day in Ireland

An Irish folktale tells of birds gathering to choose a king. A contest was arranged; the bird that flew highest would be crowned. Knowing the eagle would win, the wren climbed on his back and remained there until the eagle had spent his strength. Then the wren flew higher. On December 26, Wren Day in Ireland, young boys don costumes and carrying a holly bush and stuffed wren go from house to house displaying the bird and singing traditional songs. Adults award their efforts with a few coins. In earlier centuries, a live wren was captured and the coins used for an evening feast culminating the celebration.

Shalako Ceremonial

The Zuni Indians of New Mexico celebrate the Shalako Ceremonial, a prayer for rain, on December 1. Zunis begin preparations early, practicing dances and repainting colorful masks. There are head masks for rain spirit dancers and six giant masks with moving eyes and beaks for Shalako, the messenger of the rain spirits.

Shulawitsi, the fire spirit, begins the ceremony by carrying a burning branch into a pueblo. To represent the spirit, a boy is painted black and dotted with colorful spots. Joining masked rain spirit dancers dressed in buckskins and beads, they move through the crowd sprinkling cornmeal. Dancers dare not stumble or miss a step or they will bring bad luck to the tribe. At sunset, Shalako dancers run through the desert, visiting houses in the pueblo, praying for rain. Men of the tribe chant while the Shalakos dance. Dawn brings rest, for at noon the ceremony begins again to continue for four nights until everyone has worn a mask and danced a prayer.

Id al-Adha—Festival of Sacrifice

A three-day Muslim holiday, Id al-Adha commemorates the deliverance from sacrifice of Ishmael, oldest son of Abraham and ancestor to all Arabs. According to Islamic tradition, Allah ordered Abraham to sacrifice Ishmael (not Isaac, as the Bible says). Three times the Devil tempted Abraham, and each time he answered with stones. With his faith successfully tested, Allah provided a ram for the sacrifice. During the holiday, Muslims reenact the struggle of Abraham with the Devil by throwing pebbles at special pillars, representing the stoning of the Devil. Afterward, an animal is sacrificed. The Koran, Muslim Holy Book, directs that meat be given to the poor. With this done, the family feasts with friends and relatives.

In Senegal, Mauritania, Maki, and Gambia, this holiday is known as Tabaski. New clothing, usually blue, is worn to a celebration of feasting, singing, dancing, storytelling, and playing games. Lamb or goat, cooked over charcoal, is eaten with rice; couscous, vegetables, and sweets.

Saint Sylvester's Day

In Belgium, the last child to get out of bed on December 31 is called "Sylvester." The sleepyhead must pay a fine to his siblings, so most children arise early on St. Sylvester's Day. Switzerland and Germany also celebrate this day, honoring the death of Pope Sylvester I in 1335. Grand parties are held in the evening, New Year's Eve. Tradition says when the clock strikes 12, everyone gets a kiss.

Genjitsu

Preparation for Genjitsu, New Year's Day in Japan, begins early. In mid-December, paddles used for the game of battledore-and-shuttlecock are purchased. A traditional New Year's Day game for girls, it is similar to badminton but played without a net. Made of white wood, paddles are decorated with beautiful paintings. Late in December, decorations with special meanings begin to adorn doors and gateways. The *kado-matsu*, or gatepine, is fashioned from a pine branch, bamboo stalk, and sprig of apricot or plum blossom. The pine symbolizes long life; bamboo prosperity, uprightness, and constancy; and blossoms strength and mobility.

During the last day of the year, the house is thoroughly cleaned. Brooms are then tied with red and white string and stored. To disturb them during the holiday would frighten the spirit of good luck. A simple meal of *shoba*, thin buckwheat noodles, is served. Symbolizing long life, children try to swallow at least one noodle whole.

Awakening early on Genjitsu, the family dresses in its best attire to greet friends and relatives with the traditional, "May you grow as old as a pine." Gifts and cards are exchanged. Games like battledore, "GO" (an ancient game similar to checkers), and "Hundred Poets Game" are played.

Try "Hundred Poets Game" with your class. Print 50 cards with the first lines and 50 cards with last lines of poems well known to your children. Player reads the beginning of a poem and others try to pick the card containing the last line. Include titles and authors, too!

For more information on children and holidays around the world, write: "Big Blue Marble" Information Center, 866 Third Ave., New York, NY 10022; Information Center on Children's Cultures, 331 E. 38 St., New York, NY 10016. □

Clare Lynch O'Brien is education consultant to "Big Blue Marble," a children's television program sponsored by International Telephone & Telegraph Corporation.

DECEMBER: Bulletin Boards

LIGHTING UP THE SEASON

COVER bulletin board in white paper and draw angel holding taper. Invite kids to add ruler-sized candles with oval bases cut from cardboard and covered with small pieces of crumpled green and red tissue. Add gold-paper wicks, one each day, till all candles are lit. **Vivian Lynn**

EVERYONE can help make this country holiday tree scene. Teacher cuts out Santa, reindeer, and sled. Kids draw trees, house, and barn on colored paper then cut them out. Decorate with cotton snow and glitter. For added interest, include farm and/or wild animals. **Maribeth Peck**

HOW MANY DAYS LEFT?

COUNT AND SEE

KIDS count the days before the holidays with this bulletin board. Attach to board 12" x 2" green-paper strips in the form of a tree. Trim with ornaments cut from old greeting cards. Each day remove one card and do activity noted on back. Keep count of days left. **Marilyn Karns**

TOYS FOR GOOD

GIRLS AND BOYS

TWO or three weeks before vacation prepare your bulletin board with a cutout construction paper Santa, his sleigh, and two brown bags (open at the top). Ask the class to think of a favorite toy which Santa either brought them last year or might bring this year if they are good. After their toys are made using scraps of cloth, buttons, glitter, and colored paper, children place toys in Santa's bags. **Vivian Lynn**

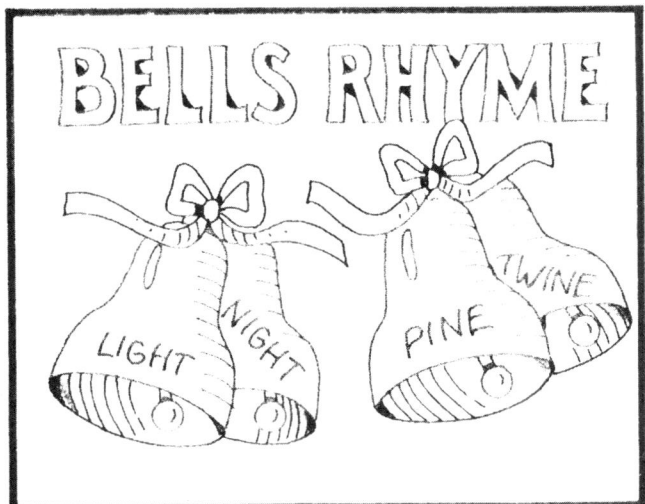

Here's a bulletin board that's decorative and instructional at the same time. Have the kids print pairs of rhyming words on construction-paper Christmas bells. These words, like *glee* and *tree*, should be related to the holiday in some way. Tack the bells on your bulletin board and label the display, "When Bells Rhyme Out On Christmas Day." CAROLYN WILHELM

Leave the finishing touches up to your kids for this holiday bulletin board. Make a large wreath from construction-paper holly leaves, then scatter individual leaves across the board. Have students decorate the wreath with cutouts depicting the gifts described in the song, "The Twelve Days of Christmas." ARLENE PACE, JUNE KLEIN, DENISE FEDOR

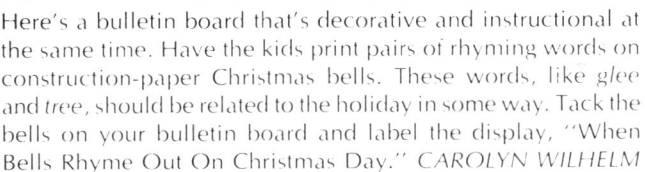

"HAPPY HOLIDAY" is a big warm greeting card on which children, teachers, and other school employees write salutations to schoolmates and friends. Choose light-colored background paper and cover a large library, hall, or cafeteria bulletin board. Then paste on a huge green-paper evergreen trimmed with cutout ornaments made from old greeting cards. With a red felt-tip pen, letter in "Happy Holiday." **Frances C. Caskey**

DECEMBER: Bulletin Boards

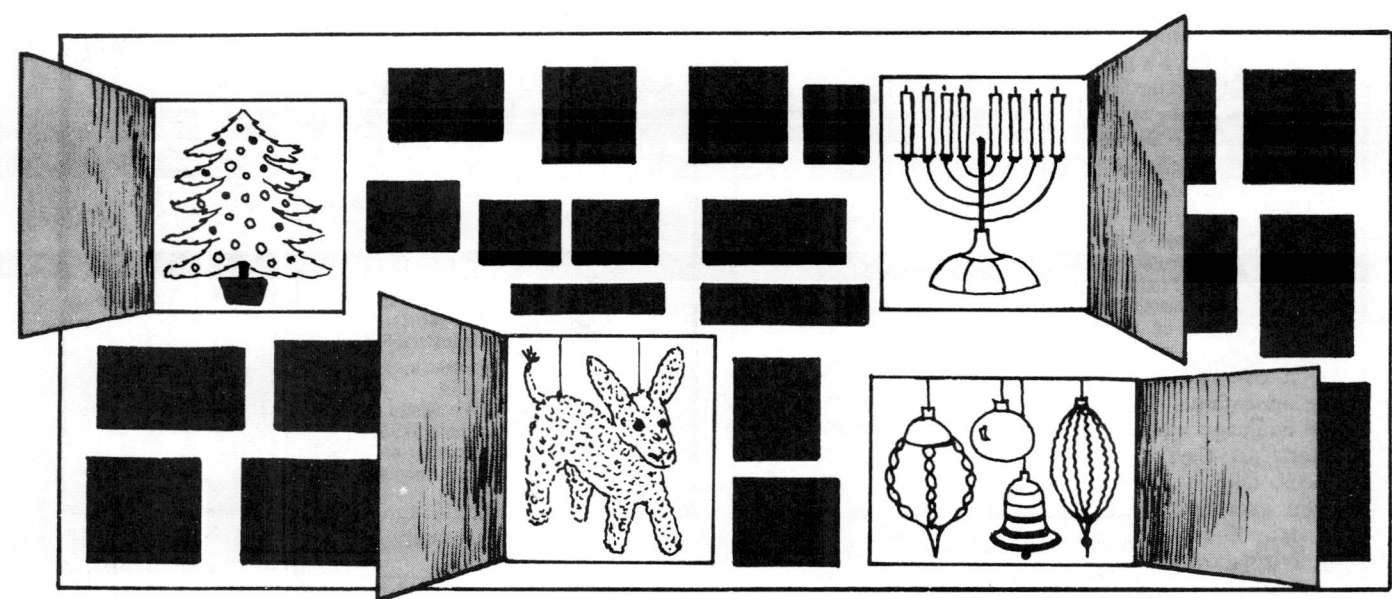

CELEBRATE December with a decoration-a-day. Your bulletin board, fashioned after an Advent calendar, becomes a fun-filled package that children take turns opening. Use two bulletin-board-sized sheets of contrasting colored butcher paper. On bottom sheet mark as many areas as there will be days of school in December. Fill each area with a drawing of a scene or object, or with holiday pictures cut from magazines. Then place top sheet under it and, with carbon paper between, draw doors around items. Remove top sheet and cut door openings. Attach top and bottom sheet to board, closing doors with colored pins. Open one door each morning. **Kitty Karp**

GREET your school family with a "yummy" door decoration this holiday season. The large candy cane is cut from white poster board, striped with red paint, and signed by the kids. Green holly, sporting a white-lettered greeting, broadcasts your seasonal message. **Kris Tice**

WARM red-paper hearts proclaim holiday love and good wishes. Each student cuts out a heart (or as many as he wishes), turns it upside down, and writes the name of a person he loves. Tree is built (pinned) from the bottom up. **Carolyn Wilhelm**

This year, "bear" down on your class and get them ready for Christmas. Use a background of bright red construction paper. Cut the bears and the tree trunk from brown construction paper and the fir branches from dark green paper. Use real Christmas ribbon to go around the bears' necks and to attach colorful ornaments to the tree. Make the star and the hammer head from aluminum foil and cut all letters and dates from green construction paper.
MABEL HELDSTAB

DECEMBER
15
"Christmas
is
coming"

Use your bulletin board this Christmas to display a peaceful winter scene that all your students can contribute to. Start with rolling hills of white construction paper against a dark background, lightened with chalk dust "snow." Now have each child draw his family's house, cut it out, and tack it on the board. Fill in with fir trees, a church, and skaters. Finish the scene with Santa's sleigh and team of reindeer.
MARIBETH PECK

This year, celebrate the start of winter with a happy snowman on your bulletin board and lots of "snowflakes" your students can make themselves. The snowman is made from circles of white paper chains, and his hat and scarf are cut from red construction paper.
DOROTHY JOHNSON

Don't just have your students draw pictures of Santa this year. Instead, let them create their own construction-paper versions of him, then hang them for display on your bulletin board. Use a plain, white background and mount each figure on green construction paper.
MARIBETH PECK

JANUARY

"Should auld acquaintance be forgot . . . ." That's the sound of millions of Americans greeting the new year with a song traditionally sung at this time every year. "Auld Lang Syne" was written by Scottish poet Robert Burns, who was born on the 25th of this month in 1759. It's a song about friendship. What better way to ring in the new year?

In the classroom, basic skills are like old friends—not to be forgotten. After the holiday vacations, January is the perfect time to give those skills a boost. This chapter is devoted to ways you can help your students brush up on the basics *and* brush away midwinter blues. It tells how to motivate readers by having them read traffic signs, menus, recipes, labels, maps, timetables, directories, and more. And math skills are in the bag when you pack drill games in portable pouches. The basics don't have to be a bore; in fact, these ideas will have your students begging for more!

Red letter days

ANNUAL JANUARY EVENTS
These special events usually occur in January, but the exact dates vary from year to year.

School Nurse Day (fourth Wednesday)

Chinese New Year (a movable feast always between January 21 and February 19)

1 It's **New Year's Day**—time to make your New Year's resolutions. Also, **Betsy Ross** was born in 1752. Although no one knows if it's true, history and tradition credit her with sewing the first official American flag.

2 **Isaac Asimov,** scientist and science-fiction writer, was born in Russia in 1920.

3 Attention sippers and slurpers! The **first straws** (made of wax paper) were patented in 1888. Also, the person credited as the world's greatest ballerina, **Anna Pavlova,** was born in 1885.

4 **Utah** was admitted to the Union in 1869. It was our 45th state. Also, **Jacob Grimm,** best known for *Grimm's Fairy Tales* (written in collaboration with his brother Wilhelm), was born in 1785.

5 Scientist **George Washington Carver** died in 1943. Also, in 1905, the **National Audubon Society** was formed. Make a birdfeeder in class to celebrate.

6 In 1912, **New Mexico** became our 47th state. Also, American author, poet, biographer, historian, and folklorist **Carl Sandburg** was born in 1878.

7 What's today? Elementary, my dear Watson! It's **Sherlock Holmes's** birthday! Some people believe that this famous detective really existed and was born on this date in 1854. Others believe he was a character created by Sir Arthur Conan Doyle in 1887.

8 In 1935, the "king of rock 'n roll," **Elvis (Aron) Presley,** was born in Memphis, Tennessee.

9 "The Seeing Eye" organization, which first trained dogs to guide the blind, was incorporated in Nashville, Tennessee, on this day in 1929.

10 **Buffalo Bill Cody,** a genuine buffalo hunter and a U.S. Army scout, died in 1917. He was best known for his Wild West Show that dramatized the Pony Express ride, a buffalo hunt, and other events of the old west.

11 **Alice Paul,** called the author of the Equal Rights Amendment (ERA), was born in 1885. She presented the first version of an equal rights amendment to Congress in 1923.

13 "Oh Susannah," "Jeanie with the Light Brown Hair," "Way Down Upon the Swanee River"—these are among America's best-loved folk songs. But while America hummed these tunes, the composer **Stephen Foster** died on this date in 1864 in obscurity with 38 cents to his name. Today is Stephen Foster Memorial Day.

15 Civil rights leader and winner of the Nobel Peace Prize, **Martin Luther King, Jr.,** was born today in 1929. Also today, the first cartoon showing a donkey as the symbol of the **Democratic Party** was drawn by Thomas Nast in 1870.

16 In 1962, two 15-year-olds discovered two huge teeth buried in the ground in Hackensack, New Jersey. Later, scientists uncovered the rest of the five-ton **mastodon** that had died there 7,000 years ago.

17 "A penny saved is a penny earned," said **Benjamin Franklin,** born in 1706. This great American made his mark on the world as an inventor, scientist, statesman, writer, and patriot.

19 The patent for the first **neon sign** was awarded in 1915.

20 **Inauguration Day** is the day on which the newly-elected president of the United States is sworn into office every four years.

21 On this date, in 1648, **Margaret Brent** became the first woman in America to ask for the right to vote. It took nearly three centuries for her request to be granted across the land!

23 In 1849, the nation's first woman doctor, **Elizabeth Blackwell,** earned her M.D. in New York.

24 "Thar's gold in them thar hills!" James W. Marshall accidentally discovered gold while building a sawmill near Coloma, California, in 1848. Efforts to keep the discovery quiet failed and the **gold rush** was underway!

25 The **world's largest diamond,** the Cullinan, was discovered in South Africa in 1905. It weighed 3,106 carats!

26 Our 26th state, **Michigan,** joined the Union in 1837. "The Sound of Music" was based on a story written by Maria von Trapp who was born today in 1905. Also, Mary Mapes Dodge, who founded the **first great children's magazine,** *St. Nicholas,* was born in 1831.

27 The **first tape recorder,** the Wireway, was built in 1948. It's also Wolfgang Amadeus **Mozart's** birthday! One of the world's greatest music makers, he was born in 1756.

28 In 1973, the **Vietnam War** cease fire was signed.

29 **Kansas** became our 34th state in 1861.

30 **Franklin Delano Roosevelt,** our thirty-second president and the only one to serve more than two terms, was born in New York in 1882. In 1933, the Nazi era began in Germany when **Adolph Hitler** became the German Chancellor.

31 It's a grand-slam day! **Jackie Robinson,** the first black major league baseball player, was born in 1919. And in 1974, the New Jersey Division of Civil Rights ruled that **Little League** baseball teams must let girls play ball.

JANUARY: Bright Ideas

Illustrations by Mila Lazarevich

WEATHER FORECAST GAME

In each sentence, find a word a weather forecaster might use.

1. Did you enjoy your ride in the Thunderbird?
2. Do you like spicy food?
3. Is the Doc old?
4. The cloudberry grows in the northern hemisphere.
5. Did you go to the clearance sale?
6. Mt. Rainer is in the Cascade Range.
7. She walked along the pleasant winding path.
8. Haile Selassie was an emperor of Ethiopia.
9. Do you like white rice?
10. A dryad was a nymph in Greek mythology.
11. Was he really an old fogy?
12. Brighton is a city in England.
13. August is the eighth month of the year.
14. Heather is grown in England and Scotland.
15. Was it a mistake?
16. Yes, Mogul may refer to a Mongolian.
17. Sunnyvale is a city in central California.
18. The stormy petrel is a black and white bird.
19. Warmongers advocate war instead of peace.
20. Do you prefer a milder flavor?
21. Did you ever ride a snowmobile?
22. How many snapshots have you?
23. Have you ever caught a lightning bug?
24. Admiral Dewey defeated the Spanish fleet in Manila Bay.

Key: 1. thunder; 2. icy; 3. cold; 4. cloud; 5. clear; 6. rain; 7. wind; 8. hail; 9. ice; 10. dry; 11. fog; 12. bright; 13. gust or gusty; 14. heat; 15. mist; 16. smog; 17. sunny; 18. stormy; 19. warm; 20. mild; 21. snow; 22. hot; 23. lightning; 24. dew.   ALETA SLATER

YOU NAME IT

Have your students play a challenging and exciting identification game that leads them straight to the reference books. Display pictures, with problem-answer sheets attached, one at a time. A typical problem might be: "What animal lived in this

shell? Give both its common and scientific names." Kids may not guess, but must research the answer within a time limit. All students' answers are visible, as they use the same piece of paper, and any number may answer in the same way (this sometimes shows that independent thinkers can be right). After two days, answers are checked. If anyone has found the right answer, challenge them with another more difficult problem!
SANDRA FREY

WANTED: GOOD WRITERS
Writing want ads can help children become aware of their use and will provide practice in clear, concise written communication. After studying newspaper want ads, have pupils write their own for the following situations:
1. You want to find your lost black kitten.
2. You are seeking a job cleaning yards.
3. You have found a lost collie puppy and are looking for the owner.
4. You want to sell your old one-speed bike.
5. You want to buy a used stereo.
6. Your family is going to have a garage sale.
GENEVIEVE BYLINOWSKI

STUDY DIALS
Make a number of double cardboard dials or disks with a small circle on top of a larger one. Fasten together at the center with a brass fastener and use to teach the words for numerals 1 to 12. Write words on the large circle; numerals, out of order, on the smaller. The child selects a number and turns small circle until it matches the right word.

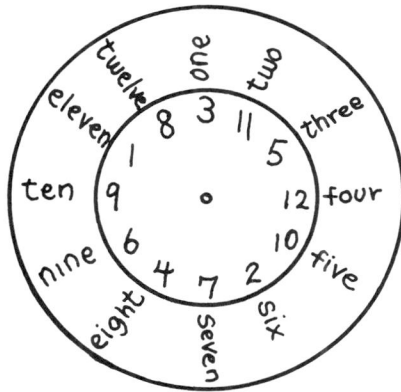

Do the same for numbers 13 through 24, 10 through 120 by tens, 5 through 60 by fives, 2 through 24 by twos, and so on. Dials are also excellent for reviewing Roman numerals. Put Arabic numerals on small circle, Roman on the larger. FLORENCE RIVES

A BRIGHTER JANUARY
Add some sparkle to this long month with these language arts activities.
A diary is an excellent way for students to write on a continuing basis. Supply each with a notebook and schedule a definite "writing time," the first or last 10 minutes of the day. Kids can comment on weather, describe the day's events, or fantasize. Stress complete sentences, good choice of words--in one or two paragraphs. Diary time should be time for reflection, and after a few days students will look forward to it.

Have the class research people born in January. Each selects a subject, does research, writes a report, and makes a nice cover. Display these reports on a bulletin board with the caption "They Had January Birthdays." Here are some to start with: Paul Revere, Betsy Ross, Jacob Grimm, George Washington Carver, Carl Sandburg, John Hancock, Albert Schweitzer, Martin Luther King, Jr., A. A. Milne, Lewis Carroll, Franz Schubert.

Have students write a seasonal story. Have titles available, but suggest kids write their own. Stories can vary in length but they should be edited and recopied. At the end of the month, compile stories into anthologies.

Have each student find a different poem about snow and read it to the class. They'll have fun browsing through anthologies, and they'll stop to read countless other poems!
HELEN MILLS

LET'S GO SHOPPING
Provide extra practice in adding and subtracting dollars and cents by using egg-carton "stores." Place a toy grocery item (found in toy sections of most stores or dollhouse supply catalogs) in each section of carton. Write the price of each item in its corresponding position on a paper diagram pasted to inside lid of carton. Children then work in

JANUARY: Bright Ideas

pairs. One selects a few items from the carton, writes their prices down, and totals them. The partner adds the same prices and they compare answers. If they agree, the shopper uses play paper money to pay for

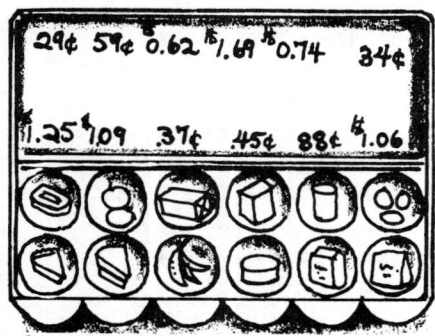

the purchase, subtracting the price, and figuring out correct change. The partner also checks this step; then they change places. This is one math assignment children love! JEANNINE MANN

PROUD TREE
As a remedy for the late winter slump, make a "proud tree" bulletin board to encourage your students to keep doing their best work. Tack a large brown tree on the board, with plenty of branches and a thick trunk. Then make leaves from green construction paper to serve as symbols of work well done. When students have done especially well in any area of study, give them a leaf to put on the tree. On the leaf, enter the child's name, date, and brief description of the work completed. Whenever you award a leaf, announce the achievement to the

class. At the end of the year, give children their leaves to take home as symbols of academic achievement. You'll find that once a few students have acquired leaves, the whole class will work to fill the tree, and you'll have an attractive bulletin board display. CYNTHIA WHITEHURST

FOR THE BIRDS
Bring to school your old box of stale circle-shaped cereal--Fruit Loops, Cheerios, and so on. Have your primary kids thread them on short lengths of colored yarn, string, or twine to hang from tree branches for the birds. They are colorful, easy to do, inexpensive, and will increase children's awareness and appreciation of the food needs of birds. JO FREDELL HIGGINS

PARTNERS IN MATH
Partners make math proficiency easier. Try this procedure. Monday, introduce a new concept; desks are then pushed close and partners work together. Tuesday, pupils work alone; if they have trouble they consult partner. Wednesday, work alone; partner checks work and points out mistakes. Thursday, work alone;

teacher corrects and partners determine why answers are wrong. Friday, work alone; teacher corrects and records marks.

Each week a math family is reviewed; for example, 12. Work for that week: addition, subtraction, or problems in combinations of 12.   ROSALIE BECK

GET THE MESSAGE
For alphabetizing drill, pass out copies of this short puzzler. Print the words at the left in alphabetical order on the lines at the right. Now copy the circled letters in the blanks at the bottom to receive a secret message.

violin   _ _ Ⓞ
fox   _ _ _ Ⓞ
wedge   _ _ Ⓞ
cub   _ Ⓞ _ _ _
foxy   _ Ⓞ _ _
dew   _ Ⓞ _
cube   _ Ⓞ _ _
under   Ⓞ _ _ _
early   _ _ Ⓞ _ _
fee   _ _ Ⓞ _
erase   _ _ _ Ⓞ _ _

_ _ _ _ _ _ _ _ _ _

Correct answer: Beware of dog.

ISOBEL L. LIVINGSTONE

HANDY EXERCISE
For a hand exercise to strengthen muscles and improve coordination, let children attach a dozen spring-type clothespins to a coat hanger. Then have them remove one pin at a time and hold it in that same hand until they have removed and held as many as they can without

dropping one (and without touching pins with other hand or other parts of the body). A young child may be able to remove and hold five or six pins; with practice, this might be increased to 8 or 9. Older kids may hold as many as 10 or 12. When a pin is dropped, pupils should begin again using the other hand.
FLORENCE RIVES

TYPE TO SPELL
I've found that a great way to reinforce spelling words is to have a typewriter available in the room. Children take turns spelling out each of their words on the machine whenever they get a chance. This manual activity is just what some kids need to help them remember the position of letters within words. If your high school offers a typing course, you might ask your superintendent if you could have one of the old typewriters. Or pick one up at a garage sale.
THOMAS BERNAGOZZI

HIGHS AND LOWS
I requisitioned 24 cheap thermometers for my fourth grade class to use in science experiments. Then one day when we had a big snowfall and the students were fidgety, I used them for what became a highly successful lesson. The assignment was this:
1. Lay thermometer on your desk. Don't touch bulb. After two minutes record the room temperature on your paper.

2. Hold your palm against bulb two minutes. Record the temperature.
3. Breathe on bulb for two minutes. Record the temperature and compare results with a neighbor's.
4. Place thermometer in snow outdoors while you count to 60. Record the temperature.
5. Push thermometer down into snow and count to 60. Record temperature
6. Hold thermometer under your arm for two minutes. Record temperature.

You can't imagine the excitement as kids watched that mercury fluctuate!
FERN WOOD

SUPERMANIA
Why not take advantage of your students' interest in Superman by trying some of the following activities?
Super Science
1. Have kids research flying. Discuss what one might see, hear, feel, and smell while flying.
2. Kryptonite is a make-

believe metal from the planet Krypton, Superman's birthplace. Have kids research and discuss different metals, magnets, and radiation.
Super Social Studies
1. Suppose Krypton hadn't exploded? Let kids write a travel brochure for the imaginary planet.
2. Have kids plan the settlement of Krypton by earth people. They must decide who can go on the expedition, the criteria for selection, what rules need to be created, what supplies should be taken, and so on. What problems might arise?
Super Language Arts
1. Write an original Superman story on a duplicating master, but leave out all punctuation. Give kids a copy and have them fill in the missing punctuation.
2. Cut out a Superman comic strip and remove all dialogue with scissors. Back the comic on oaktag or poster board and have kids write their own dialogue.
ROSEMARY HARMON

TAPE TIME
If you have access to some tape recorders, try this neat activity. Divide the class into teams. Pass out exercise sheets and tell kids they may use any facilities on the school grounds. The goal is to be the first team finished with the most correct answers. Some sample activities:
1. Record eight rhyming words.

JANUARY: Bright Ideas

2. Record the sound of sticks breaking.
3. Record the name of our eighth president.
4. Record five words with long e sounds.
5. Tape a discussion on some area of current events.
SALLY STEMPINSKI

SAVE THAT CALENDAR
Use these activities to squeeze some overtime out of last year's calendar. Your kids can:

1. Cut calendar apart and arrange months in order.
2. Find and list important holidays in each month.
3. List months with 30 days, 31 days, and 28.
4. Paste months on four charts, grouping them by season. Then use drawings to show weather and holiday motifs for each season.
5. Cut numbers apart and arrange them in sequence.
6. Circle all odd numbers in red and all even numbers in blue.
7. Cut out numbers and use them to make flash cards or other number games.
8. Use one color to circle all the numbers used when counting by twos, another color to circle numbers used when counting by threes, and so on.
9. Put numbers in a box to use in making classroom decisions. For instance, the team captain who picks the highest number from the box take his or

ACROSS:
1. What we coast on in January (plural)
3. We often have a snow ----- in January
7. We celebrate New ----- Day in January
9. Baby bear
11. To place
13. Poems
14. White flakes that fall in January
15. Conjunction
16. Lubricants
18. Part of the body (plural)
20. Abbreviation for advertisement (plural)
21. Chew and swallow
22. We make snow ----- in January
24. Shelters for animals
25. We throw snow ---- in January
DOWN:
2. New Year's --- comes in January
4. --- the season to be jolly
5. In January, we get new ---------
6. Baby flower
8. Constellation of stars
9. We drink hot ----- in January

10. ----- ring on New Year's Day
11. Sound made while sleeping
12. To squirm
17. Girl's name
19. Male
22. Part of a fish
23. Large body of water
MILDRED GRENIER

ANSWERS:
Across:
1. sleds
3. storm
7. Year's
9. cub
11. set
13. odes
14. snow
15. and
16. oils
18. arms
20. ads
21. eat
22. forts
24. barns
25. balls
Down:
2. day
4. Tis
5. calendars
6. bud
8. Leo
9. cocoa
10. bells
11. snore
12. twist
17. Ida
19. man
22. fin
23. sea

her team up to bat first.
10. Cut between the number
rows, horizontally. Tape
strips together to use as
a number line for
computing. CONNIE ZANE

MELT-AWAY MATH
Let personal snowmen help
your kids master addition-
subtraction number facts.
Duplicate a snowman for
each student, then section
and number the body into
different parts. Make a
work sheet testing a group
of addition or subtraction
facts for each section.
As kids complete the first
one correctly in the time
allotted, have them cut off
section one of their snowmen
and move on to the second
sheet. Whenever there is
an error, students must do
the problem over. See who
can "melt" his or her
snowman first by cutting
off all the sections!
LINDA PAKL

A PUZZLING TASK
Try this easy-to-execute
art idea to lift your kids
out of the post-holiday
doldrums. Give children
crayons and sheets of
9" x 12" newsprint. Have
them draw any kinds of
pictures they choose--in
only five minutes. As they
draw, distribute pieces of
manila paper the same size

as the newsprint. When
time is called, have every
child get out a pair of
scissors and cut each
picture into five or six
random sections. Now have
each child place his or her
pieces on a neighbor's desk
so everyone is left with a
new puzzle to assemble and
paste into place on the
manila paper.
BARBARA C. WESSINGER

YOUR BEST ANGLE
Teach angle measurement
with your overhead
projector. Use a black
grease pencil and a clear
plastic protractor to draw
the angle on the overhead.
Then project the image on
a screen where everyone
can see it. Place the
protractor on the angle
so they can see both the
angle and the numbers on
the protractor, and
demonstrate how to read
the measurement. Repeat
this procedure several
times, erasing the angle
each time. Then give

students a work sheet
where they measure
different angles. It is
most effective to teach
acute and right angles
first, then obtuse and
straight angles. When
students have become
competent, mix the
various angles and
change their positions
on the paper. Put them
on a slant, rather than
up and down.
ARLENE PAGE

FOLD AND DRAW SNOWFLAKES
Create snowflakes from
carbon and thin white
paper. Put carbon face
down on paper. Fold
together into quarters.
Near the center of one
corner, draw one and a
half sections of a
snowflake. Inside these,
draw simple designs.
Unfold, for a complete
six-point snowflake.
RICHARD LATTA

JANUARY-JUNE PREDICTIONS
Begin the new year by
recording your students'
predictions for the rest
of the school year. Then
seal up predictions and
put them away to be read
in June. Have your class
decide what kinds of
predictions to make. Some
should relate to the kids
themselves, some to class
activities, and others to
outside events. For
example: Will anyone child
break a bone? How many
library books will the kids
have read? Who will win the
Super Bowl? Make this a
group activity with the
majority vote deciding what
to list.
SANDRA J. FREY

JANUARY: Brush up on basic skills

EVERYDAY READING

Most things in life, from emergencies to daily living, call for everyday reading skills. Here's how to help your kids develop them.

You open the door of your home and see a magnificent geyser gushing water all over the front yard, threatening to start a flood. It's a broken water main! You'd better do something, and fast. You reach for the telephone book, look up the water company, make the call, and in a short time the situation is under control. While you probably didn't think about it at the time, you were using your everyday reading skills to solve a problem. These are skills we all use regularly. We read traffic signs, menus, recipes, labels, signs in buildings, newspapers, maps, timetables and directories, credit card information—the list is almost endless. It's a kind of reading that kids should practice, because it means solving the real-life problems they'll be confronted with the rest of their lives . . . or drowning in that geyser. And you can help them develop the skills that are important to successful everyday reading with these tried-and-true techniques.

Directories and timetables

It's a brutally windy spring day; your entire house is shaking. And then you hear it–shingles being torn from the roof by the wind. What can be done, who can be called?
● That sort of emergency—like the geyser—brings the phone directory into play (in this case, as you try to find somebody to repair your roof). To prepare your stu-

dents to handle such emergencies, first have them read the directory's alphabetical index and table of contents. Then introduce them to the guide words on the upper corners of each page. What pages would they turn to if they wanted to find emergency numbers? Where would they call to report a problem with service or to seek information about a bill—or to take care of the roof? Have them find a correct number to call.
● Next, introduce them to the Yellow Pages and have them determine where a specific section can be located, using the guide words on each page. (You might start with ''Roofing Contractor.'') Have them look up various subjects, and let them know that *doctors* might be found under *physicians; lawyers* under *attorneys;* and that other titles might not be described as kids think they should.
● Now is a good time to direct attention to the long-distance rates listed in the directory. Have students determine the times when the rates are lowest and when they are highest; also the cost on three-minute calls and cost per minute after that. Have them distinguish between the different kinds of long-distance calls—station-to-station, person-to-person, collect, direct dialing—and the cost involved with each.
● The reading of timetables has much in common with the reading of directories—in both cases information is being sought. *Mom is coming in on a late flight tomorrow.*

What time will it arrive? (Will she get home before the roof is fixed?) What time will she leave from wherever she is? Are there baggage limitations on the flight? Is she flying first class or coach and what is the difference in cost? All that, and much more, can be found by your kids in airline timetables (but not always the cost, however). And trains—which specific trains have full dinner service? Which ones have sleeping cars? How long does it take the train to go from one point to another? You can seek similar information from bus schedules.

Maps and signs

You're new in town, and after having walked around in circles for an hour or so, you're frustrated. You stop in a corner store and buy a map of the city, and your problems are solved . . . so long as you can read the map.
● Obtain a detailed map of an unfamiliar city. As your kids examine it, ask them to name at least three places of interest designated on the map (often marked in red). Ask them what directions they would be going in to reach each of those places from a specified location on the map. What streets or major routes would they use? How far would they have to go (making use of the scale of miles found on the map)?
● The scale-of-miles chart is only one of the many aids to be found on maps. Obtain copies of a state road map, and introduce

your students to such features as indexes, graph coordinate areas, population approximations, and the like. Ask such questions as, What is the largest city located in the E-2 coordinate area? What is the population of (any city)? What major river crosses the B-5 area?

● As people use road maps to travel about the country, they also need to understand the various traffic signs they will encounter. Many that formerly contained only words are now being converted into pictorial symbols. You can help your kids understand both the words and the symbols by cutting and pasting replicas of the old signs on one set of cards. Then do the same with picture symbols of the new signs. (The symbols can be found in your state's driver's manual.) Mix the cards in each group and have students draw cards and practice matching the words on the old signs with their picture symbols.

● Signs in public places also should be understood by your kids; like "No Admittance," "No Trespassing," "Violators Will Be Prosecuted," "Danger," and the obvious restroom designations. To help in this area, prepare a set of cards containing various sign wordings, and have students read each and explain its meaning. Or you might make a booklet of definitions. Ask students to read the definitions from this booklet and supply the appropriate names of the signs.

Newspapers

Big brother backed the family car over little brother's bicycle. Goodbye bicycle! What can be done to solve the emergency of brokenhearted little brother?

● Why, turn to the classified ads in your local newspaper, of course. First, have your kids look at the newspaper index and find out to what page they would turn to find the classified section. (While they're reading the index, have them also figure out what pages they would turn to for the crossword puzzle, the comics, the beginning of the sports section, the editorial page, and so on.)

● Have them search the classifieds for answers to such questions as, How many bicycles are for sale (for little brother's sake), and which one is the best buy? Under what category are they listed? What is the first ad under any specific section attempting to sell, and for how much?

● Then let students write their own ads, first checking how much each word (or sen-

tence) costs. Have them keep within the limits of a budget, say $20 or so. Also, have them check out the help-wanted section, clip the jobs that appeal to them most, and write letters of application for the jobs. This obviously can lead into a discussion of careers.

● No use of a newspaper would be complete without students doing their own article writing. After they've read the various sections of a newspaper, let students try their hand at news stories, sports features, editorials, interviews, and so on. You might even start your own class newspaper.

The financial world

Jake was an anachronism in today's world of plastic money–he didn't have a credit card, primarily because he didn't know how to go about getting one.

● There are a lot of Jakes in the world when it comes to finances and forms. What they don't realize is that it's not all that involved. All Jake has to do is obtain a credit-card application and fill in all the information required. Get some forms for your students. Have them read the questions and supply the answers for an imaginary applicant—how long the applicant has lived at his or her current address, nearest living relative, age, marital status, and so on.

● Obtain a travel-expense record from an automobile club or employer. Have the kids read and explain the various entries required—food and entertainment charges, hotel bills, transportation, ticket prices, and so on. Then have them list hypothetical expenses for each item. Have them also compute expenses for each day of this imaginary trip.

● Collect a variety of forms—income tax, credit, loans, licenses, college admissions, and job applications. Help your students to first read and understand the questions, and then fill in the answers. Remind them that in many cases their answers will have a great deal to do with success in what they are seeking through the forms.

The consumer world

The Sunday paper was checked and rechecked. "The coupon section is missing!" the irate shopper screamed. "That's gonna cost me a fortune!"

● Coupons have become great instruments of saving in recent years; the discounts *do* add up. And often there is a lot of writing on them. Have your kids determine what the different material found on the coupons

means. There's information for the storekeeper and the customer regarding cash value and discounts, expiration date, number and size of the product that must be purchased to get the discount, and so on.

● Just as the good shopper takes advantage of coupons, he or she also understands the value of checking around when looking for a particular service—auto, TV, stove, refrigerator, or washing machine repair (roof repair, too), for examples. Have your kids read ads for such services and explain why they would use one over another; they should consider quality of service, immediacy, cost, and so on.

● Speaking of cost, you can also help your kids learn to read the meters and gauges that record the amount of water, gas, and electricity that come into the home, and then to understand what the symbols on bills regarding them stand for. Have your kids bring in paid-up stubs for water and other utility bills. Go over them, explaining how the various units add up to the various cost amounts. Use this to show how conservation can indeed save money.

● Likewise, money can often be saved by the close reading of labels. Take labels from various containers of a product liked by most of your students. Have them compare the weights and prices of the containers. Is it always more economical to purchase the largest size? That involves unit pricing—comparing the sizes and prices of different containers of the same product. Devise a worksheet on which you list various products, the size or weight of each container, the cost of the product for its various sizes, and then the cost per unit (ounce, pound, kilogram, liter, whatever) with each size.

● While you're on the subject of food, you might try using menus with your kids. Get some from your local restaurants and ask such questions as, Where would you look if you wanted to order a hot dog (hot sandwiches)? What is the least expensive drink on the menu (small glass of cola)? What desserts are available? If you have just $2.50 and order the ham and cheese sandwich, what can you afford to have to drink? What does "no substitution" mean? (You can't change the food combinations listed for certain specials.)

The activities in this feature come from **Dorothy Zjawin**, an INSTRUCTOR contributing editor from Jersey City, New Jersey; **Nancy M. Longnecker,** a fourth grade teacher in Abingdon, Maryland; and **Randall A. Pelow** and **Sally A. Chant,** authors of *The How-To Book of Survival Reading.*

JANUARY: Brush up on basic skills

Math Packs!

Drill? It's in the bag when you pack these 14 terrific math games

Denise Beverina and Dorothy Zjawin

Get twice as much fun out of math class with math packs—kid-size games calculated to develop important math skills. They're easy to make and exciting to play. But the real news is that each game (game board, flash cards, and game pieces) fits into its own little pouch—a plastic sandwich bag—ready to go anywhere. Kids can pull them out any time—when they have finished their work, in the lunchroom, on the bus; and most importantly, at home with parents.

To keep track of the math packs, devise a simple checkout system. When games go home (and you'll be surprised what a popular activity this is with parents) you might send home a slip a parent can sign, indicating that the game has been played. Record the fact the next day.

Kids will get good practice with the games that follow. Or, pack your own, using supplementary materials on hand. When learning is this much fun, your kids will say that math is in the bag!

Bingo Here's a well-known game that's easy to adapt to include math skills. First, make bingo cards. (Each card should be divided into 25 squares with a random numeral written in each square.) In a sandwich bag, pack the Bingo cards; markers (you could use old buttons or plastic bread fasteners); a deck of flash cards, each with a math problem written on it; and directions on how to play the game.

Directions: Each player gets a bingo card. Then each, in turn, picks a problem from the problem card pile. If the answer to the problem is a number on a playing card, cover it with a marker. The first player to cover five spaces in a row across, down, or diagonally calls out *BINGO* and wins.

Cover-up Don't let your students hide their math skills! This is a variation on the game above that will give your kids even more opportunity to show off their calculating know-how. Use the same materials you needed to play Bingo.
Directions: Same as with Bingo, except first player to cover entire card wins.

Bing tag If you need an exciting game to teach your kids basic math functions, this game is it! You'll need several laminated grid game boards with numerals 1-6 written over squares along the top and down one side, and a pair of dice.
Directions: Each player takes a turn rolling the dice, then writes the answer for the problem (multiplying or adding the two numbers rolled) on the answer card in the correct square. The first player to complete one row across, down, or diagonally correctly wins the game.

Pen the pig Just try to prevent your kids from hogging this one! To play, construct a laminated game board made up simply of a squared off area of dots arranged in rows, perhaps $10'' \times 10''$. Add flash cards with problems on them, a crayon, and written directions.
Directions: This is a game for two people to play. Take turns working the math problems. Draw one line between two dots each time you answer a problem correctly. Draw the lines only across or down. The object of the game is to see who can pen the most pigs. If you draw the line that finishes a square, you have penned a pig. Put your initials in that square. If you have penned a pig, you get to draw another line.

Climb the ladder Step right up and try this game. What skills will your kids master? With *Climb the ladder* the sky's the limit! In this game bag you'll need to pack laminated game boards of ladders sketched with only dots where the rungs will go, flash cards with problems, a crayon, and written directions.
Directions: Pick a problem card from the problem pile. If you answer the problem correctly, draw one rung on the ladder. The first one to reach the top of the ladder wins.

Factor challenge Do your kids dare to tackle the *Factor Challenge?* To find out, get 25 $3'' \times 5''$ cards or slips of paper. On each card, write a number such as 35, 36, 130, 8, 24, 60, 4, or 2.
Directions: Place all of the cards face down

on the table. Each player takes one turn by drawing a card and trying to name all possible factors of the number shown on that card. Scores, or number of correct factors given, are written on a separate sheet of paper. Play ends when all cards have been used. The winner is the player who has named the greatest number of factors.

Build-a-problem Here's an easy way to review the steps involved in solving a multiplication or division problem. Take six (or more) 3″ × 5″ cards or slips of paper and on each card, write one part of the solution to a multiplication or division problem. Shuffle the cards.
Directions: Players, as a group or as individuals, try to put each set of cards in sequence, from the first part of the problem to its solution.

Number spill No child will be able to resist *Number Spill.* You'll need to do a bit of preparation for this game, but the multiplication practice it provides will be worth it. Collect the following: caps from milk or soda bottles, transparent tape, one or two sheets of paper, one large empty juice can. First trace 20 or more circles around milk or soda caps on a sheet of paper. Write a number or fraction in each circle. Cut out circles, and tape each to a milk or soda-bottle cap.
Directions: Each player takes turns placing all caps in the juice can, shaking them up, and dumping them out. Player then multiplies any two caps that are facing up. Each correct answer counts as one point. First one to score 10 points wins.

Choose your points The point of this game is that it allows each child to work at his or her own pace. At the same time, it challenges each student to do his or her very best. In the plastic bag, put 25 (or more) 3″ × 5″ cards or slips of paper. Write a different problem on one side of each card. Write point values on the opposite sides, assigning higher point values to more difficult problems.
Directions: Place all cards, their problems face down, on the table. Players take turns drawing a card worth the number of points

they wish to work for. Correct answers earn the number of points shown on a chosen card, and the card is turned over. If the player answers incorrectly, he must return his card and wait for his next turn. When all cards have been turned over, the player with the highest score wins.

Personalized Problems Test your children's creativity as well as their math skills by encouraging them to make up their own math problems. Paper and pencils are all your kids need to play.
Directions: Give each group the first sentence of an arithmetic problem and encourage each player to add other details and find a correct answer. Or have the first player make up the first sentence and succeeding players add details until the problem is complete. The last player reads the whole problem and joins the group in trying to solve it. (*Variations:* Use situations familiar to pupils, such as family outings, hobbies, or topics from social studies and science. Or pretend that the problems are the type that a computer might put forth.)

Fractured calendars Any day is the perfect day to pull out this calendar game that makes fractions fun! Just round up an old calendar, pencils, and paper, and you're ready to play.
Directions: Choose any month on the calendar to work with. Beginning with the first two weeks, make up two or more fractions using days directly above and below each other. Try reducing these fractions and finding the smallest or largest fraction. Or simplify improper fractions.

Fraction mix If your kids are mixed-up about fractions, give them further practice with *Fraction Mix.* You'll need 25 3″ × 5″ cards or slips of paper and a felt-tip pen. Write a different fraction on each card.
Directions: Place the whole deck face down. Each player picks up two cards. Then players take turns trying to form the lowest (or highest) whole number or decimal number by multiplying or adding the two fractions.

Top this equation Nothing can top this

game for teaching kids how to write equations. To play you'll need 3″ × 5″ cards or slips of paper. On separate cards, write numbers, signs (+, −, ×, and so on), and symbols (such as Δ, O, and □). Be sure to make at least 10 to 20 sign and symbol cards.
Directions: Shuffle the cards and deal four cards face up. On each turn, a player tries to form an equation, such as *48* + *99* =, (= signs are free to each player, not counted in the deal), using any three of the four cards. Players should try to create the equation which has the highest number as the answer. If a player's cards are all symbols, signs, or numbers, he or she misses that turn. However, a player may use any symbol to represent any sign. That is, a player who turns up a Δ, for example, may choose to add, multiply, or divide any two numbers he or she holds. After each round all players turn their cards face down and receive four more cards from the dealer. Play continues until all the cards are exhausted or it is no longer possible for each player to obtain four cards each. At the end of the game, players total their equation answers, and the player with the highest score wins the game.

Hidden figures This game proves that there's more to a picture than first meets the eye. Cut out two-inch photographs of items such as refrigerators, motorcycles, television sets, clocks, record albums, furniture, and modern art paintings from old magazines and catalogs. Then paste each picture on separate 3″ × 5″ cards to make about 24 playing cards.
Directions: Shuffle the deck of 24 cards; place them face down on the table. Have players take turns picking one card from the deck and identifying as many "hidden" geometric figures (triangles, circles, squares) in the picture as possible. Each figure counts as five points. When all the cards are used, the player who has scored the most points wins. □

Denise Beverina is an elementary guidance counselor at McGuffey School, Washington, Pennsylvania.

Dorothy Zjawin is a contributing editor for INSTRUCTOR.

JANUARY: Bulletin Boards

Here's a sunny way to bring in the new year. Cut a large sun from yellow construction paper and place it in the center of your bulletin board. Have kids write their resolutions on white construction-paper clouds and arrange them around the sun. Cut letters from black construction paper. *SUZANNE SERDEN*

When interest in schoolwork begins to wane, try this bulletin board idea to motivate your kids to finish their work quickly. The clown's balloons contain numbered doors that open to expose "special" activities for those who've finished their work. *DIANE R. PRAY*

Use this colorful clown to remind your students of proper etiquette and consideration for their classmates. The clown should be cut from white construction paper and decorated with different-colored circles. Outline with a black felt-tipped pen. Use real balloons if possible, or cut them from construction paper and attach them to the clown's hands with string. With a black felt-tipped pen, write manners across the balloons that you'd like to encourage in your students. *SARAH B. TOPKINS*

HELP children develop word-attack skills by using a manipulative bulletin board. Eye-catching words cut from magazines and newspapers surround title and attract attention. Plastic point-backed letters are used to spell out words pictured on cards found in pockets at sides. Children pick a card, tack it to their work area, sound out the word, and place the appropriate letters below it. To check, turn over card and compare answers. Vary board for other skills. **Darlene L. Cutshall**

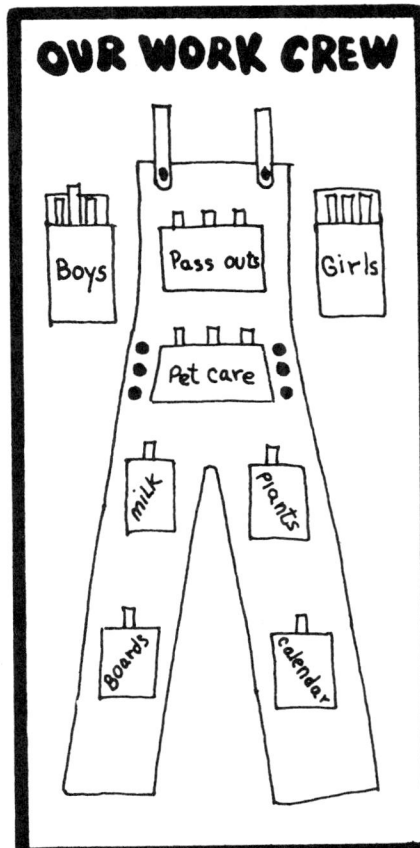

WORK PANTS signal the children about their jobs on the class work crew. Draw a four-foot-long pair of work pants on white roll paper. Cut out and attach to a bright paper-covered bulletin board. Cut out paper pockets, staple them in place, and label with jobs. Make cardboard name tags for crew pockets. Or use real bib overalls, patchwork pockets, and tongue depressor name tags for a more durable center. **Karen Smith**

DO math with child-made mittens cut from colored paper, attached together with yarn, and placed in box below board. Numbers are drawn on board and problems on mittens. Children tack mittens to board, matching problems to sums. Adapt mitten match to other study skills. **Joan Thames**

DECORATE the cat's pajamas! From tagboard, cut out a large cat wearing pajamas. Draw circles on him, printing an answer on each. Cut out same-sized colored-paper circles; on each, write a problem and answer, front and back; and arrange around cat. Children pin problems on cat's answers. **Mary Fay**

JANUARY: Bulletin Boards

YOUR entire class will become eager participants when you invite them to join "Cool Cat" (cut from colored paper or furlike cloth and attached to a contrasting paper-covered board). Cat welcomes all deserving papers and posts them under his picture. Change papers often so all students have the opportunity to have work displayed.
Sandra Frey

LET the dinosaur introduce children to new math skills. Make him from construction paper and attach to bulletin board covered with bright paper. Place fact sheet at left for pupils to refer to when beginning studies. Adapt title to other skill areas and value situations—"Roar through School—Study Hard," ". . . the Civil War," ". . . Dental Health Week."
Mary Lue Summerlin

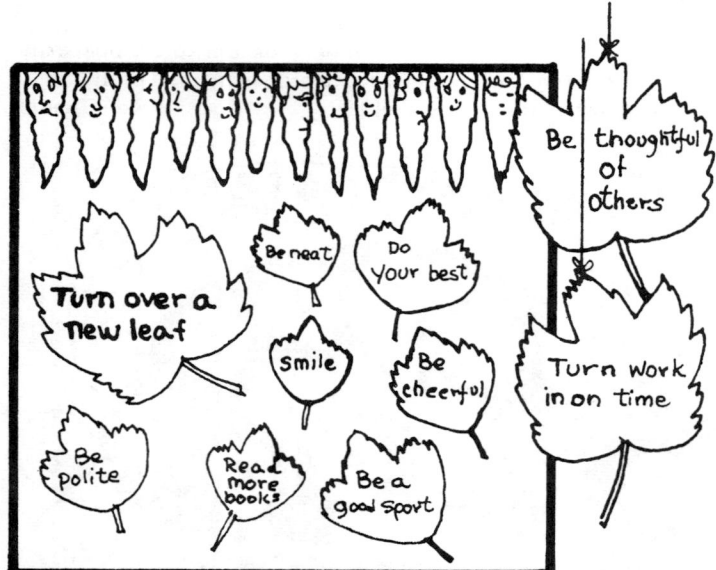

ZERO in on the New Year with a student-made bulletin board and leaf mobiles. Cover board with blue paper—the kids take it from there. Leaves and icicles are cut from white poster board. New Year's resolutions are printed on both sides of leaves. Draw faces on icicles for board's border. Tack leaves to board and hang from ceiling. **T. H. Mathre**

COMBINE a New Year's celebration with a lesson on telling time. Cut clock with movable hands from brown paper. Discuss New Year's fun. Then have each child make a mouse, to "run up" the clock, from two paper strips (one long, one short), curved, and pasted together. Add features. **Vivian Lynn**

"See what I can do!"—games for the class. *Rhyme Time, Mary Fay* (left): Prepare notched word cards as illustrated. The notches hold missing first-letter cards which are kept in pocket at bottom. Players match cards to pictures. *Words We Know, Ann Schmid* (rt.): Daily, a child selects, illustrates, and adds to board a word he'd like the class to learn. Related games which reinforce reading follow. Periodically board is cleared by an auction.

Here's an enchanting bulletin board display to get your kids interested in reading fairy tales. Use a dark blue background trimmed with yellow and make the castle from brown, orange, yellow, and green construction paper. Surround the castle with book jackets from famous fairy tales, and cut letters from yellow construction paper. — *CAROL E. FREELAND*

Use this bulletin board to encourage primary kids to learn counting to 100. Place numbers in increasing order on a white construction-paper ski slope, then give each child a miniature "skier." As kids master counting to each number on the slope, they may position their skiers accordingly. Give "gold medals" to those who reach the top. — *PATRICIA SAUTA*

All-by-myself bulletin boards offer exciting avenues for individual creative expression. *Cook Up a Story, Sandra Frey* (left) invites a child to write his own story with words appearing in the chef's hat. Change words as often as needed. *Snow Means, Betty White* (right): Begin with "skeleton" picture squares over single-word captaions. Students draw pictures to correspond with captions. Or let children choose other "snow" words to illustrate; add them to display. Some might want to write stories, instead of drawing.

FEBRUARY

Let's hear it for February! It might be a short month, but it's certainly long on opportunities for learning. Why do we say that? Because anything is possible in February. First of all, it's a love month, a time for warming hearts and declaring sentiments. It's also a patriotic month in which we salute two of our country's greatest presidents. February is a midwinter energizer, a joke month, a giggle month—and it's a great time for learning.

We want to make sure you get the most out of February. So in this chapter, you'll find lots of ideas for mixing laughs and learning. Start the ball rolling with any one of the many bright ideas that follow, then jump into six full pages of February fun and frivolity. After that, there are spare-minute learning games, a miniteaching unit on a nutty subject, and bulletin boards to perk up your room. So get going—February will be over before you know it!

Red letter days

ANNUAL FEBRUARY EVENTS
These special events usually occur in February, but the exact dates vary from year to year.
National Children's Dental Health Month
Afro-American History Month
Chinese New Year (always between January 21 and February 19)
George Washington's Birthday Observance (third Monday)
Purim (a movable Jewish feast in either February or March)

1 Poet and playwright **Langston Hughes** was born in 1902.

2 Today is **Groundhog Day!** According to a legend brought to the New World by German and British immigrants, if a groundhog sees its shadow on this date, we're in for six more weeks of winter. If not, spring is close at hand!

3 What do popular American artist **Norman Rockwell** and famous American writer **Gertrude Stein** have in common? They were both born on this date in 1894 and 1874 respectively.

4 **Rosa Parks,** "the mother of the modern civil rights movement," was born in 1913.

5 **Belle Starr,** "bandit queen of the Old West," was born in 1848.

6 **Ronald Wilson Reagan,** the 40th president of the United States, former governor of California, and former movie star, was born in 1911.

7 Outstanding English novelist **Charles Dickens** was born in 1812. *David Copperfield, A Tale of Two Cities, Great Expectations,* and *A Christmas Carol* are just some of the books that have made him famous.

8 In 1861 the **Confederate States of America** were formed.

9 **Paul Lawrence Dunbar,** called "Afro America's first great poet," died in 1906.
Also today, the **U.S. Weather Bureau** was established in 1870.

10 Do, re, mi, fa, so, la! The **first singing telegram** was introduced in New York City by the Postal Telegraph Cable Company in 1933.

11 **Thomas Alva Edison** was born in 1847. During the next 84 years, he created more than 1,000 inventions. Can your kids name some of them?

12 In 1809 **Abraham Lincoln,** our sixteenth president and the first to be assassinated, was born in Kentucky. He is especially remembered for his Emancipation Proclamation (Jan. 1, 1863) and his Gettysburg Address (Nov. 19, 1863).

13 The **first public school** in America, the Boston Latin School, was established in 1635.

14 It's **St. Valentine's Day!** Celebrate with a kiss!

15 American reformer and advocate of woman suffrage, **Susan B. Anthony,** was born in 1820. In 1872 she was arrested for voting—a criminal act at the time if done by a woman. In 1979, she became the first American woman to have her picture on an American coin—the Susan B. Anthony dollar!

16 Give a big hand to the man behind the famous wisecracking puppet Charlie McCarthy. This well-loved ventriloquist, **Edgar Bergen,** was born in 1903.

17 **PTA Founders' Day** is celebrated to honor Alice McLellan Birney and Phoebe Apperson Hearst, who founded the National PTA in 1897, and Selena Sloan Butler, founder of the National Congress of Colored Parents and Teachers in 1926. Both organizations merged in 1970.
Also, famed contralto **Marian Anderson,** the first black person to sing at the Metropolitan Opera, was born in 1902.

18 It's a day for firsts! Mary, **first queen of England,** was born in 1516. The **first 3-D movie** was shown in 1953. And the planet **Pluto** was first sighted in 1930.

19 Astronomer **Nicholaus Copernicus** was born in 1473. He discovered that the sun, not the earth, is the center of the solar system.

20 Today is **Frederick Douglass Day** in honor of this famous anti-slavery leader and orator who died in 1895.
Also, **John Glenn** became the first American to orbit the earth in 1962.

21 **Jerrie Cobb,** the first woman to be tested to be an astronaut, passed her 75 examinations in 1960.
Also, **Lucy B. Hobbs,** the first woman to earn a degree in dentistry, was graduated in 1866.
Politician **Barbara Jordan** was born in 1936.

22 "First in war, first in peace, and first in the hearts of his countrymen . . ." That was **George Washington,** first president of the United States, who was born in 1732. His birthday is legally observed on the third Monday of the month.

23 **W.E.B. Du Bois,** black scholar and author, was born in 1868.

24 American artist **Winslow Homer,** famous for his paintings of the sea, was born in 1836.
Also, the **Gregorian calendar** was instituted in 1582. It had been determined that the widely used Julian calendar was 10 days off (11 minutes and 14 seconds off each year). Pope Gregory XIII declared the calendar invalid and introduced a more exact replacement based on the solar cycle of 365 days divided into 12 months. Today it is the most accepted calendar system in the world.

27 American consumer advocate and attorney **Ralph Nader** was born in 1934. Also, actress **Joanne Woodward** was born in 1930.

29 It's **Leap Year Day!** This day only comes once every four years because it takes the earth 365 ¼ days to revolve around the sun. Those four one-quarter days make a whole day once every four years.

FEBRUARY: Bright Ideas

MULTIPLYING HEARTS

Third graders can be motivated to work harder on their multiplication facts by allowing them to create and decorate individual February trees. Trees can be made by blowing through a straw at a blob of thinned, black tempera placed near the bottom of a sheet of white paper. Add cutout pots to cover blobs. Everyday from then on, give a one-minute test on whatever number family is being studied. As a child gets all the multiplication facts in a family correct, he or she gets a red heart-shaped sticker for his or her tree. When all the number families are mastered, give kids metallic gold hearts to top their trees. RUTH MORRIS

VALENTINE PEOPLE

Combine pipe cleaners, cutout hearts, and scraps of packing foam to make stand-up valentine figures. Sandwich pipe cleaners between two identical

hearts and glue them in place to form neck, arms, and legs. Draw features with a red marker on white heart face. Use a line of individual stick figures, each labeled with a different letter, to spell a valentine message. Encircling a globe, they might read, "Love makes the world go round." LILIAN RUEBECK

ADJECTIVELY SPEAKING

How many adjectives can your class use to describe a valentine? Run through the letters of the alphabet with them. This is a great way to study and explore adjectives and synonyms! Why not offer a heart-shaped box of candy for the longest list of valentine adjectives? Start off with this pattern poem.

V is for velvet and
     vivacious,
A is for ample and
     audacious,
L is for lacy and lavish,
E is for easy and elfish,
N is for nameless and
     notable,
T is for tender and
     terrible,
I is for ideal and
     inocuous,
N is for namelss and
     notorious,
E is for endearing and
     especially--you!
HELEN MILLS

VOCABULARY SHAPE-UP
To add a bit of February mystery to vocabulary work, draw Lincoln's profile on a duplicating master and disguise it with a number of shapes, inside and outside the outline. Type definitions of words in each of the shapes, and give students a list of the words defined with instructions to copy them in the same space with the appropriate definitions. Star some words on the list so that when all the shapes in which starred words are placed are colored black, they will form a black silhouette of Lincoln on a white background. This same activity can be used at any time of the year if you substitute appropriate drawings. SANDRA J. FREY

GEORGE WASHINGTON HATS
Materials needed to make a Washington hat are one sheet of wallpaper from sample book, a cardboard pattern for hat made in the shape of half a circle, scissors, stapler, and ribbon. To make, have each child trace a pattern for three half circles. Cut a paper strip to form headband and staple together around head. Staple half circles to band. Add ribbon ornament to one side of hat. These make fine hats to wear to lunch on Washington's birthday.
HELEN KITCHELL EVANS

A TEAM APPROACH
To dramatize the four steps necessary for long division, choose a team of four children to work on one example. The first child does the division, the second multiplication, the third subtraction, and the fourth the bringing down. Then the team repeats its work as often as necessary.
ISOBEL LIVINGSTONE

SORTING SYLLABLES
Prepare numerous word cards using words from textbooks you use. Label four boxes (such as cigar boxes) "One-Syllable Words," "Two-Syllable Words," "Three-Syllable Words," "Four-Syllable Words." In free time, let children sort the word cards by placing them in the right box. They must be able to pronounce the words or look them up in the dictionary to place them in right box. After child has placed the cards, someone checks to be sure they are correct. Children in middle grades especially like this activity; it helps them pay more attention to words in general and to syllables in particular and improves spelling.
FLORENCE RIVES

NEW USES FOR OLD BOOKS
When picture books wear out, the pictures can be used in many enjoyable activities. Tear the pages apart and trim, then roughly categorize the pictures and they're ready to use.

At the kindergarten level, the teacher may hold up a picture and ask children to name all the things they see. This sharpens perception of objects, shapes, sizes, and colors. As children begin to read and write, each selects a picture and writes two or three lines about it. Staple pictures, with stories underneath, to colored paper and display on the classroom or library board.

As children begin to do independent work, give them a set of pictures and let them create their own stories. Have them write a title and underline the main word. Vocabulary,

FEBRUARY: Bright Ideas

comprehension, and sequencing are made stronger. To help them understand actions within a story, ask them, "What is happening in that picture right now?"

Finally, use one set of pictures with an entire class by having each child write one sentence about the picture in front of him or her. All pictures are then gathered and rearranged into a sequential order.
GEORGE BOOKS

BRIGHT BEGINNINGS
Have some fun with language skills. Discuss beginning consonant sounds by creating expressions in alliteration. List these starters on chalkboard:
Jumping Jupiter
Talk Turkey
Stuffed Shirt
Mad Money
Snappy Swinger
Winter Wonderland
Great Guns
Make a class list of others the kids create.
DAVE BLOOM

THIS THING CALLED LOVE
What day could be better for a lesson on values than February 14? You will find that a talk about love and its basic meaning is one of the most important discussions you and your class will ever have. There may be a few giggles at first, but kids quickly grasp the idea that love involves many feelings--consideration, concern, happiness, understanding, respect, and so on. Culminate the

discussion with a bulletin board displaying heart montages. Use cutout pictures of loving actions bearing personalzied statements such as, "Love is not yelling at your sister when she spills her milk." Title the display, "Love Is An Active Verb."
ELFRIEDA PIERCE

SWEET ASSIGNMENT
For a quick creative writing assignment kids can really get their teeth into, buy a bag of the candy hearts that have

short phrases printed on them such as "true love," "hi, cutie," and so on. Let children pick one or two hearts, then use the words on their hearts in stories or poems.
BRENDA McGEE

VALENTINE GET-TOGETHERS
Have students make heart puzzles to reinforce skill in such areas as alphabet recognition, rhyming words, and opposites. Upper grades will enjoy using similar devices to practice math facts, synonyms, states and their capitals, and so on. If two adjoining classess make these puzzles, they can trade in mid-February. Trace hearts on sturdy paper. Draw zigzag lines

through middles and write puzzle clues on each half. For longer use, laminate before cutting apart. Mix all pieces in a box or large envelope and put kids to work mending those broken hearts!
CONNIE ZANE

COLOR YOUR WORDS
When you introduce new spelling words, try using colored chalk to emphasize difficult spots. For instance, write the word friend on the board, then ask a student to trace over the tricky "ie" with red chalk. Likewise, have a student emphasize the first "r" in surprise, and so on. This simple device will help impress correct spelling on your kids minds.
ISOBEL LIVINGSTONE

SPECIAL SPELLING WORDS
To add interest to your weekly spelling word list, add one student's name to it. Your kids will look forward to having their names presented as spelling words, and it's a good way for children to learn unusual ways of spelling common names.
JOAN KNUTH

LIKE LINCOLN
Try this February writing

project in your class this year. Have kids carefully research Lincoln's likes and dislikes, character traits, appearance, and background to find out what they might have in common with him. Then have them write brief compositions detailing these points of similarity. TRUDY AMES

CREATE A PROBLEM
One day there was an abundance of colorful ads in the morning paper, so I brought them to school and passed them out to my primary children. I told them to cut out two or three things they would like to buy and gave each a certain amount of play money. They quickly figured out how much their purchases would cost and whether I had given them enough money to buy the items. Not a pupil figured wrong! I then had them write out the problem they had just completed and mount the ad along with it on construction paper. This activity showed that creative thinking can be used in math and gave the children a better grasp of problem solving techniques.
JACQUELINE ARMIN

BETTER SCIENCE DISPLAYS
Boards for mounting science projects such as insect or leaf collections can be obtained just for the asking from fabric stores or departments. Inside all bolts of fabric are rectangular-shaped boards made of cardboard or plastic foam. They're

usually discarded after all the fabric is sold. These are ideal for use in displays, as they are strong enough to be hung on strings or propped up against tables or shelves. They can be used as is, spray-painted, or covered with cloth. Objects can be glued, taped, tacked, or held with straight pins to the boards.
TALIS BYERS

UPLIFTING MESSAGES
For room-brightening Valentine decorations, you can't beat Valentine kites. Children should think up their own ideas for designs. Use crepe paper, string, and scrap paper for tails on large red, pink, or white construction paper kites. Brainstorm for suitable sayings such as "Love Is in the Air," and letter them somewhere on designed kite. EILEEN ETNA

BOTTLED BOATS
Here's a fun art project that lets kids use their imaginations as they learn about ships past and present. Have each child draw the outline of a bottle on light blue construction paper or poster board, 8" x 11". Bottle should fill most

of the page. Now draw bottle caps with black crayons or felt-tipped pens. Boats should be drawn centered inside the outline of bottle, but before drawing them have kids research various types of sailing vessels from history or present day, to make models as authentic as possible. For foaming waves, kids can paste tufts of cotton along bottoms of boats. Finally, have each child cut around bottle outline, then cover with clear plastic wrap. Use this activity to accompany a unit on sailing, Columbus, or any facet of history.
JANE K. PRIEWE

TELL AND DON'T SHOW
Here's a variation on the Show and Tell game that helps develop listening skills, retention of information, and deductive reasoning. On Show and Tell day, have children deposit their objects in a large bag or box. Then choose one student to stand and describe his or her object without showing it. When student has finished, put all objects on a table and have kids guess which one has just been described. Or, have the class ask questions about the object after it's been described; this way the object won't be seen until one of the children guesses what it is. The first one to guess correctly is the next to describe his or her object.
Another possibility is to assign categories for

FEBRUARY: Bright Ideas

show-and-tell objects. You could have kids bring in things that are red, things that begin with a certain letter of the alphabet, things that fit in your pocket, or things that come from foreign countries. Often you'll find that the child's family will get involved in searching for an appropriate object. JOSEPHINE LAZZARO

IDEAS ON WHEELS
An ordinary red wagon can be the answer to lots of otherwise messy classroom projects. You can get one from a student, toy store, antique dealer, or discount house. After cleaning it thoroughly, try some of the following ideas.
1. Load all your classroom plants into the wagon. This way, you can give them the light they need by wheeling wagon around to follow the sun. They won't drip over your windowsill, either!
2. For special holidays, use the wagon to hold your centerpiece, jack-o'-lantern or Christmas tree. It can be moved around the room so all can enjoy it.
3. Use wagon to transport items such as play props, art projects, library books, and so on.
4. If you have classroom pets, load them into wagon now and then to visit other rooms in your school.
5. Place corrected tests and worksheets in wagon and choose one student each week to distribute them. NICKI KLEIN

JUST-FOR-FUN HOLIDAY GAME
The object of this game is to get Baby New Year from his home, around the board and through the different holidays. After he passes Christmas, he becomes Old Father Time. Use colored buttons for markers, a spinner, a score sheet, and 18 cards or slips of paper. Players move buttons the number of spaces shown on spinner and must land by exact count to earn 100 points. Players may pass an opponent's button, but no two buttons may rest on same space unless it is a holiday. The first to get 1,200 points and go into Father Time's house wins.

When a player lands on a space marked with a clock, draw the top card from card pile and follow instructions. Shuffle cards at start of each game. Place used cards on bottom of the stack. Sample instructions for cards follow, but let your kids think up their own too: (1) For sending a Valentine to every classmate, go to nearest holiday. (2) For sending Valentines only to your friends, lose a turn. (3) For always being truthful, take an extra turn. (4) For being too stubborn to admit doing anything wrong, go back 10 spaces. Lose 25 points. (5) Take 50

extra points for sharing your Easter eggs. (6) Lose a turn and 25 points for peeking when Mom hid Easter eggs. (7) Advance 10 spaces and collect 25 extra points for taking down the flag before sunset. (8) Lose 50 points for dragging flag on the ground. (9) For marching so snappily in Fourth of July parade, collect 25 points and advance 7 spaces. (10) Go back 10 spaces and lose 10 points for not marching in Fourth of July parade. (11) For helping Dad on Labor Day, advance to the nearest holiday. (12) Lose a turn and 75 points for getting lost in the park on Labor Day.
JANE K. PRIEWE

SURPRISE BOXES
A good way to get kids to do mundane tasks around the room is to use individual food containers from fast food places. After cleaning each carton, glue in a slip of paper that may say, "Surprise-- you get to pick up all the paper," or "Surprise-- you get to straighten up the bookshelf." Once a day put a pile of boxes on a table for kids to choose from. Besides the ones for chores,

"FAST TASK TABLE Take your pick"

there are also boxes for being first in line for lunch, for captain of a team, and so on. Children look forward to "duty lottery" because there is a chance they might get a good surprise!
NANCY K. METHNER

SHAPE-UP GAME
This game helps young children review familiar geometric shapes. Cut several shapes from oaktag and put a string through each so children can wear shapes around their necks. Have children with shapes stand in line; another child should be caller, still another will bounce a ball. The caller tells the bouncer to bounce the ball X number of times in front of the square. The bouncer goes to the person with the square and bounces the ball that number of times. And so on with other shapes.
LORRAINE LEE

PARTY TIME
Give your kids an old-fashioned Valentine party and they'll love you for it! Start by inviting your class with one giant accordion-folded paper invitation, shaped like a heart.
Play familiar games like "Drop the Handkerchief," only in place of handkerchief, substitute a red, heart-shaped beanbag. Or play "Mail the Valentine" by decorating a jar with a top opening that looks like a mailbox. Give children paper hearts

held by clip-type clothespins and have them try to drop their clothespin valentines into "mailbox" opening. They can remove and keep the hearts from pins which make a direct hit. Count hearts to add score.
Provide a "Make your own valentine" activity by assembling a variety of materials, and let each pupil construct a valentine to take home. Refreshments might be red gelatin parfaits with whipped cream and a candy heart topping, or heart-shaped cookies with red juice or Kool-Aid.
JULIANNE FITZ

TAKE A LETTER
Here's an idea that will get your kids interested in writing business letters. Divide your class into groups of three or four, and have each group form a fictitious company with members acting as its chief executives. Each group must think of a name and address for its company, and must then design letterheads and matching envelopes. Pass out a list of businesses and addresses to the whole class; each child must choose an executive from the list and write him or her a letter of praise, complaint, or suggestion. In return, the executive must answer back, using the company's letterhead. Check each letter before it's sealed in envelope for "mailing."
ANNETTE V. WERLE

FEBRUARY: Fun and frivolity

A fun story for primaries by Frances B. Watts

Grover Groundhog's Boom-bangers

MEADOWBOG was a quiet, cozy small town for small animals. The homes there were so little that no one bigger than a skunk or a beaver could find suitable living quarters. The Meadowboggians liked the peaceful atmosphere of small town life. And most of the time the town was safe from the large wild beasts of the forest.

One morning some of the animals were shopping early at Pat O'Possum's General Store. Suddenly, Meadowbog was rocked by a series of loud explosions. BOOM-BANG! BOOM-BANG! They rushed from the store. "What is it?" they cried. "Hunters?"

"The noise came from the direction of Grover Groundhog's cottage," said Doctor Raccoon. "Perhaps he's had an accident." He picked up his doctor's satchel and raced off. The others followed him.

On reaching the cottage, everyone piled in through the back door. To their surprise, Grover

was seated at the table, quietly eating his breakfast cereal. "Good morning," he nodded.

"Are you all right?" asked Doctor Raccoon.

"I'm very well, thanks," replied Grover, calmly spooning his cereal.

"Then what was that terrible racket we just heard?" inquired Mrs. Hop-Hare. "My ears are still aching."

"Oh, you must be referring to my Boom-bangers," Grover replied.

"Boom-bangers?" asked Clarence Chipmunk.

"It's a cereal I invented," Grover explained. "Some cereals, when you first pour milk on them, snap and pop. My cereal booms and bangs. It's a rousing way to start the morning. A good waker-upper, that's for sure."

The visitors shook their heads and exchanged knowing glances. Grover was an odd sort. He was forever puttering about with rather ridiculous inventions.

For example, he had invented harmonicas for humming birds, jump ropes for grasshoppers, and bath bubbles for bullfrogs. Nice inventions, but not really needed or wanted.

Presently Pat O'Possum said, "Sure, and it's a noisy way to start the day, Grover. The quieter-type cereals that I sell at the store are much easier on ears and nerves."

"But not as jolly and exciting," said Grover.

The animals sighed but said no more. If Grover chose to eat Boom-bangers for breakfast, that was his right. But they also had the right to think that Grover was a bit feather-brained. They all returned to the general store, grateful that their own brains were made of more sensible, sturdier stuff.

Grover found his Boom-bangers so rousing and delicious that he ate them every single morning at seven o'clock. As he poured milk on his cereal, immediately the booms and bangs echoed all over Meadowbog. It was an eye-opener, all right. No one could possibly oversleep. No one was ever late for work or school. Even Mr. Creep-turtle, who slept late, was up and at it after Grover's cereal boomed.

Despite all these advantages Grover's Boom-bangers soon grew very unpopular. On Sunday mornings, many Meadow-boggians resented being boomed out of bed. Mrs. Hop-Hare complained of frequent ear-aches. Small owlets hooted, fox puppies howled, and baby mice squeaked every time Grover fixed breakfast. Furthermore, the beavers claimed that the Boom-bangers shook the very foundations of their dams.

A lot of grumbling, muttering, and protesting sprang up. Grover Groundhog, the animals decided, had the right to invent and eat Boom-bangers, but he had no right to disturb the peace. Finally, a meeting was called at Meadowbog Town Hall. The meeting was held at eight o'clock on a Thursday night. When the meeting came to order Grover was given a choice—either stop eating Boom-bangers or leave town. "Hmmm," Grover said thoughtfully. "I like Meadowbog, but I also like Boom-bangers."

Just then Black Bart, Meadowbog's lookout crow, came winging through the window. He gave a piercing caw, "Wolf-alert! Wolf-alert! Wild Wolf from Windrock Mountain is heading this way!" Then with squeaks, squeals, shrieks, and screeches, the animals quickly scrambled to their homes. Very shortly, Wild Wolf loped into Meadowbog. He bayed and bellowed, then he hunched himself on the steps of Pat O'Possum's General Store, waiting until he'd had a taste of at least one Meadowboggian.

The hours crept by. At daybreak, the trembling animals, peeking from their windows, saw that the wolf was still there.

Then all at once, at seven o'clock, the familiar sound of BOOM-BANG shattered the silence. And wonder of wonders! Those watching from their windows saw Wild Wolf streak off toward Windrock Mountain. A few minutes later, Black Bart cawed, "All clear! All clear!"

Soon the animals gathered at the general store. "Wild Wolf must have thought Grover's Boom-bangers were hunters' guns!" they cried. They laughed, slapped knees, and whacked each other's back with glee. Then someone noticed that Grover Groundhog was not in the crowd. Everyone rushed off to his cottage.

Grover was seated at the table calmly eating Boom-bangers. "Good morning," he nodded.

"Grover, you're a hero!" Doctor Raccoon exclaimed. "Your Boom-bangers scared off Wild Wolf!"

"That's good," said Grover, spooning his cereal. "This morning I was going to try to invent something to chase him away. Now I won't need to."

"Whatever made you think of pouring milk on your Boom-bangers?" asked the doctor.

"I wasn't being clever," said Grover. "It was seven o'clock. Wolf or no wolf, I was hungry. So I fixed breakfast."

The animals had all considered Grover a featherbrain. Yet, in the face of danger, he'd been the only animal to keep cool. "Sure, and we hope you'll decide to stay in Meadowbog," said Pat O'Possum at last. "You're a fine citizen, Grover."

"Well, I do hate the thought of my Boom-bangers disturbing the peace," he said hesitantly.

Right then and there, earaches, lost sleep, crying babies, and shaking beaver dams seemed unimportant. "Stay, Grover," they begged. "We need you!"

So Grover did. And, as far as anyone knows, he still eats Boom-bangers for breakfast! ☐

Valentine Day

2 parts (round)

words and music by **Leah Patt Rivenburg**

I'll give you my heart and sweet sug-ar kiss - es,

Val - en - tine, Val - en - tine. I'll give you my love and

lots of good wish - es, if you 'll be mine.

FEBRUARY: Fun and frivolity

A lesson from Abe Lincoln

Jane W. Krows

BECKY stood in the doorway of the general store in the village of New Salem. Her walk from the cabin seemed long on that hot day, and her bare feet were dusty from the dirt street. She had come to buy some things for her mother at the Lincoln-Berry store.

At first Becky thought the store was empty. She stood with the bucket of eggs her mother had sent in payment for the supplies she wanted. "If there is enough left over," her mother had said, "get some calico for the quilt you are making."

Becky walked into the store and put her bucket down near the wooden counter. Then she saw a man get up from a bench, a book in his hand. She thought he would never stop unfolding his long legs. When he finally did, he stood towering over her, looking down at her with friendly eyes.

"Are you Mr. Lincoln?" she asked.

"Yes, little lady, I am Abraham Lincoln, but everyone calls me Abe. How did you know my name? I don't believe we have met before."

"I'm Becky Cobbins. My brother saw you wrestling Jack Armstrong," Becky said. She looked up and down at the tall thin man. "You don't look strong enough to whip Armstrong," she said, "but my brother said you did."

"Oh, I've a strong back, but I've always heard, 'a strong back, a weak mind'," he answered. "So, I'm trying to strengthen my mind. What can I do for you?"

She stood staring at the book he had put on the counter. "You can teach me to read," she said.

"I meant, did you want something from the store?"

Becky's eyes dropped to her bare feet. "I clear forgot what I come for,"
she said, pulling a small piece of paper from her apron pocket. "Ma wants this, but I can't read what it says, and here are the eggs she sent."

"Your ma wants tea and brown sugar and a piece of calico for a quilt if there's enough left from the eggs," Mr. Lincoln said. "Don't you go to school?" Mr. Lincoln asked as he reached for the tea.

Becky watched as he weighed the tea. "Pa says it's foolishness for a girl, and Ma says it's too far for me to walk in winter."

"Does your father read?" Lincoln asked as he weighed the sugar.

"No, but Ma reads and writes," Becky said. "She grew up in the East."

Next, Lincoln put some bolts of cloth on the counter. "Let's see now, three yards ought to about make you a new dress and leave over a few scraps for your quilt," he said.

"But I'm sure there was not enough from the eggs to buy that much," Becky worried aloud.

"I'll bet you can't figure either," Lincoln smiled.

"I can't," Becky admitted.

"Then let me do it," he said.

Becky looked at the patterns. She could not take her eyes off the yellow print with the tiny roses. "I would like this," she said, "but I don't know what Ma would think."

"I'll make a deal," Mr Lincoln said. "Three yards of yellow flowered print if you will come once a week and sit in my store wearing your new dress so others can see what three yards of calico can be made into."

"That would be a pleasure," Becky said.

"But there's one more thing." Mr. Lincoln pointed to a shelf of books. "While you sit you must be reading one of these books."

"But I can't read," Becky said.

"You will learn. You can teach yourself. I did, with a little help, and I will help you."

When the dress was finished, Becky came to the store once a week and sat on a straight chair with a book in her hands. Sometimes she sat on the little wooden porch.

At first the book said nothing to her. Then she saw the word *girl* under the picture of a girl, the word *boy* under the picture of a boy, and the word *dog* under the picture of a dog.

"I can read," she told Mr. Lincoln that day, a big smile on her face. "I can read girl, boy, dog, and chair."

"Very good," Abe said, "but you must learn more and more words."

Summer wore on. Sometimes Becky got tired sitting in the chair. She got tired of looking at the book. Sometimes she wished she had never seen the yellow dress or Mr. Lincoln. But she was proud of the words she had learned.

One day Mr. Lincoln was waiting for her when she arrived. "Look, I have signed you up for the fall session in Mentor Graham's school. I have gotten your parents' permission for you to go. All you need is a pair of good walking shoes and a warm shawl, and here they are." He reached beneath the counter and brought them out.

"But I can't pay for those," Becky said.

"You have paid for them," the storekeeper insisted. "While you sat in your yellow flowered dress, I sold all the material from that bolt and ordered two more."

"Is that enough?" she asked.

"Not really," Lincoln said, "but I will consider everything paid in full when you take one of these big books home and read it through." □

Mulligan's Monstrous Mailbox

by Florence Boutwell

A special delivery from the heart comes to a thoughtful neighbor in this unusual valentine story.

Mr. Mulligan is my best friend. I spend most of my Saturdays with him. Once my mom said I shouldn't bother Mulligan so much. So I asked him, "Mr. Mulligan, do I bother you when I hang around on Saturday?"

Mulligan said what I knew he would say. "Ted, fourth graders are my favorite people." His voice was soft and kind and I knew he meant it.

So every Saturday I'm at Mulligan's house. In the spring, I help him plant his garden. In the winter, we mostly do indoor work. Sometimes we just sit in his workshop. He carves animals out of small blocks of wood, and I look through his old *Popular Mechanics* magazines.

That's what we're doing today. Mulligan is telling me about the old days. "The street was just a wagon trail," he says. "See that shiny red, white, and blue mail truck coming down the street? Nothing like that in the old days. Hee, hee, hee." (I like Mulligan's laugh.)

The mail truck is stopping at the corner, in front of a row of eight silver mailboxes. It is a cool February day and the mailbox lids stick as the mail carrier opens them. At the end of the row is a mailbox that is almost knocked down. The name on the side in black letters is *George Mulligan*. The mail carrier passes it by.

"Guess you didn't get any mail, Mr. Mulligan."

"Never do. That's why I never bothered to fix my mailbox after the heavy winds knocked it down a few weeks ago."

"Gee, Mr. Mulligan," I say. "That's probably why you don't get any letters. The mail carrier can't get to your mailbox."

Mulligan keeps carving, but I'm not looking at *Popular Mechanics*. I'm thinking.

"Mr. Mulligan, I'll help you fix your mailbox." Mulligan lays down his carving. He looks thoughtful. Finally he says, "Why not? Can't do any harm. And while we're doing it, let's do it right. That old one is pretty rusty. We'll build a new box. One out of wood. We'll fix the prettiest, biggest mailbox on the street."

"A-l-l-right!" I say. "Al-l-right, Mr. Mulligan! Hey, if it's going to be so big and great, let's call it Mulligan's Monstrous Mailbox!"

There are deep smile wrinkles around Mulligan's eyes. They get deeper and he laughs, "Hee, hee, hee! Mulligan's Monstrous Mailbox!"

"I'll bet you'll get some packages in Mulligan's Monstrous Mailbox!"

"I don't know," Mulligan says. "Appearance isn't what counts. It's having writing-minded friends that fills a mailbox."

Mulligan has everything we need in the workshop. Lumber, nails, and paint. We use one of his birdhouses as a pattern and build a mailbox three times the size of the rusty little one. It's in the shape of a house.

When the mailbox is finished, Mulligan looks at it with pride. "If I don't get any mail in it, we can pull it down and put it in the garden for the birds."

I paint it red and Mulligan letters *George Mulligan* on the side.

I carry it down to the corner and Mulligan loads his shovel, hammer, nails, and a bucket of cement in the wheelbarrow. We dig out the old post, pour cement in the hole, and set the post in the cement.

"Nothing will knock this over," Mulligan says.

"Better than the others," I say. "Best looking mailbox on the block."

Mulligan shakes my mom's mailbox. "How would your mom like some cement around hers, Ted?"

"Hey, great! While you're doing that, I'll drive a few nails in the others."

The next Saturday, I'm sitting in the workshop with Mulligan when I see the mail carrier stuffing the boxes. There seems to be a lot of mail today. It reminds me of Mulligan's Monstrous Mailbox.

"Been getting any mail, Mr. Mulligan?"

"Nope," he answers.

But just as he says this, I see the mail carrier place a letter into the monstrous box.

"Al-l-right, Mr. Mulligan," I yell. "A letter!" We put on our jackets and dash to the mailbox.

I open the lid to peek inside. It's dark in there, but sure enough, in the back of the box sits a large white envelope. I snatch it out and give it to Mulligan. "It's a card," he says. "It's a valentine card!" He reads the message and grins.

"Let me see," I beg. And Mulligan hands it over. Inside the card, under a huge red heart is a message. It says: "Thank you so much for being neighborly and fixing the mailboxes."

The card is signed by all the people in our block. Even Mr. Villa who never talks to anybody, Mr. and Mrs. Joyall who work and don't have much time, and, of course, my mom.

"That's a real special valentine, Mr. Mulligan," I say.

"You're right, Ted. Real special. It's from my friends. Yes sir. And all because of Mulligan's Monstrous Mailbox. Hee, hee, hee!"

Mulligan decides we should make a frame for the valentine. We hang it with his other souvenirs in his workshop. "It's a first, Ted," he says. "It's the first real letter that was put in Mulligan's Monstrous Mailbox."

FEBRUARY: Fun and frivolity

Guess Who?

2 or 4 parts (round)

words and music by **Leah Patt Rivenburg**

Shut your eyes, now guess who sends this Val-en-tine to you?

To___ you, my___ love. To___ you, my___ love.

Presidential activities

George Washington (1789-1797)

1. George Washington was responsible for many historical "firsts" during his years as president. For example, the Bill of Rights was ratified in 1791, the states of Kentucky, Vermont, and Tennessee were admitted to the Union, and the Supreme Court met for the first time. Play detective for the afternoon and discover other historical firsts that occurred during Washington's presidency. Or invent other, less spectacular events that might have taken place. Then pretend you're Washington and write a state of the union speech, capsulizing these historical events.

2. The National Mint was established during Washington's presidency. Choose one of his many accomplishments as president and use it as the theme in a commemorative coin design. Share your design.

3. Washington considered only the best candidates for appointment to his cabinet. Invent a dialogue that might have taken place between Washington and one of his top advisers over appointing Thomas Jefferson secretary of state. (It was largely due to the influence of congressional leader James Madison that Jefferson was eventually offered this position.)

4. As president, Washington interpreted the Constitution quite literally and used it as a detailed guide to government. Choose a portion of the Constitution that existed then and write a literal statement summarizing the way Washington might have interpreted it.

Abraham Lincoln (1861-1865)

1. Thanks to the newly invented transcontinental telegraph, Lincoln was able to receive messages at the White House from as far away as Sacramento, California. Research the invention of the telegraph and the telephone we know today. What would life be like without these forms of communication?

2. Pretend that you are an urban worker or small farmer living in Lincoln's time. Because of the Homestead Act of 1862, you have finally obtained some land of your own. Your 160-acre plot on the semiarid plains is difficult to farm. Write stories or journal entries about your family's struggles and efforts to farm the land.

3. During his term in office, Lincoln signed the Conscription Act, making all white males, 20-45 years of age, eligible for the draft. Draftees could avoid service, however, if they were willing and able to pay $300 for a substitute. In spite of this provision, a vast number of men enlisted in the Union forces, while many others rioted against the draft in our country's major cities. If possible, find examples of arguments for and against the draft during Lincoln's term and compare them to contemporary protests concerning the draft. Also, you'll probably find words like *loyalty* or *patriotism* mentioned in these arguments. Use these words in stories, poems, cartoons, and posters related to the draft issue.

4. As of January 1, 1862, the first income tax bill became effective. This bill was responsible for 3 percent deductions on incomes over $800. Taking the role of schoolteacher, soldier, storekeeper, railroad worker, or others, state your reaction to this new legislation. Or write a speech that Lincoln might have delivered had he chosen to defend this bill. How do you think the public would have reacted? Make up letters to the editor, protests and petitions, sample income tax forms, ads for income tax preparers, articles against tax dodgers, and so on. Then compare our present income tax system to its earlier days. Find out how our government uses tax money now and compare it to the way it was used in Lincoln's time.

5. The transcontinental railroad was first chartered during Lincoln's term in office. Pretend that you are one of the first passengers, and write several journal entries describing your adventures and impressions. Or write a letter to a friend describing a particular incident that occurred during the trip, such as a snowstorm or a flood on the tracks. What part did you play in the incident?

Groundhog Rock

Moderato

Words and Music by Dorothy E. Kemp

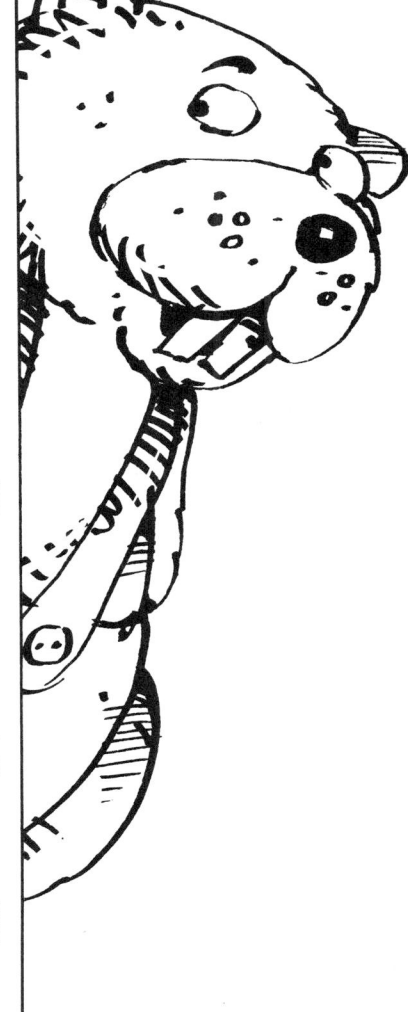

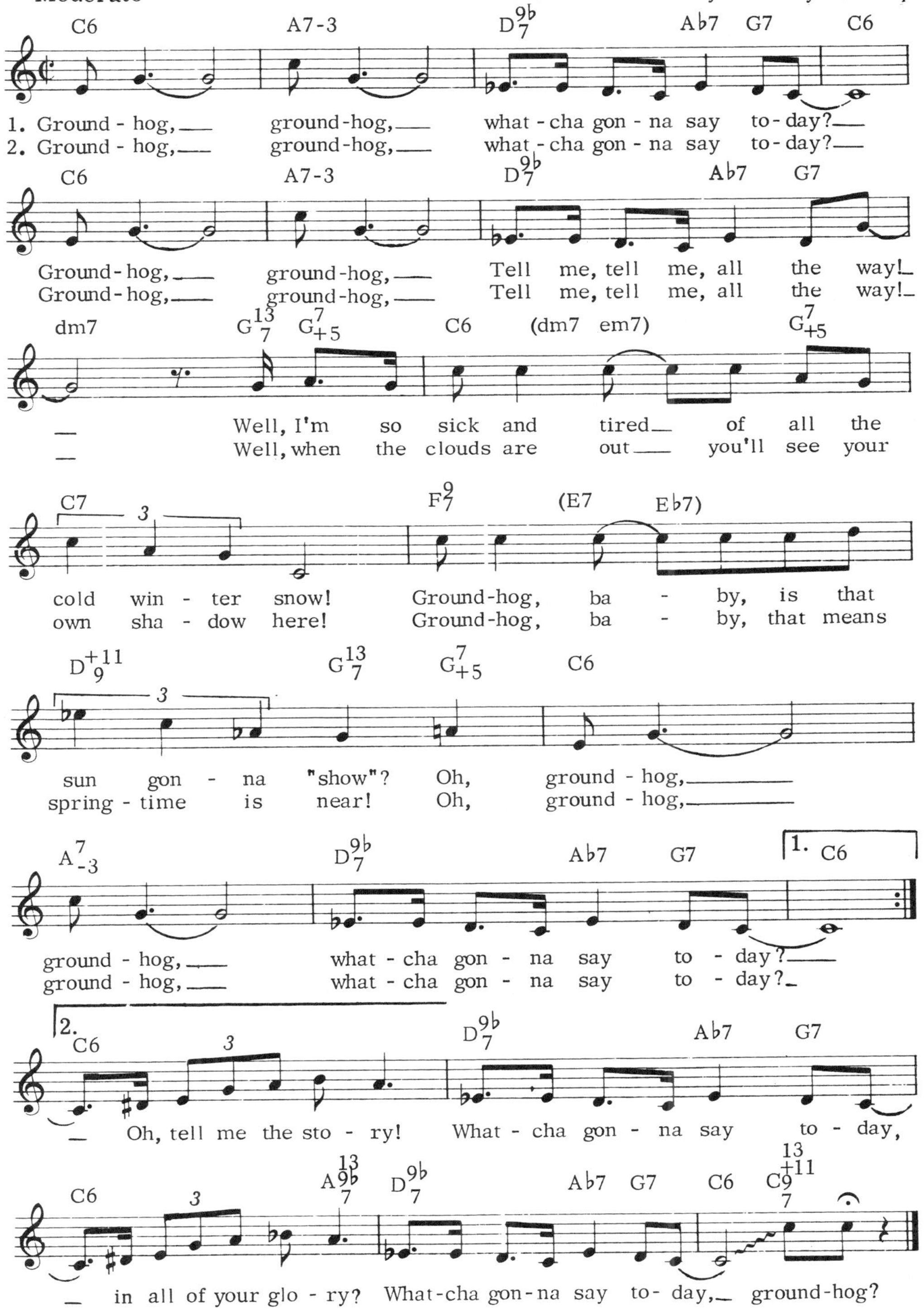
C6 A7-3 D9b7 Ab7 G7 C6
1. Ground - hog, ground-hog, what - cha gon - na say to - day?
2. Ground - hog, ground-hog, what - cha gon - na say to - day?
C6 A7-3 D9b7 Ab7 G7
Ground-hog, ground-hog, Tell me, tell me, all the way!
Ground-hog, ground-hog, Tell me, tell me, all the way!
dm7 G13 7 G7 +5 C6 (dm7 em7) G7 +5
Well, I'm so sick and tired of all the
Well, when the clouds are out you'll see your
C7 3 F9 7 (E7 Eb7)
cold win - ter snow! Ground-hog, ba - by, is that
own sha - dow here! Ground-hog, ba - by, that means
D+11 9 3 G13 7 G7 +5 C6
sun gon - na "show"? Oh, ground - hog,
spring - time is near! Oh, ground - hog,
A7 -3 D9b 7 Ab7 G7 1. C6
ground - hog, what - cha gon - na say to - day?
ground - hog, what - cha gon - na say to - day?
2. C6 3 D9b 7 Ab7 G7
Oh, tell me the sto - ry! What - cha gon - na say to - day,
C6 3 A13 9b 7 D9b 7 Ab7 G7 C6 C13 +11 9 7
in all of your glo - ry? What-cha gon-na say to- day, ground-hog?

FEBRUARY: Beat the blahs!

Spare-Minute Learning Games

Dorothy Zjawin

MATH

Number search Draw a grid, 12-squared, on the chalkboard. Fill each space with either an addition, subtraction, or multiplication problem (without answer), making sure that some will have the same answers. Ask the children to examine the grid and find two examples, when worked, that give the same answer.

Another number search activity is counting legs. Add together all the chair and table legs. How many are there? What else in the room has legs? People, of course! Multiply to get the number of people legs. Are there pets in the room? Do they have legs? Add them for a total count. What is the grand total number of legs in the room?

Auction math Collect pictures of items (refrigerators, TVs, cassette recorders, toys, cars, books, clothes, and so on) from magazines. Cut them out and paste each item on a 3-x-5-inch card. Underneath each, write its monetary value.

Then hold an afternoon auction. Give each pupil $5,000 in pretend money to spend. Display the auction items 10 minutes before auction time. Hand out pencils and paper and begin. Caution your buyers to start bidding at a lower price than each expects to finally pay. After each purchase, buyers subtract cost from their allotted $5,000. Also, they can make as many purchases as they want so long as their money lasts. Compute monies left over at the close of the sale.

Secret Codes Have each pupil make up his own secret code, using numbers instead of letters. For example, number 1 for A, 2 for B, 3 for C, and so on. Start the ball rolling with this message: 14/15 19/3/8/15/15/12 20/15/13/15/18/18/15/23 (No school tomorrow). Ask the kids to make up their own secret messages.

Follow me Draw a dragon on the chalkboard. Divide it into 12 sections. In each section, write one part of a simple math problem—3 $\times$ 8 + 5 — 10 + 4 $\times$ 6 — 2 + 39 + 2 — 11 + 6 = ? Children solve the problem, starting at the tail, finishing with the answer at the head.

Math bingo Give each child an 8-by-11-inch sheet of paper. Have them fold it into sixteen squares and copy one math example from the board (6 $\times$ 4, 10 + 8, 3 — 2, and so on) in each square. When paper boards are finished, call out the answer to one problem, giving the kids time to find the example that fits the answer and place a marker on it. The first child to cover a horizontal or vertical row, wins. To check, repeat answers and compare with winner's examples.

READING

How to make it Write directions on the board for the children to follow for either a simple folded toy or a game. Children must read and follow the directions to complete their project.

Picture this Write the following sentences on the board. Have everyone read them, and then draw a picture showing their interpretation.
Time was running out.
He followed his nose.
He had a nightmare.
There's a rainbow tree in my yard.
I saw a giraffe-cat!
There are dog willows on the pussy willow tree.
The tulips are dancing and singing.

Word scramble Using a list of reading or spelling words, mix up each word's letters. For example, the word *tree* may look like *eetr*. Write scrambled words on the board, and challenge class to unscramble them.

Picture stories Display action pictures cut from magazines and newspapers. Ask the children to write a three- or four-line story about one.

Onstage Divide the class into four groups. Have each group choose or make up a story. Give them paper and crayons with which to make character cutouts. Then groups present their improvised puppet shows.

Story fill-ins Make up or shorten a favorite story. Write it on the board. Omit words which describe or name colors, and list these words next to the story. As the children read the story, they fill in the blanks from the word list.

Now hear this! Let pupils make up a written advertisement for a favorite book, toy, record album, or piece of clothing. Invite them to illustrate ads if they wish.

And they lived happily ever after Ask children to write a different ending to their favorite story, illustrating it with cutout or drawn pictures.

Personal dictionaries Have kids write individual word lists which include words each must learn to read and also those words each would like to learn. After their lists are complete, have them alphabetize them. To make dictionaries, place two or three words on a sheet of paper, give definitions, and illustrate them (optional). When the inside pages are complete, cover with heavy paper and decorate.

Fancy words Let students decorate large lettered words. Use words, such as *Love, Dog, Heart, Hand*.

Word collage After choosing opposite words like *hot* and *cold*, have pupils make a collage by drawing or pasting cutout pictures on a large piece of construction paper. On a smaller sheet, invite them to describe their creation in writing.

FEBRUARY: Mini-teaching unit

Uncommon explorations with a common object:

The Nut

WALNUTS, peanuts, almonds, cashews, hickories, piñons, hazelnuts, chestnuts, and more have provided food for mankind since before recorded history. Nuts can provide your class with hours of uncommon learning explorations, too.

1. Challenge kids to list as many different kinds of nuts as they can in a limited time. Can they find a nut for every letter of the alphabet?

2. Have students guess which five states grow the most nuts (California, Texas, North Carolina, Alabama, and Virginia). What types of nuts are grown in your state? Visit a nearby nut farm.

3. Ask students to bring in many different kinds of nuts. Compare them and derive a class definition of "nut." How does that definition compare with those from the dictionary, the encyclopedia? Do some nuts have more than one name?

4. Introduce a different nut to the class each day for two weeks. Compare colors and textures of nutshells. Examine each with a magnifying glass. Then classify them according to characteristics, such as texture, size, color, shape, and uses.

5. Send for the free brochure "Mr. Peanut's Guide to Nutrition," containing information on the role peanuts play in the four basic food groups. Send to: Educational Services, Standard Brands, Inc., PO Box 2695, Grand Central Station, New York, NY 10017.

6. Give each child an English walnut and a black walnut. Divide and label the chalkboard into two areas: Alike and Different. Have students list as many items in each column as they can.

7. Make a nut tree. Cut a half circle from heavy construction paper. Fold the corners to form a cone and paste. Glue largest nuts around the bottom of the cone and let dry. Keep gluing rings of nuts. Let each ring dry before adding the next.

8. True or False: The coconut, the largest seed in the world, travels thousands of miles across oceans without salt water penetrating its shell. (True) Research and discuss.

9. Man isn't the only animal who eats nuts. The nuthatch, a small tree-climbing bird found in many parts of the United States, wedges nuts into the cracks in bark and cracks (hatches) them open by repeated pecking. Find a photo or film of the nuthatch. Invite kids to watch for one around home and in parks during the winter months.

10. George Washington Carver was a scientist who found many new uses for peanuts. Challenge students to identify new uses they see for peanuts. Then read about Carver and compare your peanut creations with his.

11. Many students don't know that nuts are so high in protein they can, in a balanced diet, take the place of meat. Call your local agricultural extension agent or health food store for nut recipes.

12. Pick four or five different kinds of nuts, weigh each on a metric scale, and find calorie content for each. Does the number of calories vary in proportion to the nut's weight? If so, why? If not, make and test hypotheses explaining the calorie values of different nuts.

13. **Some nuts are poisonous! Warn your students that unknown nuts can be dangerous.** For example: cashews before roasting, horse chestnuts before being made into flour and used in baking.

14. Nut stew is a staple food in parts of Africa. In some places in Europe, bread is made from chestnut flour. Try this recipe for still another way to eat chestnuts. Place in saucepan, cover with cold water, and season with a pinch of salt and celery flakes. Cover and simmer 45 minutes to an hour. Drain, cool, and serve.

15. Is a nutmeg a nut? (Yes) Bring in a whole nutmeg and ask kids to guess the best way to eat it. Then, with the help of cocoa or applesauce, show them.

16. Nuts in music. After reading a summary of Tchaikovsky's *Nutcracker Suite,* play the music. Ask students how well it tells the story.

17. Make finger puppets from nutshells. Paint funny faces with felt-tipped pens and use yarn for hair.

18. Ask a horticulturist how to grow a nut tree. Make plans to plant one at your school on Arbor Day.

19. Have students bring nutcrackers from home. Compare them. On what principles do they work? (Fulcrum) Find ways to open a nutshell, keeping the meat intact.

20. New Year's greetings! Put a note or piece of dried fruit inside a walnut shell; glue back together. □

Martha Sayre is assistant project director of the Early Child Care Center, Lexington, Kentucky.

FEBRUARY: Bulletin Boards

MIX AND MATCH—a favorite learning center for your primaries. Attach a cutout paper painter to the bulletin board. Next to "painter," place a bucket holding 11 paint stirrers, labeled with color words. On a ladder, place 11 colored-paper paint buckets. Children must match colors—stirrers to buckets. This setup is very adaptable to other subjects.   **Vivian Lynn**

MAKE your bulletin board a drill center for all subjects. Alphabetizing is illustrated. Place words randomly on board; repin them alphabetically. Math and science work well also.   **Richard Latta**

LIVEN up your reading corner with a colorful display. Depict a large marching character surrounded with footprints, containing titles of various books on display nearby. Invite kids to read a book. Then each traces his footprint, writes his name and the book's on it, and displays it.   **Leonard J. Basile**

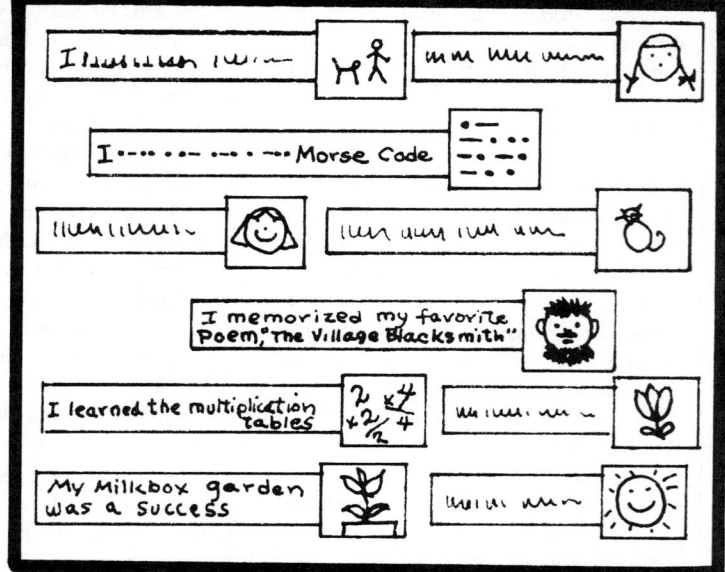

FACE open house and parent conference time confidently after producing the above bulletin board. Have each student list the 10 outstanding things he's learned during the year or the quarter. Together, at a brief conference, select one that is the most important. Then using colored paper, each child writes his out, illustrates it, and then displays it.   **Darby Anderson**

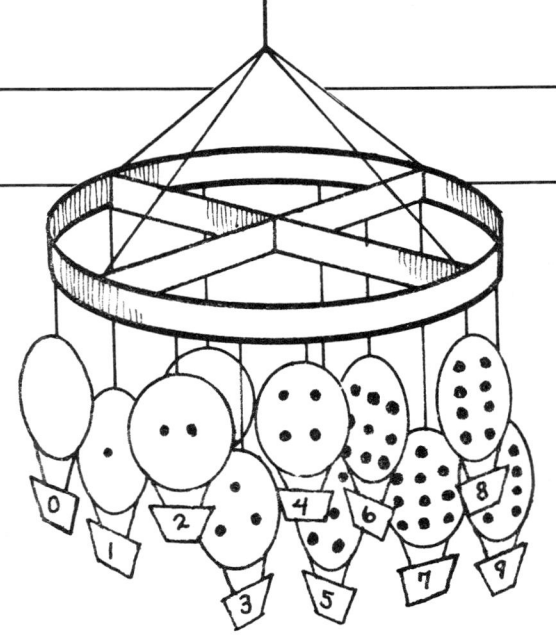

PIQUE interest in math with a number mobile. Cut two ten-inch tagboard strips, staple together at center, and fold out to an X. Cut another strip long enough to encircle X and staple ends. Fold back X ends for tabs and staple to circle. Attach dot cards to circle with thread. Dot cards can be any shape—clowns, kites, shirts, or balloons as shown. (Devise dot facts for grade level.) For other ideas, see *Instructor*'s August issue, page 112. **Mary Lou Alsin**

ALL grade levels can create this valentine garden. Cover board with yellow paper. Draw figure on background or cut parts from paper, assemble, and attach in place. Kids cut heart-shaped cards, decorate with cut paper and paint, and attach to board in a gardenlike display. Strips of twisted green crepe paper become flower stems. Suggest cards be made for family members, relatives, friends. On Valentine's Day, cards are "picked" and taken home. **Vivian Lynn**

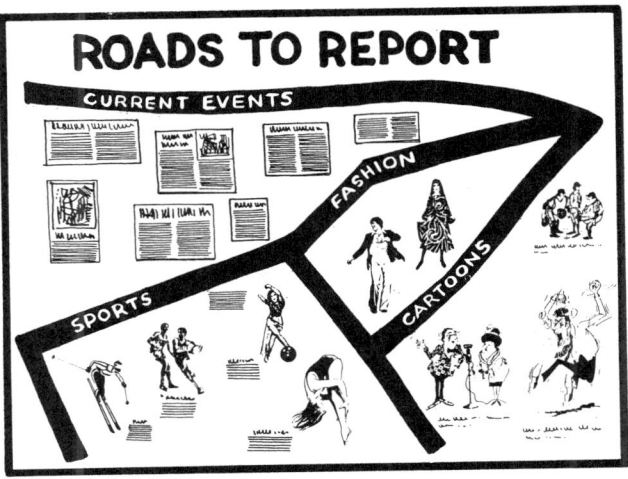

MIDDLE and upper graders develop good health habits through study, discussion, and this bulletin board, featuring popular characters. Draw or cut characters from magazines and newspapers. Write personalized tips on cut colored paper and attach as shown. Study diet, the yearly physical, fresh air/pollution, physical and mental health, play/safety. **Elizabeth Carroll**

THIRD-GRADE current events reporting becomes exciting with a "Roads To Report" bulletin board. Students cut out daily newspaper articles, pictures, ads, and so on and attach them to appropriate labeled spaces—sports, fashion, cartoons, current events. Great for developing individual interests, reading and reporting skills, and awareness of world happenings. **Lynn S. Bryant**

DATELINE

MARCH

Did your students know that March used to be the first month of the year? It's true. Not in America, but in ancient Rome. It wasn't until 45 B.C. when Caesar reformed the calendar that January became our first month and March our third.

Where did the name *March* come from? The Romans, again! March was the time for waging war in ancient Rome so for good luck on the battlefield, the Romans named the month in honor of the god of war, *Mars.*

For a long time this month was called *Martius.* In English, it became *March.* What other words come from the ancient Roman myths? Have your students do some research on the subject. They'll be surprised to find that everything from the names of planets to the names of sink cleansers are influenced by Roman names.

What else is in store for you and your students in March? Just turn the pages to find out.

Red letter days

ANNUAL MARCH EVENTS

These special events usually occur in March, but the exact dates vary from year to year.

Red Cross Month

Youth Art Month

Girl Scout Week (the week of March 12, the day the Girl Scouts organization was founded in 1912)

Shrove Tuesday (always the day before Ash Wednesday)

Mardi Gras (the last feast before Lent, Mardi Gras is properly limited to Shrove Tuesday, but it has come to include the preceding two weeks)

Ash Wednesday (the first day of Lent—40 days to Easter Sunday, not including Sundays)

Easter (a movable Christian feast always on a Sunday—between March 22 and April 25)

Passover or Pesach (a movable eight-day Jewish feast usually in March or April)

Purim (a movable Jewish feast in either February or March)

National Poison Prevention Week (third week in March)

National Music in Our Schools Week (first full week of the month)

National Wildlife Week (the week including the first day of spring)

First day of Spring (March 20 or 21)

National Energy Education Day (1st day of spring)

1 Ohio, our 17th state, and **Nebraska,** our 37th, were admitted into the Union in 1803 and 1867 respectively.

2 Theodor Seuss Geisel, better known as **Dr. Seuss,** was born in 1904. Read *The Cat in the Hat* to celebrate!

3 **Florida** entered the Union in 1845 to become our 27th state. Also, **Alexander Graham Bell,** who invented the telephone, was born in 1847.

It's **National Anthem Day**—the anniversary of the American adoption of the "Star Spangled Banner" as our national anthem in 1931.

4 **Vermont** became our 14th state in 1791.

5 First to fall in the struggle for American independence was **Crispus Attucks** who was killed in the Boston Massacre on this date in 1770.

6 "Remember the Alamo!" **Alamo Day** commemorates the day the Battle of the Alamo ended in 1836. Davy Crockett and 186 other courageous Texans were killed as they tried to defend their compound in San Antonio against the large Mexican Army.

7 Race car driver **Janet Guthrie,** the first woman to qualify at the Indianapolis 500, was born in 1938.

8 **International Women's Day** is celebrated in honor of all women, but especially working women around the globe.

9 **Amerigo Vespucci,** the Italian navigator for whom America was named, was born in 1454.

It's also the day the first patent for false teeth was awarded in 1822.

10 **Harriet Tubman,** a former slave and a prominent abolitionist who led more than 300 slaves north to freedom through the Underground Railroad, died in 1913.

12 The **United States Post Office** was established in 1789.

13 **Uranus** was discovered by Sir William Herschel in 1781.

14 Eli Whitney received a patent on his invention, the **cotton gin,** in 1794. This machine made it possible to separate cotton from the seed about 50 times faster than by hand.

15 Beware the Ides of March! **Julius Caesar** was assassinated on this date in 44 B.C.

Also, **Maine,** our 23rd state, was admitted to the Union in 1820.

16 Comedian **Jerry Lewis** was born in 1926.

17 May the luck of the Irish be with you! It's **St. Patrick's Day** in honor of the patron saint of Ireland who died in 493.

20 In 1852 **Harriet Beecher Stowe** published her classic story *Uncle Tom's Cabin,* which did much to develop Americans' sympathy for slaves.

Also, *Sesame Street's* **Big Bird** celebrates his birthday today!

21 German composer **Johann Sebastian Bach** was born in 1685. Also, Mexican **Benito Pablo Juarez,** symbol of Mexican resistance to foreign intervention, was born in 1806.

22 Congress overwhelmingly approved the proposal of the **Equal Rights Amendment** (ERA) and submitted it to the states for ratification in 1972.

23 "Give me liberty, or give me death!" cried **Patrick Henry** in 1775 as he spoke out in favor of arming Virginians in case of war with England.

25 **Ishi,** the last Yana Indian, died in 1916.

Also, writer **Flannery O'Conner** and feminist **Gloria Steinem** were born today in 1925 and 1936 respectively.

26 American poet **Robert Frost** was born in 1874.

27 **Edward Steichen,** celebrated American photographer, was born in 1879. Also, the **United States Navy** was created in 1794.

28 The **first picture book** just for children was written by Johann Amos Comenius, who was born in 1592.

Also, the **first washing machine** was patented in 1797.

Today is also the anniversary of the accident at the nuclear power plant on **Three Mile Island** in Pennsylvania, which threatened a meltdown in 1979.

29 Janet Aitchison, the world's **youngest author,** was born in 1969. When she was five and a half years old she wrote a story called *The Pirates' Tale,* which was published first in a magazine and later as a book.

Also today, in 1969, **Niagara Falls** stopped falling. Honest! Tons of ice jammed the river's entrance near Buffalo damming the river for almost 30 hours.

30 The **first pencil with an eraser** was patented in 1858.

Also, Dutch painter **Vincent Van Gogh** was born in 1853.

MARCH: Bright Ideas

Illustrations by Mila Lazarevich

SPELL TO WIN

Here's a spelling game that is colorful, fun, and very instructive. Buy or make an assortment of cardboard letters in upper- and lower-case. Make sure each set is a different color. Now divide your class into four groups and give each group a set of letters. Designate four children to serve as the judges for each group. Now give each judge a flag to match his or her team's letter color. Choose one spelling word. From their set of letters, members of each team must select the ones that spell that word. Then members must stand in the correct order, holding the letters. The first group to spell the word correctly gets one point. Judges must watch their groups carefully and as soon as a word is correct, raise their flags to alert the teacher.
JOAN LINCOLN

CREATIVE CAREER CONTEST

Here's a way to introduce kids to a wide variety of careers they might be choosing from in the future. Start by setting up a "career corner" in your classroom. You'll need an area that's free from distractions, a table, chair, paper and pencils, and a good vocational book for reference.

Now select an object of your choice, such as a pumpkin, a magazine, or an article of clothing, and place it on the table. Kids are to go to the career corner, one at a time, and list all the occupations that might be associated with the sale, production, or utilization of the chosen object. The student who comes up with the longest list is the winner.

Here are some "spin-off" activities to accompany the career contest.
1. Pretend you are involved in one of the occupations you have listed. Write a letter to an imaginary friend describing the work you do.
2. Write a "want ad" for the career of your choice

to appear in the local newspaper.
3. Write a poem or limerick about one of the careers listed. Describe a typical day on the job.
JILL P. GANN

RHYME TIME
Try a sequential approach to the writing of rhymed verse. First, list four to six rhyming words. Now draw two lines and place one of the rhyming words at the end of each line. The two rhyming words you choose should have some related quality that might make an interesting kind of thought.

_____bug
_____rug

Now have your kids decide what words to place before the rhyming words. Ideas may range from those that are funny or serious to those that are just plain ridiculous. For instance:
  A skinny green bug
  Ate up the shaggy rug
Next have children work with two pairs of rhyming words, then three.
BARBARA K. SHELLENBERGER

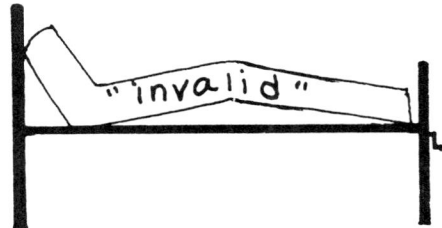

GIVING WORDS HOSPITAL CARE
Sketch a hospital bed on your chalkboard. Each time a child misuses or mispronounces a word while reading aloud, he or she must put the word to bed

in the "word hospital." After the "word doctor" has heard the word read and pronounced properly three or four times, the child may remove that word from the bed to make room for another one.
SHIRLEY SHRATTER

PUZZLING ILLNESS
When a student in your class is ill and absent for more than a few days, try making a get-well puzzle. Have your kids write "We miss you" or "Get well soon" in the center of a square of posterboard and sign their names around it. Now cut the board into puzzle pieces, put them in a bag, and ask someone who lives nearby to deliver the gift to the sick child.
MARGARET SHAUERS

SHAMROCK FESTIVAL
Here's a manipulative bulletin board display with a St. Patrick's Day theme. Use it to reinforce basic multiplication skills. Start with a light-colored backgound, then cut large leprechaun's face from construction paper. Place the leprechaun in the center of your board, under the heading, "Shamrock Festival." Now make some green construction paper shamrocks. Using a black felt-tipped pen, print one multiplication equation across the front of each shamrock. Now cut apart each shamrock so the first part of the equation is on one piece and the answer on the other. Tack only the beginning pieces to your

bulletin board surrounding the leprechaun. Collect the answer pieces and place them in a large envelope tacked to the bottom left-hand corner of the bulletin board. Students are to take turns going to the board and selecting answer pieces from the envelope. They must then match the answers to the appropriate pieces on the board, so complete shamrocks result.
PAULA J. PLOWEY

EGG COLLAGE
This variation of the Easter egg uses small pieces of paper that can be saved from other art projects or cut from old magazines. Draw the light outline of an egg with a design. Choose colors and paste pieces close together, filling in each area. Mixing magazine pieces with plain colors adds interest. TALIS BYERS

EATING OF THE GREENS
To stimulate interest in vegetables and encourage good nutritional habits, why not celebrate "The Eating of the Greens" for St. Patrick's Day? Gather together green vegetables such as lettuce, cabbage,

MARCH: Bright Ideas

raw spinach, green pepper, celery, parsley, and dill pickles. Slice and arrange them attractively, then have children select their party snacks from this "green" buffet. To accompany the snacks, serve green fruit-based punch. Plan your taste treat for the end of the day, then watch as kids return two or three times to a table that packs a punch with a crunch! This is an activity parents will applaud as well.
CAROLE SILEA

EXPRESSIVE SPEECH GAME
People often ascribe human qualities to animals and insects and birds. Have children complete each sentence by choosing the creature that best fits the saying.
1. Wise as an...(owl)
2. Peaceful as a...(dove)
3. Courageous as a ... (lion)
4. Quiet as a...(mouse)
5. Playful as a...(pup)
6. Stubborn as a...(mule)
7. Innocent as a...(lamb)
8. Slippery as an...(eel)
9. Eager as a...(beaver)
10. Sly as a...(fox)
EDWARD R. WALSH

THE EASTER EXPRESS
If you enjoy giving your kids a surprise for Easter, here's an easy but fun way to do it. Have each student bring in a colorful egg carton. Cut off the lids to save for another project. Now tape black cutout wheels to the cartons or attach with paper fasteners, then add Easter grass. Make a large train engine and

caboose out of colored construction paper. Cut two of these and staple one on each side of the two end cartons. Place the engine on a table and as each student remembers to bring in an egg carton, add another train car. Place caboose carton at the end. For your Easter party, fill each piece of the train with treats.
PHYLLIS MARCUS

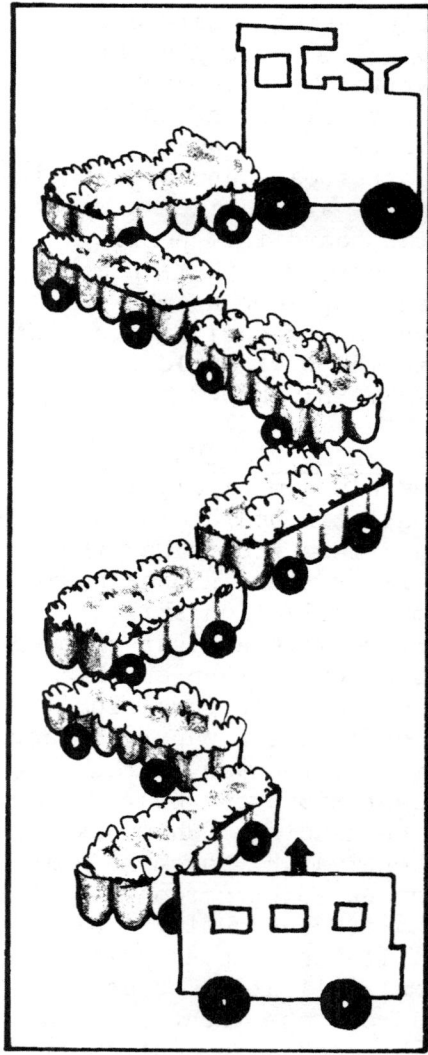

LOOKING AHEAD
After school pictures are taken and returned, most teachers are given a long

strip of black and white proofs or a few extra class composites. Here is a career education idea that uses photos in an intriguing way. Have each child trace around a dime or penny somewhere on a sheet of manila paper and then cut out the circle. (Very young children may need help.) Then ask each child to make a picture of an adult doing a specific job. Tell them to use the holes for the faces of their people, but put hair or hats around or over the holes. Now have each of your students tape his or her picture to the back of the drawing so that the face peers out of the hole. Mount the pictures on a bulletin board display with the caption, "What will you be in 1993?"
JOAN THAMES

A BUNCH OF GOOD EGGS
Students aren't the only people in your school who need a little positive reinforcement from time to time. So do teachers, aides, and other staff members! Here's a perfect springtime moral-booster. Cut out a stack of paper eggs and write short comments about fellow staff members on them. Pin eggs on the bulletin board in your faculty lounge. Leave blank eggs on a table for others to write "praise-o-grams."
CONNIE ZANE

OVER THE RAINBOW
For an art project for St. Patrick's Day that's different from the usual shamrocks and leprechauns,

try making rainbows! Start with some research, discussion, and a bit of folklore about rainbows. What do your kids dream of finding at the end of their rainbows: cars, famous people, pets, bicycles? As they watercolor their desires, be sure they keep the proper spectrum in order--red, orange, yellow, and so on.
GERALDINE DeSALVO

DIVIDE AND CONQUER
Room dividers can solve many discipline problems and provide for a well-managed, comfortable atmosphere in your room.

Hang large, colorful pieces of muslin or heavy material from wooden dowels to section off a particular area of the room. Next, add traffic signs made with dowel sticks, blocks, and colored tagboard. Signs might read, Quiet Zone! Serious Studies Only! or Caution--Testing Zone.
JULIE A. McDONNELL

STUDENT "TEACH" SHIRTS
Many physical education student teachers are assigned to the elementary level for such a short period of time that they find it very difficult to learn the names of their children. It's helpful if classroom teachers ask

all parents to send to school a plain white tee-shirt, at least two sizes larger than their child. A big heart can be traced on the front of the shirt and children can then color the path that blood travels through this major muscle, which is so vital to any physical activity. Kids can then print their names on the backs of their tee-shirts, to be worn in all physical education classes. Since the shirts are big, they can be slipped on over regular clothes just as one would wear a paint smock to art class.
ROSALIND K. KOCIUBA

FIND THE PLACE
For a quick test to help you spot those children who have difficulty with place value, duplicate the chart that follows. Ask kids to supply numbers which come before and after the given numbers.

Before	Given	After
	999	
	909	
	800	
	1,021	
	750	
	1,001	
	4,099	
	310	
	9,909	

ISOBEL LIVINGSTONE

WINDOWS OF THE MIND
This art project adds to further self-awareness and exploration in language arts. Give your children window frames. (These may be actual small, wood frames or cardboard strips stapled together to suggest frames.) Direct

students to paint scenes they would most like to see if looking out real windows. This causes each child to remember his or her most cherished sight or to visualize a much-desired moment. When frames are placed over the scenes, kids can preserve their dreams, visually speaking. As a follow-up activity, ask each child to write about his or her scene.
PALMYRA ANDREWS

SPRING GREETING
Practice cutting circles without patterns by making this simple card. Draw and cut out two circles. Paste large circle on the card. Draw eyes and beak on small circle and paste to a paper loop. Paste loop to body. Add crayon legs and grass and paint chick. BEATRICE BACHRACH

MARCH: Bright Ideas

HANDY REMINDER
What do a handshake and an informal letter have in common? Each is a friendly gesture. So use a simple hand tracing to help kids remember the five parts of a friendly letter. Very young students may enjoy giving each part a personal name, such as Heidi Heading, Gary Greeting, Brent Body, Cathy Closing, and Suzie Signature. To carry this learning device one step further, stories may be written about the job each character does. Suzie Signature's story might go like this: "My name is Suzie Signature. I am a very important part of a letter. Without me a letter can be a mystery, but with me the mystery is solved. I can make people very happy when I'm part of a letter. I travel long distances sometimes just to be heard from. Don't forget me!"
TALIS BYERS

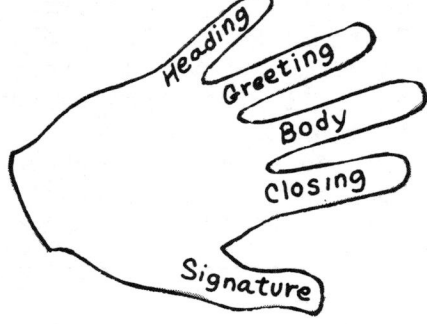

PLASTIC SLATES
Have your kids make their own slates from transparent gripper report covers for practice in all subjects. One cover yields two slates. Cut cover at the fold and tape each half to a piece of colorful oaktag the same size. Use 3/4" tape along all four sides of each half. Dark crayon or felt-tipped pens will mark the surface and a soft cloth will erase the marks.

    These slates can be used effectively in arithmetic, language, spelling and phonics, or review in science or social studies.
ANNE M. CORBETT

TRIPLE LAYERED DESIGNS
A pair of pointed scissors and three sheets of the same-sized construction paper are all you need to produce open designs with a layered look. Poke or stab into each sheet of paper at random and cut interesting shapes. Use straight-line shapes (rectilinear) or shapes with curved lines (curvilinear) or try a combination of both. Be sure to poke into the paper and not cut in from the edges. When substantial areas of paper have been removed from each piece, stack all three sheets together and staple them. Add a fourth sheet for backing if desired.
JOAN MARY MACEY

THE LIST GAME
Keeping kids busy while you take attendence or count lunches can be a problem--but not if you teach them to play the "List Game." Write a different topic for list-making on your chalkboard each morning, such as green things, wet things, happy things, and so on. The student who can write the longest list during attendence time is the winner for that day. Use some of the most unique lists as inspiration for imaginative short stories and poems.
KATHIE PIPER

CARD SHARK MATH
To make math drill fun, all you need is a deck of ordinary playing cards with the Jacks, Queens, and Kings removed. Keep the aces to represent the number one. Shuffle and deal them, two at a time, to each of two players. At a given signal, players turn over their cards; the first one to call out the correct sum of the two cards is the winner and gets to keep the cards. The big winner is the one with the most cards at the end of the game. To increase difficulty, deal more cards to each player. To practice subtraction, have students call out the difference between their highest and lowest cards. Multiplication can also be practiced this way. From this drill students learn that knowing a sum enables them to give answers much faster than they could by counting. SANDY HOUSTON

NO E's ALLOWED!
Try this challenging word game. The letter e is probably used more than any other letter of the alphabet. Can your kids think fast enough to avoid using it? Choose two teams.

One team asks the other team questions involving a one- or two-word answer. The trick is to answer without using the letter e. For example: What two words stand for parents? Father and mother would be incorrect answers. Ma and pa, on the other hand, would be correct, as would mom and dad. The first team to get caught using more than five e's has lost the game!
DAVE BLOOM

RULE OF THUMB
Here's a way to help primary kids become more independent about choosing library books they can read themselves. Have them pick out a book, turn to the middle, and read silently. While reading, each child should put a thumb on the table. Every time a word is missed, a finger should be put down. If all fingers go down, on one page, the book is too difficult.
CECILY PURCELL

DECORATE FOR MARCH
In the month of blustery winds and swooping kites,
make your room reflect the great outdoors. Cut fleece-shaped clouds from doubled pieces of white construction paper. Cut thin, curving shapes from a double cloud and paste or tape pale blue tissue on the back of one piece, over cutout areas. Paste clouds together and hang where light can shine through blue "linings." Make kites in the same way: cut kites all shapes, colors, and sizes from doubled construction paper. Cut out patterns on kites. Line with thin, contrasting colored paper and paste matching pieces together. Add tails made by tying scraps of lightweight tissue or paper toweling at two-inch intervals on a piece of colored yarn. Hang kites and clouds overhead to add the breezy touch of March to your room.
JANE K. PRIEWE

LUCKY IS...
Try this St. Patrick's Day activity in creative writing to show your kids that lucky events may have unlucky counterparts. Start by having each child make a large green shamrock from construction paper, then a slightly smaller white one. Now have the kids mount their white shamrocks on top of the green ones for an area to write on. Each child is to print one lucky event and its unlucky counterpart across the front of his or her shamrock. Some examples are:

1. Lucky is finding a hamster; unlucky is when it bites!
2. Lucky is seeing King Kong; unlucky is King Kong seeing you!
When all the shamrocks are completed, arrange them on your bulletin board or scatter them around your classroom walls.   BRENDA McGEE

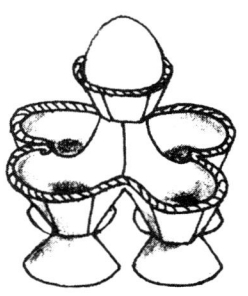

TIERED EGG HOLDER
Cut four connecting cups from a papier-mache egg carton. Cut and glue four separate sections to the bottom of the connecting cups for legs. Cut one more cup and glue to center of four sections. Glue yarn around edges.
JAMES W. PERRIN, JR.

AIRY ANSWERS
Have children write the following short rhyming riddle as a handwriting exercise and illustrate it as an art activity. Can your class think of other good subjects for March riddles?

A bird with no song,
You go flying along.
A bird with no wings,
You make use of strings.
A bird with no feather,
Will you fly forever?
Answer: A kite.
MARY R. PALMER

MARCH: Strike up the band!

A Salute to Music-in-Our Schools Week

Tips for the Tuneless

"I'm so tone-deaf that I don't know if a band is playing the 'Star Spangled Banner' until the audience stands up. How can I ever teach music to my students?"

This teacher is not alone in her feelings of inadequacy when it comes to the subject of music. Many others like her are insufficiently prepared to tackle this area of the curriculum due to a lack of musical ability or proper training.

If you fall into this category, it doesn't mean your case is hopeless. There are many ways to enrich the lives of your students through joyous, aesthetic, and valuable musical experiences—even if you're a nonmusician. Following is a list of ideas to start you on your way. Try any or all of them—they're sure to bring new harmony to your music curriculum.

1. Set up a music center in a corner of the room. Start with a record player equipped with one or two sets of earphones and some inexpensive recordings of classical and popular music. Add colorful pictures of instruments and musicians and leave a scrapbook open with scissors and paste nearby so students can add pictures at their leisure. From your school library, create a display of attractively illustrated books on music and composers, including the plots to operas and ballets. Now, when individual students have finished class assignments, they can delve into the world of music on their own—without disturbing others.

2. If you can't carry a tune—and even if you can—it's always fun to sing along with records. Folk songs are the simplest, and there are many excellent collections available. Artists like Burl Ives, Pete Seeger, Ed McCurdy, and others have recorded lots of material that's suitable for children. In addition, a number of music book series include records that provide accompaniments for varied songs of good quality.

3. Invite "guest artists" to visit your school or classroom. You'll be surprised to find that many of your students' parents, relatives, or friends are fine performing musicians (some may even be professionals) and would be happy to demonstrate their particular talents. If your students are of varied ethnic backgrounds, these performances could feature music from different cultures and be related to studies of other countries.

4. Get acquainted with the resources of your local library or curriculum media center. Numerous recordings and tape cassettes—some with accompanying filmstrips—and films on music are available to teachers on a loan basis. Many fine lessons can be based on these materials, whether or not you have any previous knowledge of music.

5. Music education films can be ordered directly from businesses and manufacturers, often for little or no charge. For example, films of the Leonard Bernstein Concerts for children can be ordered from the American Telephone and Telegraph Company, 195 Broadway, New York, New York.

6. Sometimes commercial films deal with musical subjects or are based on musical productions. Among these are *Fantasia,* *Song of Norway, The King and I, Oklahoma, Oliver,* and *The Wiz.* If any of these are being shown in your community, take your class to see them, to culminate discussions, reading assignments, or listening sessions focused on the music.

7. Educational television is an obvious and ready source. PBS programs have included numerous concerts and ballets as well as fine instructional series. Among the most successful has been "Music Is . . . ," a series of ten 30-minute music appreciation lessons using animation and live performances. Videotapes of this series, produced by WETA-TV, Washington, D.C., have been prepared for distribution to New York state schools, free of charge, by Association Films, 1815 North Fort Meyer Drive, Suite 107, Arlington, VA 22209. Guides to the program, including lesson plans and review questions, have been issued by the New York State Department of Education.

8. Commercial television is also a good source of musical experiences. Subscribe to a suitable television guide so you can be aware of upcoming productions in time to send announcements to parents, suggesting that they watch the shows along with their children.

9. Finally, read professional journals and union publications carefully. You'll be sure to find advertisements for musical games, ready-made materials, visual aids, and additional resources. Also, a number of companies offer free films, booklets, posters, and other materials.

Ruth Zinar is an associate professor of music education at York College of the City University of New York.

Give 'em Rhythm

If each of your students seems to be marching to the beat of a different drummer, maybe it's time to give all of them a little training in the elements of rhythm. Hands-on experience with musical accompaniment is the best approach, but there may not be room in your school's budget for the purchase of instruments. Well, don't let that stop you. Here are all the instructions you'll need to make inexpensive, easily constructed rhythm instruments that will have your children tapping and clapping to beat the band!

Maracas. To make this particular variety, you'll need one empty soda can, one half-inch wooden dowel that's about nine inches long, 1/16 cup of popcorn or dried

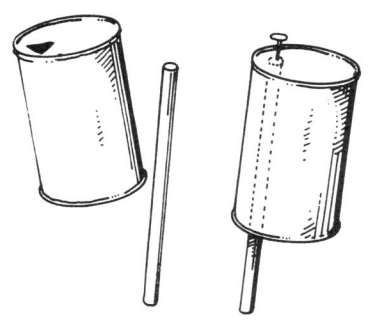

beans (you can also use the aluminum rings from the tops of several soda cans), one ribbed nail or screw, and clear plastic tape. Fill the bottom of the can with popcorn or beans. Insert the dowel into the "flip top" opening until one end rests firmly on the bottom of the can. Now turn the can upside down and drive a nail or screw through the aluminum bottom, securing the dowel into place.

Make one or two of these simple instruments for each child in your class. Then let the kids decorate their maracas with colored construction paper or paints so each instrument is given a personal touch.

Note: If you use the newer aluminum cans with environmentally safe "no throw" opening tabs, you'll find that the hole will be the ideal size for your half-inch dowel. However, if you use the older models, with U-shaped openings, you may have to wrap aluminum foil around the dowel where it protrudes from the opening so beans or popcorn kernels don't fall out during use.

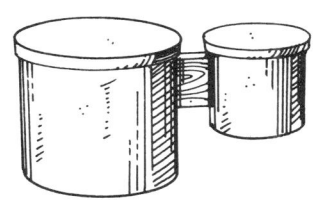

Bongos. Kids love to bang away on percussion instruments. Here's one you can make with two tin cans of different sizes, plastic lids, or a piece of inner tubing stretched across the tops of the cans, a small wooden stick or dowel, and a few screws. Punch a hole in each can, about an inch below the top. Now insert a screw into each hole, place the wood between the cans, and drive the protruding screws into the wood to hold it in place. These "bongos" may be painted, decaled, or decoupaged. If you feel really industrious, try adding a third or fourth can for a more sophisticated sound.

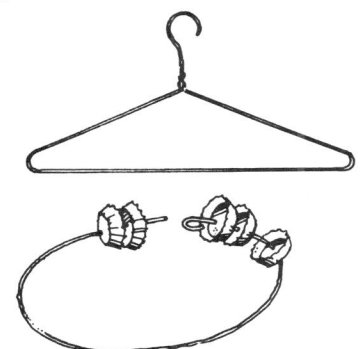

Tambourines. Below are instructions for making two different types of tambourines. Try them both to determine which is best suited to your needs. The first kind requires 10 or 15 bottle caps, one foot of strong wire (a straightened coat hanger is perfect), and clear plastic tape. With a hammer and a large nail, make holes in the centers of the bottle caps. Now bend the wire to form a curved shape and, using a pair of pliers, make a hook at one end to keep the caps from falling off once you place them on the wire. When they're all assembled, make another hook at the remaining end and join the two hooks together. Wrap with plastic tape for safety. If you use bottle caps of assorted sizes, this can be a very colorful instrument.

The second type of tambourine is especially simple to make. All you need are two heavy-duty paper plates, eight bottle caps, and paper fasteners or six feet of heavy

yarn. Put all the bottle caps in one plate. Cover it with the second plate so you've created a flying saucer effect. If you choose to use paper fasteners, push them through both plates at two-inch intervals. If you'd rather use yarn, punch holes in both plates at one-inch intervals. Now thread the yarn through the holes, circling the plates twice for extra strength. Because construction is so simple, you might want your kids to make their own tambourines. Have them decorate their instruments in a combination art and music project.

Gong: You can use this instrument as a stop-start signal or to help your class explore the vibrating qualities of musical sound. You'll need two feet of strong rope and the large metal lid from a commercial dry-cleaning detergent barrel. (These can usually be obtained from your local laundry or dry cleaner. However, if this isn't possible, the lid from a five-gallon bucket of paint or tar will suffice.) Use a hammer and thick nail to punch two holes into the rim of the lid. Now thread one end of the rope through each hole and tie the ends together.

If properly planned, the construction of these rhythm instruments can be an excellent rainy-day activity or art project for your students. In addition, you can integrate them into other areas of your curriculum such as social studies. For instance, when teaching a unit on Mexico, you might want to introduce the song "Mexican Hat Dance" using homemade maracas.

Don't consider these instructions absolute. Use your own imagination to elaborate on the instruments, and involve your students in the process, too. Then sit back and let your class strike up the band—you'll be pleased with the results!

Ripley Marston is an instructor of elementary physical education courses at the University of Northern Iowa in Cedar Falls, Iowa.

MARCH: Intergalactic activities

CLOSE ENCOUNTERS
OF THE CLASSROOM KIND

How to use science fiction in all subject areas

I would feel very good if someday they colonize Mars when I am 93 years old and the leader of the first colony says: "I really did it because I was hoping there would be a Wookie up here." George Lucas.

Film producer George Lucas, you just might get your wish because science fiction is the rising star on the teaching horizon! From *Star Trek*'s Mr. Spock to Stanley Kubrick's "Hal," intragalactic forces are working their way into every subject in the curriculum and for teachers and kids of all ages.

Why has science fiction become so popular? *Star Trek, Star Wars, Space: 1999, 2001: A Space Odyssey,* and *Close Encounters of the Third Kind* have, of course, contributed to the attraction. But teachers have also discovered that science fiction gives their students an opportunity to work their imaginations in ways which are creative, entertaining, and socially significant.

There are various kinds of science fiction. Science-fiction writer Isaac Asimov makes three categories: gadgets, adventure, or sociological stories. Donald Wollheim, author of *The Universe Makers: Science Fiction Today* (Harper and Row) lists four branches: imaginary voyages, future predictions, remarkable inventions, and social satire. And all of these themes offer exciting voyages in your classroom exploration.

But why teach science fiction to elementary students? Science fiction is no longer considered "out of this world" or pure fantasy; the best combines scientific knowledge with good writing. As Asimov points out, sci-ence fiction is a worthwhile educational device. Today's children, who may face more changes in the future than any other generation, are made aware that the future offers a wide range of possibilities and choices.

How to get started

Unless you were raised on Buck Rogers or Flash Gordon, odds are your students know more about science fiction than you do. The best way to become familiar with this subject, then, is by reading short stories and novels yourself. Try authors like Robert Heinlein, Isaac Asimov, Ray Bradbury, or Poul Anderson, Next, contact local or school librarians, bookshops, and science-fiction enthusiasts to gather suggested materials for kids. (At the end of this article you'll find "The Science-Fiction Library," a listing of novels, short stories, films, records, and cassettes suitable for nine- to thirteen-year-olds, prepared by Lahna Diskin, associate professor of English, Trenton State College, New Jersey.)

Start your study of science fiction with these activities:

1. Each day read a portion of a science-fiction story, leaving students in suspense until the next day.
2. Display books, calendars, and posters of scenes from *Star Wars, Star Trek,* and other science-fiction stories. Set up materials in a library corner or in an interest center.
3. Use simulation board games that are science fiction oriented to get kids thinking "sci-fi."

Language arts encounters

Reading science fiction is a fascinating way to begin challenging students to imagine the unimaginable. Science-fiction literature is an excursion into unknown frontiers which can excite your students. At the same time, it enhances children's vocabulary, improves their oral expression, and increases their curiosity about science. But science fiction and the language arts are compatible in other ways. After you've read some science-fiction stories try these activities:

Write a different ending to a science-fiction story you've read.

Develop a dictionary of words related to science fiction and include such words as *androids* and *light-years.*

Play "hangman" or other vocabulary games using terms, names, places, and facts in the stories.

Write a class science-fiction story. The first player makes up a line about a new planet, for example, and writes it down. He passes it to the player behind him. The next player, in turn, adds a story line, and so on, until the last player has had a turn.

Divide the class into groups to assemble a specified number of sentences that describe the world in 500 years. Illustrate the story and bind into a book.

Sponsor a debate about science-fiction issues, such as UFOs, alien life in outer space, man vs. machine, or the likelihood of space colonies.

Dramatize stories or pantomime a character, such as Captain Nemo.

Write "A day in the life of . . ." one science-fiction character.

Make murals, dioramas, and booklets about stories read.

Read science-fiction stories or novels by one particular author. Then do a drama, radio play, booklet, mural, or guessing game based on these stories. Or make a videotape with sound effects and artistic scenes.

Think up your own science-fiction book of records based on the stories you've read. For instance, who was the tallest creature? What was the most bizarre effect?

Investigate myths—old and new. Look at the popular works of J. R. R. Tolkein or others. Then suggest students create "far-out" myths.

Try some story starters. *What if . . . people could visit an event in the past?* (What would happen?) *What if . . . everything stopped moving? Permanently froze? Disappeared?*

Science treks

There are many ways science and science fiction interact. (Writers Jules Verne and H. G. Wells were scientists in their own rights!) Try different science experiments or problem-solving activities. For example,

In a subject like astronomy, speculate about space colonies! Would it be possible to discover a new planet? What kind of life might be on the planets you've studied? Stage interviews between aliens from outer space and "earthlings." Questions can range from the obvious "Why are you so shiny and purple?" to social matters like "Will we get along?"

When studying the human body, students may be interested in bionic people and the far-reaching effects of heart transplants, bone and blood replacements, and so on. Ask students: What would happen if a person's body contained many artificial internal organs? Would this person still be considered a human being? What would he be able to do that most people couldn't? (Science fiction has already considered many of these often chilling effects. Take a look at the original *Frankenstein Monster,* for instance.)

Set up interest centers on robots. Read, for example, Isaac Asimov's novel, *I, Robot* (Doubleday). Then suggest students write their own descriptions or make robot models.

Inventions like the automobiles, light bulbs, and telephones were all considered science fiction 100 years ago. Now we think they save people time and change their lives. Make a list of other inventions (airplanes, bicycles, calculators, cameras, clocks, computers, paint, paper, and so on). Rate these conveniences according to those "most necessary" and "least necessary." Which ones are at the top of the list?

Think up new inventions. Look around your community. What "invention" could replace one already in existence? Would time or effort be saved? How much fuel, if any, would this invention take? How will new inventions change the world your students will live in? Answers to these questions could be the basis for new science-fiction stories, puppet plays, or models of new inventions.

How could changes in natural events affect the future of Earth? Discuss, for example, what would happen if endangered species suddenly began to multiply for no apparent reason. Or if an animal that is habitually shy gradually lost its timidity. Or what would happen if people took their pets or other animals to another planet?

Weather is another subject of interest to science-fiction fans. Talk about the following possibilities.

Suppose you could control the weather? A storm is heading your way. But a large device is invented to blow it away. How could its use affect nearby regions and other parts of the world?

Or imagine an invention which could automatically regulate local conditions. One day, the device breaks down and people are forced to contend with very hot weather. What would happen then? What if the device could not be fixed? How would this affect people who have been accustomed to year-round comfort? What advantage could dome cities offer? In addition to writing answers, students could build imaginary models, dramatize an event, or make other scenes by using paper-mache.

Figure out new ecosytems. Nancy Broz at Moorestown (New Jersey) Middle School, had students spend three weeks designing new ecosystems. A team of 100 students divided into groups. They spent the first week reading stories and viewing films; the second week planning their ecosystems; and a third building their environment right down to the models for sewage, shelters, food, and so on. They presented these to the rest of the class, wrote descriptions of them for a newspaper, and voted on the best one. One group even came up with "Life in a Blade of Grass," complete with a transportation system!

Solve environmental problems. Suppose trouble is brewing because of the litter floating in space. Certain kinds of litter are even clumping together. Under the right conditions, these clumps explode, scattering pollution far and wide. Distant neighbors become irritated by these explosions and threaten to take action. What might happen?

Many scientists have found the subject *time* particularly fascinating in science fiction. For example, look at H. G. Wells's story *The Time Machine.* (Older students might also enjoy this movie.) Ask: If you had a time machine in your class, where would you go? Or what if you could live 1,000 years? Or what if the time machine helped you see into the future?

Investigate the origins of scientific words and terms. In science fiction, many of these words are make-believe. But learn the meaning behind the names and why they are appropriate.

Turn a large cardboard box into a weird invention called "The Ask It Machine." Ask each child to write a question related to science. These may be about terms, objects, travel, and so on. Divide the class in two teams Each player gets one turn to pick a question from the weird machine and answers it in fact or in fiction. The only rule is that the answer sound plausible. If it is too "wild," the other team may answer it or choose a different question.

Far-out social studies

Science fiction isn't limited to speculation about science and technology. In most of these discussions, people are involved. For example, Alvin Toffler warned of the effect of rapid change in the future in his book, *Future Shock* (Random). But for children to gain any understanding of the con-

MARCH: Intergalactic activities

cept *change,* they must understand both "past" and "future" changes in their own lives.

Have children list the 10 most important changes in their lives. Then list 10 changes in their parents' lives and then their grandparents' lives. What about their future children's lives? What changes might these people experience?

Ask students: What do you remember happening in the past that you least expected? How were you involved? Could you have done something about it beforehand? Would you be better off if this particular event had not happened? What do you feel will happen to you in the future?

Look for the effects of change in various science-fiction stories. Ask students to observe how change affects them by looking for examples of it in their own neighborhood. For example, on the way to school notice if a building has been torn down or a new traffic light set up. Record these changes. Or go on a walking tour of the local area. What changes are there?

Ask: How will your city look years from now? 50 years? 100? 500? What kinds of changes will take place on your street? What new features might be added? What kinds of changes would help the neighborhood?

Construct a display of your neighborhood as it looks today and then how it could look tomorrow. Title it "Our Changing City." Include other pictures, models, dioramas, word cards, and stories.

Talk about energy. What energy needs will we have in the future? What changes will have to be made in life-styles in the future? What if there was an entirely new energy source? What if we ran out of energy? Or, what if all our energy problems were solved by space solar stations? What kinds of changes would take place?

Explore the outer limits in "pretend" situations. For example, suppose the earth was visited by aliens? How would these aliens look? What "first impressions" would you have of them and they of us? Write an imaginary dialogue. (Then speculate how

you would communicate if neither spoke the same language.)

Plan an expedition to a distant galaxy. What would you take? How would you prepare?

Simulate a different environment in your classroom. Make the atmosphere of the room look different. What kinds of scenery, customs, language, recreation, communication, music, food, machines, vehicles, clothing, and other aspects could you invent? The more research, thought, and creative efforts, the more "realistic" your simulation will be. This may be a long, ongoing project, but one worthwhile pursuing.

Play "This Is Your Future." Small groups of students draw their versions of what the future might be like for them—including good and bad points.

Intragalactic math

For some science-fiction authors, math is a necessary tool for constructing different, imaginary worlds. To look at the math aspect of science fiction, try the following:

Pretend inhabitants of another planet have a different way of counting. What kind of system might it be? Might it be a base five? Six? Two? How would computations be made?

Look at the nature of computers. Ask: How have they changed peoples' lives? What are some computers used for? What mathematical languages do computers use and why? Do computers all look the same? How are they put to use in science-fiction stories?

Take out your calculators! What new uses of calculators are there? How have calculators changed lives? How could they change lives in the future?

As students read science-fiction stories, they are likely to read various terms describing distances between two given places. These figures are meant to give the reader an impression of reality, but they can also be helpful in extending children's experiences with measurements. For example *length, width, height,* and *weight* are often referred to by different names in those stories. Ask students to make a list of the terms they've encountered in their reading.

After students have collected the terms above, arrange them on a chart. Make a comparison to the English or metric systems. Try simple problems using other measurements.

Invent a "measuring machine" using milk or cardboard cartons. Draw the ideas on paper first and then make machines out of sponges, empty food boxes, paper bags, pieces of cardboard, and even discards like broken calculators and clocks. Students can share these machines with each other and challenge their classmates to solve problems or play games, using different measurements.

Space-age art

Through art, children become involved in science fiction in other ways. Some of your language arts, science, or social studies projects may have resulted in various art activities —drawings, paintings, cut-and-paste projects, or models. But in addition, try these:

When a science-fiction author writes about a fantastic animal or a strange environment, he has a vision of what it looks like. But students can draw their own interpretations, too. What a surprise it is to many children to find that the character they so strongly visualized is not the same as another artist's version.

Make models of future cities. Include models of roads, cars, trains, buildings, airplanes, and so on. What new forms of transportation might there be—like the moving sidewalk?

Draw or paint robots, imaginary planets or environments, unusual gadgets and inventions, or even fantastic happenings.

Design collages that depict scenes, people, objects, and so on.

Make mobiles containing words, cards, pictures, or small models.

Create science-fiction puppets of imaginary devices, people, or animals. Use screws, clips, nuts and bolts, discarded rubber gloves, braided cloth, unusual buttons, erasers, shiny pieces of fabric and aluminum foil . . . in science fiction the possibilities are endless!

Dorothy Zjawin

MARCH: A story for St. Patrick's Day

I wish, I wish, . . .

Cyndi Young

IT had been a rough day, even by a 12-year-old's standards. Davy slipped out the back door and ran into the comforting quiet of the woods behind his house.

He should have known bad luck was in store for him when he leaped out of bed late and rushed to the bus stop . . . only to remember it was Saturday.

Disgusted, he'd stomped back into the house, slamming the door behind him. "Davy!" his mother had scolded. When he had wheeled around to apologize, he'd knocked over his mother's favorite vase. It had shattered on the floor and he'd been sent to his room in disgrace.

Davy collapsed on a fallen log and leaned back against a moss-covered maple. "I wish this day had never happened. Oh, I wish, I wish . . .'

"And what might you be wanting, lad?" said a chipper voice at Davy's shoulder, startling him.

A tiny man—he couldn't have been over three feet tall—perched himself on the log next to Davy. He crossed his green-clad legs, folded his green-clad arms, and gave Davy a quizzical glance.

"Who are you?" Davy whispered.

"Why, Davy O'Shaunessy," the little man answered. "I'm a leprechaun for sure."

A leprechaun! Davy's grandmother had often told him about such creatures. She claimed to have seen leprechauns when she was a young lass in Ireland. Supposedly, they had the power to grant wishes and make dreams come true.

"Do you make wishes come true?"

"Aye, that I do, lad. Do you be requiring something?" The little man flicked a speck of dust from his sleeve and straightened his tie. "If so, I be at your service." He took off his bright green hat, leaped to his feet, and bowed low.

Davy couldn't believe that his luck was actually taking a turn for the better. He could ask for anything—money for his father, beautiful clothes for his mother, toys for himself. He could travel. There were just too many choices.

"Well, lad?" The little man's eyes twinkled. "It's not easy to decide, is it?"

"No, it's not," was Davy's solemn reply.

"How does this sound to you, me boy? You go home and think about this tonight. Then, you meet me here, at this very spot, tomorrow afternoon at three. You can tell me your wish then."

Davy was overjoyed. He thanked the little man a dozen times, then ran for home. When he turned around to wave good-by, the tiny man in green had disappeared.

All night long Davy worried. He even went so far as to make a list of everything he had ever wanted.

Long after his mother had kissed him good night and turned out the light, Davy continued to toss and turn in his bed. What was he going to tell the leprechaun?

He woke up when the first light of dawn filtered through his window. He still had no answer.

Davy squirmed through church, and wiggled through lunch. As the magic hour of three o'clock approached, Davy was more and more miserable. At last, Davy bolted through the back door and ran as hard as he could into the woods. It was nearly three when he reached the fallen log.

"Well, Davy lad, are you feeling better?"

Davy wheeled around to find the little man standing right behind him. "I didn't hear you come up."

The leprechaun winked an eye. "Have you given any thought to our little conversation yesterday?"

Davy just looked at him for a moment, then he sighed and flopped on the log. "I . . . ," he shrugged his shoulders and sighed again. "I'm sorry. I thought and thought, but . . . ," his voice dropped. "I just don't need anything. Maybe someone else should use the wish."

The leprechaun was silent, but when Davy finally looked up, he saw the little man was smiling broadly.

"Davy," the man said softly, "you're a rich lad."

Davy just stared.

"Aye, lad, you already have a gift worth more than anything I could ever give you. Unselfishness. You're a good boy."

Davy blinked his eyes rapidly and looked down. When he looked again, the leprechaun had vanished.

Slowly, Davy trudged back to the house, dragging his feet in the dry earth of the path. Slipping through the back door, he nearly let the screen door slam. As he whirled around to catch it, his sleeve caught a statuette on a shelf next to the door. The glass object crashed to the floor.

"Davy!" His mother's voice came sharply from the next room.

"Oh, I wish . . ." Davy stopped short. "Oh, no, not that again!" □

MARCH: Bulletin Boards

ALERT students to the musical signs they'll meet along the roads of music with the above bulletin board. Make it with paper cutouts (black road, red and yellow signs, blue background) shaped like road signs. Then talk about them as stop, or rest (octagon); warning, or repeat (diamond); caution, or different notes (round). You'll be surprised how students will remember what's what! **Dorothy Thompson**

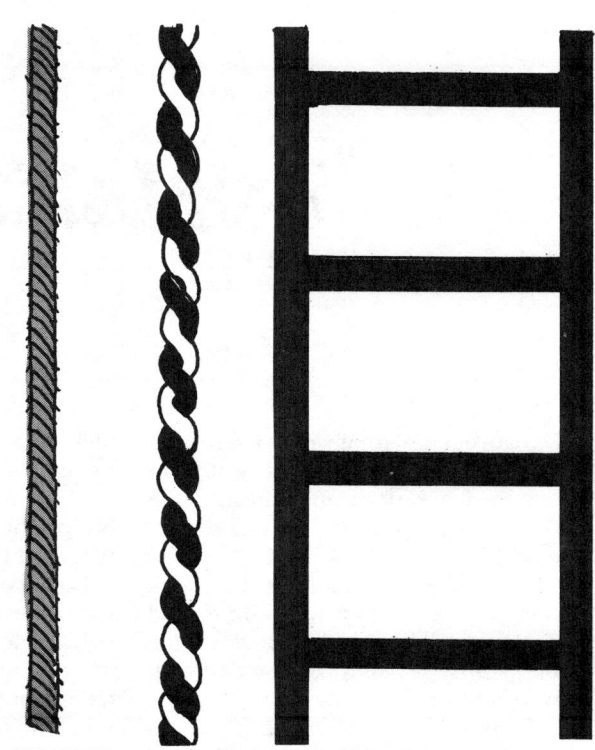

STRETCH your bulletin board/display area by using one or all three ideas suggested above—length of hemp rope (left) or braided craft cord (center) or a ladder made from cloth scraps (right). All are attached at ceiling and floor, giving ample display area for papers, pictures, and so on. **Constance B. Shaw**

STIMULATE positive self-concepts with the above board. Three days a week have children tell what other students did to help them. Write name of helper and person helped on a seasonally shaped paper (March wind, above); staple to board. At month's end, child who helped the most wins a photo of himself and those helped. **Suzanne Liddle**

LET primaries learn reading vocabulary with a fun bulletin board game devised from pictures and word cards. Draw or paste magazine pictures on individual manila sheets folded up at bottom to form a pocket (see above). Arrange on board, placing word cards with a sketched answer on back in an envelope. Children match cards and pictures placing cards in manila pockets. **Mary Fay**

BUILD a 3-D circus tent as a motivator for teaching phonics. Cut a Hula Hoop in half and secure it to the bulletin board so it projects outward from the wall. With wire, attach lightweight pieces of doweling at intervals around the hoop; rest opposite ends in the chalk tray. Make tent cover from triangular sections of felt (or crepe paper). Attach points to bulletin board above hoop, laying wide ends of triangles over hoop in a flaplike manner. Wind felt strips around doweling. Cut out felt horses and letters and attach to board under tent. Individual children add cut-paper horses and letters when they have mastered various sounds.

Helen Houser Cowles

DESIGN a Friendship Tree in celebration of National Arbor Day. Cover the bulletin board with white butcher paper. Tempera paint a brown tree as background. Then let the children finish it with individual hand-printed leaves. Prepare paint for handprints by placing green tempera in a shallow dish large enough to hold a rectangular sponge. Squeeze-fill the sponge with paint. Each child presses his hand gently on sponge, prints his hand-leaf print on a branch, and writes his name below his print.

Patricia Adams

OUR FRIENDSHIP TREE

GUESS WHAT WE FOUND AT THE END OF THE RAINBOW?

HELP your primaries to build study skills with this rainbow bulletin board. Every child has a black pot with his name on it attached to the board. As he completes various activities, he glues a gold piece to his pot. When his pot is filled, he writes his name on the rainbow and places a gold star next to it.

The rainbow is made from colored-paper strips. Pots and gold pieces are cut from black and yellow and labeled with names and activities. Remember to make enough gold pieces. For a class of 25, for example, you'll need 25 "Is neat," 25 "Shares," and so on. **Terita Gusby**

DATELINE APRIL

Come April, what's the first thing your students want to celebrate? April Fools' Day! If you're going to maintain your sanity on this silly day, better be ready. Here's your teacher's guide to April Fools!

1. If a child says, "I bet I can jump higher than a house!" don't argue. You can, too. Houses don't jump.

2. If another claims, "I can poke my head through a hole made with my fingers," believe it! All the child has to do is stick a finger from the other hand through the hole and poke his head.

3. If your favorite young artist says, "I can make this pencil write in color," it's true. He or she will take out a piece of paper and write the words "in color."

4. But if someone's always promising to do something such as clean off the chalkboard "when I get around to it" you've got 'em. Cut out a round piece of paper and print the word "Tuit" on top. Hand it to your procrastinator with a wink and don't forget to say "April Fool!"

Red letter days

APRIL ANNUAL EVENTS
These special events usually occur in April, but the exact dates vary from year to year.
Cancer Control Month
Week of the Young Child (first week in April)
National Library Week
National Boys' Club Week (week before Easter)
Good Friday (always the Friday before Easter)
Easter Sunday (a movable Christian feast, always on a Sunday between March 22 and April 25)
Passover or Pesach (a movable Jewish feast lasting eight days, usually in March or April)
Purim
Bike Safety Week (third full week in April unless Easter falls during that week; then the following week is used)
Arbor Day (in many states the last Friday)

1 It's **April Fool's Day!** (Don't say you haven't been warned!)

2 Celebrate **International Children's Book Day** in honor of Danish author Hans Christian Andersen who was born in 1805.

3 Heading the list of books to read this month is *The Legend of Sleepy Hollow.* This story about the headless horseman was written by **Washington Irving,** who was born on this date in 1783.

4 **Maya Angelou,** author and performer, was born in 1928.
Also born on this date in 1802 was **Dorothea Dix,** who spent her life campaigning to expose and improve the living conditions of the mentally ill.
Martin Luther King, Jr. was assassinated in Memphis, Tennessee, in 1968.

5 Black educator and leader **Booker T. Washington** was born in 1856. He founded the Tuskegee Institute and believed that education was the route to equality.

6 The **first modern Olympic Games** were played in Athens, Greece, in 1896.

7 It's **World Health Day** in honor of the World Health Organization's confirmation as a specialized United Nations agency in 1948.

8 Hammerin' **Hank Aaron** walloped his 715th career homerun in 1974 to beat Babe Ruth's forty-seven-year-old record.

9 The **first public library** in the United States opened in Peterborough, New Hampshire, in 1833.
Also, the **Civil War** ended in 1865.

10 Be kind to our four-legged friends. Help the **American Society for the Prevention of Cruelty to Animals** which was chartered in 1866.

11 **Gertrudis Bocanegra,** a revolutionary who fought for Mexico's independence from Spain, was born in 1765. She was called the Joan of Arc of Mexico.

12 Children's book author, **Beverly Cleary,** was born in 1916. Well-loved by children, she is best known for her two characters, Ramona and Henry Huggins.

13 **Thomas Jefferson,** third president of the United States and drafter of the Declaration of Independence, was born in 1743.
In 1870, the **Metropolitan Museum of Art** was founded in New York City.

14 Today is **Pan American Day,** which is observed to commemorate the bonds of friendship uniting the countries of the Western Hemisphere.
Also, President **Abraham Lincoln** was shot by actor John Wilkes Booth in 1865 as he was watching a performance of "Our American Cousin" at the Ford Theater. He died the following day.

15 The **Titanic** sank in 1912 after striking an iceberg.

16 Silent-film star and world famous comedian **Charlie Chaplin** was born in 1889.

18 "One if by land, two if by sea!" **Paul Revere** rode his way into the history books as he galloped from Boston to Concord to warn of the British advance in 1775.

20 Today is **Patriot's Day** which commemorates the Battle of Lexington and Concord in 1775.

21 **Charlotte Brontë,** English author best known for her book *Jane Eyre,* was born in 1816.

23 **Shirley Temple Black,** a child actress who became a millionaire by age 10 and who was later a diplomat, was born in 1928.
Also today, the great English poet and playwright **William Shakespeare** died in 1616.

24 The first **soda fountain** was patented in 1833.
Also today, actresses **Shirley MacLaine** and **Barbara Streisand** were born in 1934 and 1942, respectively.

25 Who wrote the song, "A-Tisket, A-Tasket"? Tsk! Tsk! American jazz vocalist **Ella Fitzgerald,** of course! Known as the "First Lady of Song," she was born in 1918.

26 The **Great Plague** began in London in 1665.

27 Civil rights leader **Coretta Scott King** was born in 1927.
Also, the 18th president of the United States, **Ulysses S. Grant,** was born in 1822.

28 **Maryland** became our seventh state in 1788.

29 The "separable fastener," better known as **the zipper,** was patented in 1913.

30 What a deal! The U.S. purchased almost a million square miles of territory from France in 1803 for $11,250,000. It was called the **Louisiana Purchase.** Coincidentally, **Louisiana** became our 18th state on this date nine years later.
Also, a great American tradition started today. **Hamburgers** were first introduced at the St. Louis World's Fair in 1904.

APRIL: Bright Ideas

![illustration of a rabbit in a suit walking with a cane and a basket of eggs past a house]

A BARREL OF FUN

Rain barrels are probably not familiar objects to your students; so a brief explanation of the function of these once-very-useful household items may be necessary before you start this rainy-day math game.

Use two small wooden barrels if you have them, or substitute two coffee cans covered with wood-grained peel-and-stick paper. Place the barrels in front of your room, with a sign reading, "It isn't raining rain to us, it's raining answers!" Now divide the class into two teams. Read simple math problems and call upon alternate team members to answer them. Every time a team answers the problem correctly, drop a paper raindrop in that team's barrel. After all members of a team have answered, count the raindrops to determine the winners.
JILL SWEARINGEN

COUNTING RAINDROPS

Have children hold up their fingers to indicate the number of drops, as they are mentioned in this rhyme for counting.

I see ONE of many drops of rain
Sliding down my windowpane.

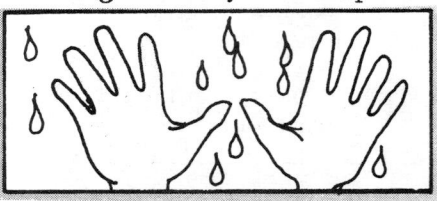

Here come TWO to join the one.
They're really having lots of fun.
Now there are THREE--
Now there are FOUR,
My, oh, my, here come some more.
I count FIVE; I count SIX:
They're doing funny circus tricks.
I see SEVEN, EIGHT, NINE, TEN.
I'll have to start all over again.
JEAN BRABHAM McKINNEY

TWO WAYS TO USE THE NEWS

The daily newspaper can be used to stimulate thinking in your pupils. Have them search the newspaper for descriptive headlines containing an action word (verb) that has a second meaning. Then have them draw a cartoon-type picture describing the headline. Examples: "Kings Beat Lakers," "Man Holds Up Market," or "48% Support Reagan." Make several papers available, and if possible, inform kids of the activity in advance so they can search outside of class for that special headline.

A good culminating activity after learning the parts of a newspaper is to have a "Newspaper Scavenger Hunt." Students work in groups of two or three. They're given a list of items to find in the paper and a time limit. Use duplicate copies of the paper on a day when additional sale ads, coupons, recipes, and so on are included. (Be sure students number their articles.) Here are some suggestions:
1. Find a good buy on dog food.
2. Cut out the letter to the editor from Tom Hunt.
3. Find a coupon for free candy.
4. Find the article that tells the latest news about the president.
5. Copy the recipe for Cheese Log.
6. Locate a lost and found ad for a white kitten.
NANCY A. CAMARIGG

SIX PEEPS
Make a line-up of six cheery chicks from a yellow plastic foam egg carton. Cut the bottom part of the carton lengthwise into two sections. Glue one six-cup section on the other, open edges together. A small rubber band placed between each hump holds the sections firm while the glue dries. Cut six pairs of orange feet and six beaks from construction paper. Use a paper punch to make paper eyes. Glue feet and beaks on all the chicks. Add a yellow wing to each end chick. And there you have it--a cheery chorus line of little peepers ready to welcome Easter.
CONNIE ZANE

COMB IT OUT
A unique tool for your elementary art corner is a common pocket comb. Have children tip yarn or string in tempera paint and lay it on glossy paper. Pick up the yarn and "comb" the scroll formed with the wet yarn into a spread-out, wispy, abstract design. This idea is fun and the

results are often quite attractive. Comb patterns into thick coatings of finger paint for a very different effect. Don't forget to wash the comb after use.
JOAN MARY MACEY

HOOK AND SHOW
Children love to show off their work, and one easy way for them to do this is for each to have a hook with his or her name printed above it. The hook may be made by bending a paper clip and taping one end with masking tape which can be printed upon with marking pen. Tape hooks on the wall, and when children finish an art project or produce a good paper, they can quickly put it on their hooks. This leaves the decision of which work to display up to the child, rather than the teacher-- an arrangement that provides an incentive to do better work and lets every child show his or her best.
ANN MARGARET BINDER

NATURAL EASTER BASKETS
Science and art join forces in this Easter activity. Have each child bring in a berry basket to line with aluminum foil and fill with potting soil in class. Pass out grass seeds and plant them ½ to 1 inch deep, then water soil and place all baskets in a sunny spot. Then have children record on an experience chart the day when the grass sprouts, amount of water needed weekly, and so on. When

APRIL: Bright Ideas

the grass has grown about two inches high, have kids make colorful handles from oaktag and staple them to sides of baskets. Have them dye Easter eggs to put in baskets, then draw bunnies to cut out and clothe with crayons, felt-tip pens, and construction paper. After bunnies are in their baskets, surround them with nutritious goodies like raisins, whole peanuts, and a wrapped slice of banana bread.   LYNN BARWELL

SMOKING BOTTLE
When warnings about cigarette smoking go unheeded, a demonstration of the "smoking bottle" says much more than words.

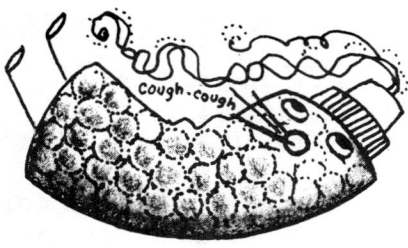

Start with a clear plastic squeeze bottle. Remove label and wash bottle; then take off the cap and fill bottle tightly with cotton balls. Snip the end off the cap and screw it back on bottle. Place a cigarette in the hole in the cap. Begin squeezing the bottle as you light the cigarette--this will enable the bottle to smoke. Continue squeezing the bottle and add more cigarettes as needed. A brown residue (tar) will begin to accumulate on the cotton. As students realize that this tar goes into their bodies, a great deal of thinking begins. KATHY PATTAK

TELLTALE NECKLACE
For art projects that must be done in small groups, make sure all your students get a turn by having them put on red yarn necklaces. Then as a child finishes with the project, the necklace is removed and another child still wearing the necklace joins the group. Just by looking around the room, you can see at a glance if anyone has been missed. Necklaces may be a class project to teach crocheting, finger-weaving, or pom-pom making.
MADELINE THEIL

RED CARPET TREATMENT
To emphasize good manners, good posture, and clean, healthy habits in your class, try designating certain months as "good manners month" and so on, and keep your students' interest by using "The Royal Red Rug." The child who shows the best manners each day (use of napkin, silverware, and so on) has "The Royal Red Rug" placed under his or her desk the next day.

The rug is a piece of bright red carpet. The same privilege is given each day of the following month for the child who displays good posture habits; the next month, for good health habits. There's no limit to the number of times a student can receive the rug, and kids will really work hard for this honor!
PATSY CAPPS

FUZZIES AND PRICKLIES
To help young children learn about getting along with others, try teaching them about warm fuzzies--something you give others when you say or do a nice thing to them, and cold pricklies--what you give someone when you say or do something unkind.
   Make a huge, warm fuzzy for your room out of a large packing box with a large punch ball tied on to the top. Over the whole

ball and box, place a nice soft, pink blanket; add cutout feet made from colored poster board and big eyes with two antennae.

To remind children at the same time of the cold pricklies they are often unaware of giving each other, give each child a cold pricklie for his or her desktop. Buy a bag of marshmallows and colored toothpicks, stick about ten toothpicks in each marshmallow and leave them to harden. Add an "evil eye" (from construction paper) on each marshmallow by sliding it down one of the picks.
PHYLLIS S. MARCUS

IT'S MAGIC
Sometimes the simplest experiment is the most effective. Have your kids obtain dirt from fields or woods. Place it in a small pot or milk carton with some pebbles in the bottom for drainage. Keep pots in a sunny place and water gently every other day. Very soon a little green head will pop up. In fact, many little plants may begin growing. It delights students to see these plants that they didn't plant begin growing, and you can be sure the plants will be suited to the soil.
VICKI HYDE

PATCHWORK ANIMALS
Here's an art project kids will love for the bright, colorful, and different pictures that result. Have them select two or three different colors of contruction paper and cut them into 1" x ½" squares. Glue squares alternately onto onto a 9" x 12" piece of manila paper. When they're

finished, the paper will be completely filled with little squares of colored paper, in a patchwork pattern.

Next, have kids draw an animal of their choice on the "patchwork paper" and cut it out. Glue the cutout on a piece of 9" x 18" construction paper and use crayons or felt-tipped pens to draw in a background. Finally, use a black felt pen to outline the patchwork animal and other important features in the picture for a really striking effect. MARLENE KARKOSA

HINK PINK
What's another name for a chubby rodent? A fat rat. What's a person who borrows a paperback and never returns it? A book crook. Or a squeeze from an insect? A bug hug. This is a vocabulary game called "Hink Pink."

It's a rhyming game that reinforces rhyming, syllabication, and defining skills, and also teaches children to put words together in new ways. It can be used in conjunction with teaching dictionary skills and use of the thesaurus--and it's fun!

To play, simply think of a rhyme such as bear chair; then define it without using the words in your rhyme (a seat for a big furry animal). A definition for glass grass might be a breakable lawn. Kids should begin with the rhyme and then figure out a definition.

When they've mastered one-syllable rhyming, you might want to go on to "Hinky Pinky" (a large cart for a fairy tale beast is a dragon wagon).

As a class activity, children write their definitions down and read them aloud. They must identify the rhyme by saying, "This is a hink pink for a large plant with an insect hive" (bee tree) or "This is a hinky pinky for a rabbit that tells jokes" (funny bunny). Children can form teams, reading back and forth and scoring points for stumping the opposite team. A good rhyming dictionary will help those who wish to advance to Hinkity Pinkity. Pasta thrown at a parade? Spaghetti confetti!
BRUCE PORELL

MIX AND MATCH
Find or duplicate two identical pictures of vocabulary words to be studied. Mount them on construction-paper cards and cover with clear

APRIL: Bright Ideas

plastic food wrap. Place cards face down on table. Children draw two cards at a time, then state what they've drawn. If a child has a match, he or she keeps the cards; if not, they're returned to the table. Student holding most pairs at end of game wins.
MITCHELL E. WALLICK

DOWN THE BUNNY TRAIL
You'll hatch a batch of eager readers with this activity that combines reading with a colored-egg hunt. Before school, hide a basket of eggs, then set up a trail of paper bunnies with clues that lead to the hidden treats. Put a child's name on the front of each bunny and the clue he or she will read on the back, such as "Look under the sink." When the child finds bunny #1 under the sink, he or she reads the name of the child who will then read that clue, and so on until each child has had a turn and the final clue locates the basket.

You can write each clue to coincide with the reading level of the child whose name appears on the front, from simple clues like "Look in the closet" to more complex hints like

"There's a bunny hidden in the encyclopedia. Look under 'rabbits'." Kids enjoy having their own bunny and individual clue. But you have to prepare in advance, so hop to it!
CONNIE ZANE

A SPRINGTIME PUZZLE
Unscramble these words and you'll find all kinds of things that make you think of spring. Then draw a picture including each one and crayon or paint it with pretty springtime colors.
1. S S G A R
2. L F O E W S R
3. H E I S S U N N
4. R B D S I
5. T S S N E
6. T T E R Y F U B L
7. E S E B
8. D S S E E
Answers: 1. grass; 2. flowers; 3. sunshine; 4. birds; 5. nests; 6. butterfly; 7. bees; 8. seeds. MARY E. MATTHEWS

CARD LADDERS
To keep vocabulary words or math facts within sight without using up needed bulletin board or wall space, suspend card ladders from the ceiling or light fixtures. Punch corresponding pairs of holes in the sides of 3" x 5" or larger cards.

String them on yarn. More cards can be added as they are needed. Instead of review facts, you might put questions or math problems on the fronts of cards and answers on the backs. CONNIE ZANE

STICHERY ON WALLPAPER
If you can get wallpaper sample books from a local dealer in your town, this stiff combination of paper and fiber can be just the thing for stitchery projects with younger children, who find it easier to work with than cloth. Have them draw designs with pencils first and then stitch them with yarn. Tangles will be minimal! LYDIA WHITE

IN THE PICTURE
This activity helps pupils develop skills in looking for details, skimming and scanning for information, and understanding questions on tests, study guides, and worksheets. Pictures from magazines are pasted to sheets of paper large enough to include ten comprehension questions. Students' answers may be written on a separate sheet of paper and correct answers are written on the back of each picture-page. The questions should be

explicit. What time is it in this picture? How many people are there? What do you think the man in front is saying? CHRIS YECKE

EASTER EGG LEARNING
The large plastic eggs that panty hose come in or the smaller ones that stores sell at Easter can be put to good use in the weeks before the holiday. These hands-on learning activities will make your kids hop to be in on the fun!

Egg-citing language arts
Print vocabulary words on slips of paper, one word per slip. Place four or five words inside each egg, then put all eggs together in a basket. Have kids choose eggs from the basket and put words found inside in alphabetical order, write their definitions, or use them in complete sentences. Or try printing words with one letter left out and have kids supply missing letter; or place several words inside each egg that together will form a complete sentence when unscrambled and taped side by side in proper order.

Math activities by the dozen
If you have 12 small plastic eggs and one empty egg carton, print math problems on slips of paper, one problem per slip, and place one inside each egg. Then put all eggs inside the carton and close the lid. Have kids take turns opening the eggs and solving problems inside, timing themselves. The first to solve all 12 in the shortest time is the winner.

Classy egg organization
Fill a large plastic egg with slips of paper on which you've printed the names of your students. Pick a name from the egg whenever you have a special job to be done by one student. Or use them to call kids up for show and tell, reading groups, or the lunch line.

To make these egg-tivities more enticing, have students decorate the eggs before you use them, using tempera paints, colored construction paper, cotton balls, and so on. CAROLYN WILHELM

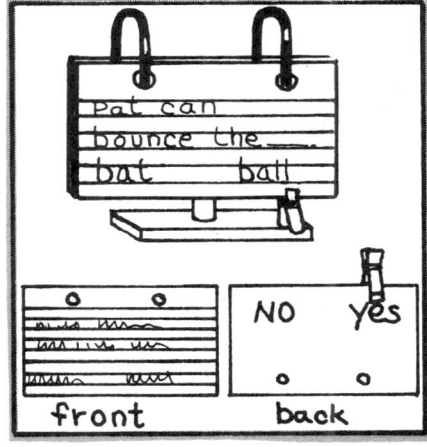

FLIP AN ANSWER
Change a revolving photo holder into your own "Review Machine." Your kids will love it! Print or type review questions on 3" x 5" cards, with two or three possible answers in a row at the bottom of each card. (Answers must be short.) Insert cards in the clear photo sleeves of your holder. After children read a question, they clip a clothespin under the correct answer. To check the answer, they flip the card to see if the clothespin is above the corresponding "yes" or "no" found on the upper back of each card. MARJORIE WATSON

COLOR ME SPRING
Here's a wonderful way to get your kids outdoors where they want to be and increase their powers of observation at the same time. Obtain color charts from a hardware or paint store and have each child select a chart with a variety of basic colors and shades. Then take the charts outside and try to match each shade with a leaf, flower petal, tree trunk, branch, grass, some dirt, or any other object found in nature. LAUREL GRANQUIST

STRING A WORD
Get a box of round tubular macaroni. Put a different letter of the alphabet on each piece of macaroni with a permanent marker. Now have students string the macaroni to make words. Have lots of vowels and much-used consonants. What a different sort of spelling drill! RICHARD LATTA

APRIL: P. E. games

Spring Shape Up

Pouf the chute

IT'S spring! Take kids outdoors and get their bodies (and minds!) in shape. Playing pouf the chute is an imaginative way to exercise. Buy or borrow a parachute. A popular starting activity is to have the kids spread out around it, grab hold of the ends, and then walk, hop, skip, or jog in a circle. Music adds enjoyment.

Next, parachute in tow, give commands, such as "walk to the left," "walk to the right." Then try sitting, kneeling, standing, and jumping and throwing it in the air. (Beats deep-knee bends!)

After a good workout, you can hang the chute for instant shade or drape it over the monkey bars to make a tent. You can even roll someone up in it, mummy style. Teachers using chutes have an additional advantage, too— by having kids throw chute up, jump under, and pull ends down around them, a whole class disappears.   **Joe Kraus**

Jog across the USA

BELIEVE it or not, our fifth graders jogged across the USA. We didn't actually take to the highway but we covered the 2,786 miles from Los Angeles to New York and learned a lot as we got our bodies in tip-top shape.

It all began as a math activity. We measured the distance around our playground—just over 2,000 feet! Next, we decided to jog around the perimeter. How far should we jog? Across California? No, farther. To New York! We set up the following ground rules: Jogging was only to be done before school and during morning recess. All joggers must have a lap punch card. Each card had 20 half-mile segments, making a total of 10 miles for a card. Joggers who ran nine laps were given a free punch on every tenth lap since our course was longer than a half mile. Student monitors would punch cards. Jogging was to be done on a voluntary basis. Fifth-grade teachers could participate.

Every day the cards were turned into the monitors. They added the daily distance to the cumulative total, and the mileage was posted on a bulletin board map. Each night we stopped in different places—Needles, California; Ulys-

ses, Kansas; Devil's Elbow, Missouri, to name a few. The places, names, and population was also posted.

Jogging-related studies included health, geography, topography, map plotting, mileage scales, national weather, and discussions on what we should expect to see as we jogged through various states.

At the end of our journey, we held a class party. Our menu included milk, juices, nuts, fruit, and Granola-type cookies. Certificates of achievement were awarded, noting each one's contribution to the total mileage of the class.

We reached our goal, New York, yet continued to jog. We have returned to Los Angeles, and are headed northwest to Oregon. One comment heard while jogging alongside a student was, "I don't need my card punched after each lap. I just love the way it feels to jog!" That makes it all worthwhile!   **Richard Jacobsen** and **Char Girard**

Create a playground

PLAYGROUNDS should be the kind of environment where children work together to make up their own games. If your playground doesn't seem to foster these creative activities, ask your kids what sort of things they'd like to have for playing on. The parents of the Linda Vesta School in Pasadena, California, did just that. Then, with permission, they constructed out of surplus tires, telephone poles, and netting, these playground structures. Once final approval was obtained, materials (telephone poles, tires, cement, pipe, netting, and tools) were secured and construction began. The school district did the site preparation (sandy base) and provided a fork lift for moving the heavier tires into position; the parents did the rest.

Four structures were built—Tire Mountain, Tire Jungle, Tire Ring Swing, and Cargo Net Climb. The large, heavy-equipment tires making up the mountain were fastened together with ⅜" bolts; firemen slide poles were set in concrete with a bolt at the bottom so it will not pull out. The bottom tires are filled with sand to keep them from moving and also to provide for soft landings.

For the jungle, 15-foot telephone poles were set five feet deep and about four feet apart. Any voids or holes in them were spackled; the poles were then covered with burlap (or fiberglass cloth) and coated with boat resin to meet safety standards. Last of all several pairs of tires were bolted to opposite sides of each pole with two ⅜" threaded rods to create tree branches.

Six telephone poles mounted in cement in a circle held the Tire Ring Swing. Eighteen automobile tires were laid out in a circle on the ground and drilled for 2" x ⅜" bolts. Drainage holes were drilled so that when they were tilted into position they would be on the bottom of the tires. The entire circle of tires was bolted together on the ground. Holes were drilled in 12 of the 18 tires to attach the chains for hanging, and the entire ring lifted approximately two feet into position for attaching chains. It is a good idea to leave excess chain in place for a while in case the kids find the ring too high. The chains were attached to the poles with ⅜″ bolts or eye bolts, and ends of the bolts hammered to insure that the nuts do not come off.

The fourth piece of equipment was the cargo net, which was suspended from a framework of 2½″ galvanized pipe. Once plans were made, the net was woven to their special specifications.

Since the Linda Vista playground was developed, other schools in the area have completed similar playgrounds, all based on the interests and abilities of each school's pupils. Your school can develop its own creative playground. Ask your kids what kind of equipment they'd like, talk to your principal, add your own ideas, contact a parent group for its help. **Penny Nicolai**

Try juggling

BET you never thought of juggling as a shape-up activity. It's a good one though because it not only helps kids develop good hand-eye coordination, it helps develop control of their indominate hand. It's easy to learn, as my third graders and I found out. Start basic three-ball juggling techniques using a beanbag instead of balls. Always start left one time, right the next, unless the child is having a dominate hand problem. If he does, have him start every time with the indominate hand until he can do it correctly. Let's begin:

Skills using one object
1. Throw and catch object using right hand.
2. Throw and catch object using left hand.
3. Throw object from right hand to left hand and from left hand to right hand. Then practice, practice, practice, and practice!

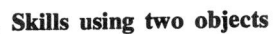

Skills using two objects
1. Hold one object in each hand. Throw up together; catch with same hand.
2. Hold one object in each hand. Throw right object to left hand and then immediately throw left object to right hand. Catch right object in left hand. Catch left object in right hand. Repeat starting with left object.

Three-ball juggling
1. Take two balls (A and C) in right hand and one ball (B) in left hand.
2. Throw ball A upward toward your left hand.
3. Before ball A reaches your left hand, throw ball B up under ball A.

4. Catch A in left hand and before B reaches right hand throw ball C under B to the left hand.
5. Catch B and start again with A which is in left hand. Continue this movement. You are juggling!

For further help try one of these books. *Juggling Book* by Carlo (Random, 1974), *Juggling Made Easy* by Rudolf Dittrich (Wilshire Book Co., 1967), and *Juggling for Fun and Entertainment* by Ron Humphrey (Tuttle, 1974).
George T. Mason

Fling a Frisbee

THE art of Frisbee knows no age. For those of you whose skills are rusty, ask one of your classroom experts for help.

Frisbee challenge involves two players and two Frisbees. Players stand five to ten yards apart and exchange discs as rapidly as they can until one of them misses. If a player touches the Frisbee but does not catch it, the opponent scores.

Frisbee golf is when a player throws from a starting line toward a target, counting number of throws it takes to reach it. (Trees, poles, benches, and so on can be targets.) After first throw, player goes to the spot disc landed and throws again; rolls count. Low score wins.

Ultimate Frisbee is fast moving on a field 40 yards by 60 yards with 30-yard end zones. Play with any size Frisbee and two teams, seven on a side. The object is similar to football—to get the Frisbee down the field and into the end zone. Game rules: Players cannot run with the Frisbee; they must throw to a running or stationary teammate. Once the Frisbee is thrown, it must be caught by the offensive team or it goes to the opposing unit. If disc goes out of bounds, the defensive team takes possession. During play, opposing team tries to intercept throws without bodily contact. Score as in football.

Johnston relay involves as many teams as you can manage. Each team has six players and one Frisbee. A marker is placed 100 yards downfield. The object is to hit the marker (using as many throws as needed) with the Frisbee and run it back as in a regular relay race.

Throw, run, and catch (TRC) is where the Frisbee is thrown in an arc, and the same player must catch it before it touches the ground. Distance is measured from the point of throw to where the catch is made.

Maximum time aloft (MTA) is played like TRC, but time of Frisbee's flight, not distance, is measured.

Frisbee for accuracy is throwing the Frisbee through a hoop or tire target fifteen yards off. Scoring: Ten points for direct flight through target. Eight points if edge is hit. Five points for passing within arms length of target.
Dennis Craig Smith

Joe Kraus is news editor for the *Daily Ledger-Gazette*, Lancaster, California; **Richard Jacobsen** and **Char Girard** teach at Emma W. Shuey Elementary School, Rosemead, California; **Penny Nicolai** is editorial director, World Features, Inc., Los Angeles, California; **George T. Mason** teaches physical education at Snow Hill Elementary School, Maryland; **Dennis Craig Smith** teaches at Westwings Elementary School, Vandenberg AFB, California.

APRIL: A one-act play

April fool boomerang

Dennis Andersen

Characters: *Mom, Dad, Brad, and Ginny—the Hooper Family.*
Setting: *The Hooper kitchen.*
At Rise: *Brad is sitting at the breakfast table eating a bowl of cereal. He isn't paying too much attention to the cereal because he's absorbed in his book.*

Ginny *(enters)*: Morning, Brad.
Brad: Morning, sis.
Ginny: Boy, that cereal sure looks good.
Brad *(hardly listening)*: Uh-huh.
Ginny: But what's that funny thing?
Brad *(still reads his book)*: What funny thing?
Ginny: In your spoon.
Brad *(too late—he swallows the spoonful)*: What are you talking about?
Ginny: Oh, no! It was a fly! You ate a *fly*!
Brad: What? Help! Mom! Dad! Help!
Mom *(enters)*: Brad, what's wrong?
Dad *(enters running)*: What's all the yelling about?
Brad: I swallowed a fly! I swallowed a fly!
Dad: Take it easy, son.
Brad: But, dad, I ate a fly!
Mom: Now, Brad, don't worry. When you were little, you ate much stranger things.
Dad: You'll live.
Brad: I'm going to be sick.
Ginny *(who has been trying to keep from laughing)*: Oh, Brad. It wasn't a fly. It was a raisin. April Fool! *(She laughs.)*
Brad *(angrily)*: I'll get you!
Mom: You'll do no such thing. But, Ginny Hooper, I want a word with you.
Ginny *(gulps down a glass of orange juice and runs out the back door)*: Oh, Mom. It's April Fool's Day.
Mom: Honestly, I don't know what we're going to do about that child. Ginny's stories are getting out of hand. She's always stirring up some kind of trouble. Even when it isn't April Fool's Day.
Dad: I've been reading all about this sort of problem in a book on child psychology.
Mom: And?

Dad: And it says that a child with an overactive imagination like Ginny's is just looking for attention.
Mom: Well, she's certainly getting it.
Dad: The psychology book says that the best cure is to agree with anything the child says.
Mom: But why on earth should we do that?
Dad: If you refuse to get upset or excited about the practical jokes and imaginary happenings—the child will get tired of the game and give it all up.
Mom: I'm not so sure it would work with Ginny but let's give it a try.
Dad: OK. Remember now—you've got to pretend to believe everything she says and not get the least disturbed.
Ginny *(enters out of breath)*: Mom! Dad! Brad! Guess what?
Mom *(calmly)*: What, Ginny?
Ginny: A UFO just landed in our backyard!
Dad *(calmly)*: That's nice, dear.
Ginny: A big, round, silver disk from outer space is sitting right in the middle of our flower garden.
Brad *(calmly)*: Gee, what a shame! There go the daffodils.
Ginny: Didn't you hear what I said?
Mom *(begins to clear the breakfast dishes calmly)*: Of course, we did, Ginny. You said a UFO landed in our flower garden.
Dad *(still reads the newspaper calmly)*: And I suppose it trampled the tulips, too.
Ginny: Of course, it trampled the tulips. And it leveled the lilies. And the gladiolas aren't so glad either. Now what are we going to do?
Mom: We'll simply have to plow it all under and start from scratch.
Brad: Just as soon as the UFO takes off.
Dad: Ginny, did they tell you when they were planning to leave?
Ginny *(very disturbed)*: I didn't talk to anybody. I came running in here the minute I saw it.
Mom: Well, that's good, dear. I've always

told you never to talk to strangers.
Ginny: Shouldn't we call the president of the United States?
Dad: The president? Now why in the world would he care about our flower garden?
Brad: Dad, if they're not in a big hurry—couldn't Ginny invite them for breakfast?
Dad: That's a great idea.
Ginny: I give up! I give up! Well, if you won't do anything about it—I'm going next door to tell Mrs. McGee. I'll bet she'll call the president.
Mom: Whatever you think best, Ginny. *(Ginny exits. The three Hoopers look at each other and laugh long and loud.)*
Dad: See, I told you it would work.
Mom: Like a charm. I'd better call Mrs. McGee and warn her. *(Mom goes to the telephone and dials.)*
Brad: Hey, Dad, this psychology stuff is neat.
Mom *(on the phone)*: Hello, Mrs. McGee. This is Mrs. Hooper. *(She laughs.)* I've got something very funny to tell you. It's about Ginny....Mrs. McGee, what's the matter? You sound very strange. Look out the window? Why? *(Mom looks out the window.)* Yes, I see. *(She hangs up the phone.)*
Dad: What is it, dear?
Mom *(with a stunned look on her face)*: Mrs. McGee just heard Ginny invite them for breakfast.
Brad: Who?
Mom: The things getting out of the spaceship in our garden!
(Dad and Brad look out the window.)
Brad: Gosh, dad, what are we going to do?
Dad: Let's set out some more food....
(Three visitors from outer space enter, sit at the table, and begin eating the cereal. Mom, Dad, and Brad look stunned.)
Ginny *(enters, sees how her family is taking the visit, then smiles)*: This is about the best April Fool's Day we've ever had. And all I had to do was tell the truth!

Dennis Andersen is an associate editor for INSTRUCTOR.

APRIL: A song for spring

APRIL: Time for a laugh

Joke Center: Where Kids Play On Words

Sue Whitesel

Does your class suffer from the blahs? Do they need something to add zest to language arts activities? My fourth-grade class did, and we found a "Joke Center" to be the perfect remedy. Not only did we learn a lot about various kinds of humor and practice many of the language skills we had been drilling for months, we had a terrific week of laughter as we shared our favorite jokes and made up new ones.

How to Set Up the Center

As a focal point for my "Joke Center," I print the following quotation by nineteenth-century American humorist Josh Billings, put it in the center of a bulletin board and surround it with a collage of laughing and smiling faces: "When you . . . laugh open your mouth wide enough for the noise to get out without squealing, throw your head back as though you was going to get shaved, hold on to your false hair with both hands and then laugh until your soul gets thoroughly rested."

I arrange numbered task cards on that or a nearby bulletin board (a folding screen will do just as well). For those tasks requiring a duplicated page, I include a "take one" folder made by covering a manila folder with colored paper and stapling the sides and bottom together. Three of my activities also require teacher-made posters for student reference. On a table I display a collection of joke books obtained from the library and from my own and my students' personal collections. Books essential to our activities described here are *Witcracks: Jokes and Jests from American Folklore* and *A Twister of Twists, A Tangler of Tongues,* both by Alvin Schwartz (Lippincott), although the task cards could easily be modified to fit other materials if these books are not available. I also include a decorated box labeled "Joke File" and a stack of index cards for the students to record and illustrate their favorite jokes. If they come from other sources, such as books or magazines, I ask that that source be noted. Other materials needed in the center are a box of old magazines, scissors, crayons or felt-tip markers and paste.

After they've had an opportunity to look over all of the activities, I ask my students to sign a contract specifying how many activities they will complete. (I require all students to do certain starred activities.) I allot one week. The number of activities can, of course, be adjusted to the grading system used, the total number of activities offered, the level of the students and the amount of time available. Our contract reads as follows:

I, ____(student's name)____, promise to complete ____ of the activities in the 'Joke Center' (including the starred activities) during the week of _____.

A = At least 10 activities thoroughly, neatly and creatively done

B = 9 activities

C = 8 activities

date _____

student _____

teacher _____

Have your students make "Joke Center" folders for their completed work sheets and the other written assignments. Provide duplicated lists of the titles of the center activities to be stapled or glued on the inside front cover of the folders so that you can initial them as the children complete them satisfactorily.

1
PUNS

Student directions: "A pun is a riddle or joke that is funny because one or more of the words has more than one meaning. Or, the word is almost the same, but perhaps one letter or letters is different. For example: 'Why did your cat join the Red Cross?' 'It wants to be a *first aid kit.*' Read the jokes on the duplicated sheet and underline the words that make each one a pun. Are some spelled differently for their other meanings? If so, note the other correct spelling."

Work sheet:

1. All the animals came to the picnic in pairs except the worms. They came in apples.

2. "I don't understand why this coffee tastes like mud," said Mr. Walker. "It was ground only this morning."

3. The goldfish did not enter the deep-sea diving contest because he felt that it was beneath him.

4. "I'm certainly hungry for supper tonight," said the old pelican, wading into the river. "Maybe a fine big bass will fill the bill."

5. "My bloodhound is a very intelligent dog," bragged Frank. "He earns his own living by picking up a few scents every day."

6. To avoid that run-down feeling, a person should always look both ways before crossing the street.

7. "Whew!" panted Jeff after he had moved the desk from one end of the passageway to the other. "That was a long hall."

8. The Spaniards supposedly were able to go three thousand miles on a galleon, but you can never believe everything you hear about those foreign cars.

9. It was not surprising that the octopus won the battle, since he went into it well-armed.

10. The sailor did not have to worry about his dirty clothes. He just threw them overboard and they were washed ashore.

11. One horse said to the other, "I don't remember your mane, but your pace is certainly familiar."

12. Ellen's dog was chewing on a dictionary until Ellen took the words right out of its mouth.

13. "I'm sorry we're so noisy," said Bob to his mother, "but it's hard to play tennis without raising a racket."

14. "I suppose it will take a lot of training before I qualify for a job with the railroad," said Scott.

15. When his mother asked Sam how he got his black eye, he told her he had been hit by a guided muscle.

2
SILLY SPOONERISMS

Student directions: "An Englishman often had trouble keeping his words straight. If he wanted to say, 'May I show you to a seat?' he said, 'May I sew you to a sheet?' This Englishman was the Reverend W.A. Spooner and words mixed up in this way became known as 'spoonerisms.' Can you straighten out the spoonerisms on the duplicated work sheet?"

Work sheet:

1. The minister introduced Elizabeth II of England as "Our queer dean."

2. At a wedding, it is kistomary to cuss the bride.

3. When he lost the game, he received a blushing crow.

4. I don't like to eat parrots and keys.

5. The kinquering congs entered the capital of the enemy.

6. I keep my icycle well boiled.

7. There's a saying, "It never pains but it roars."

8. The weather report says it will either drain or rizzle, with possible shattered scowers.

9. The pupil didn't learn anything and therefore tasted his worm's work.

Source: The spoonerisms on the work sheet came from the *Arrow Book of Word Games* by Murray Rockwitz (Scholastic).

3
CRAZY COLLAGE POSTERS

Student directions: "Cut pictures from magazines or draw a picture to illustrate a riddle. For example, take the riddle and answer, 'What is a bulldozer?' 'A sleeping bull.' To illustrate it you might glue a picture of a large machine on a piece of construction paper with a bull's head attached—sleeping of course! Use a riddle you know or make one up or get some ideas from our joke books and the joke file."

4
TWIST YOUR OWN TWISTER

Student directions: "Read some of the tongue twisters in *A Twister of Twists, A Tangler of Tongues*. Make up a tongue twister of your own. The book suggests that the best way to begin is to write a sentence in which the words each start with the same sound or the same letter. Just write down what occurs to you. If you follow the rule you should tangle a tongue."

5
TONGUE TWISTER GAME

Student directions: "Play the game as described in *A Twister of Twists, A Tangler of Tongues*: 'Only one other player is needed. Each of you makes up [or chooses] a twister. Then each, in turn, repeats the other's twister five times as fast as he [or she] can. If either of you stumbles, he [or she] loses. But if both of you do, or neither, the game goes on with another pair of twisters and another test of skill.' "

6
DAFFYNITIONS

Student directions: "Make an illustrated poster of these daffynitions:

1. *Aftermath:* That which follows arithmetic.

2. *Logotype:* That which is written on trees.

3. *Portent:* Low quality camping gear.

4. *Hereford:* Mother's car.

5. *Paradox:* Two physicians.

6. *Myth:* A female moth.

7. *Parapets:* Two poodles.

8. *Triplet:* A very short voyage.

9. *Jacks or better:* What it takes to open a bus window.

"Read the silly definitions on the posters. Try making up some new ones of your own or write down some that you have heard before. Looking in a dictionary might help. Make another poster or some illustrations for these."

7
ETHNIC JOKES

Student directions: "You have probably already heard many Polish (or Italian or German, etc.) jokes. Read some of the jokes that have been used against minority groups in Chapter 5 of *Witcracks*. Then answer these questions: How do you think such jokes as these came about? Why do you think such jokes are used? What do they say about the attitudes of people toward people of other races, creeds and backgrounds? Is it all right to tell a joke on yourself or your own group? Is that the same thing as making the joke on someone else or his or her group?"

8
TOM SWIFTIES

Student directions: "Tom Swifty jokes humorously combine a quotation and the verb or verb and adverb describing the way it was said. Make a poster of 'Tom Swifties' such as these or of some you've heard before or made up yourself."

1. "I've broken my leg," he said lamely.

2. "What kind of sand?" she asked quickly.

3. "I'll turn you into a frog," she said charmingly.

4. "But I didn't know it was an electric chair," she said crisply.

5. "You say you've struck oil?" she gushed.

6. "Watch out for the spear!" he said pointedly.

7. "I've been hit by a steamroller," he said flatly.

8. "Drop that gun," the man said disarmingly.

9
TALL TALK

Student directions: " 'Have you the audacity to doubt my veracity and insinuate that I prevaricate?' Nonsense of this sort is called tall talk. You use big words to say something simple. The above example is tall talk for 'How dare you call me a liar?'

"Try to figure out Smart Sam's Proverbs or make up some tall talk of your own. Use a thesaurus for help."

Work sheet:

1. A male human being's most highly regarded companion is a four-footed domestic animal.

2. Great unhappiness has a strong feeling of affection for companionship.

3. Direct your eyes in advance of a jump.

4. At no time do drops of condensed moisture fall to the earth except in a downpour.

5. A pair of that part of the body which contains the brain is to be more valued than half the pair."

Source: Smart Sam's Proverbs above came from the *Arrow Book of Word Games*.

APRIL: Bulletin Boards

You'll need lots of Styrofoam egg cartons for this Easter bulletin board. On a bright pink background, draw the outline of a bunny, an Easter basket, and a few large eggs. Then have your kids cut the cartons apart so the egg cups can be painted individually. They should use green paint for the grass area; yellow for the basket; red, blue, and purple for the eggs; and white, of course, for the bunny. Have the kids glue the individual egg cups to your board, filling in the outline you've drawn.

CAROL ANN CHODAN

Looking for a good way to motivate your students to work a little harder? Try this attractive bulletin-board display that's perfect for Easter but can be used any month of the year. Start with a light pink background trimmed with dark blue or green scalloping. Then, from construction paper, cut a yellow baby chick popping out of a large, white egg as in the illustration at right. Place the chick in a corner of your bulletin board beside the words, "Don't Be an Egghead; Scramble for Good Grades."

PAM STRANGE

Here's a manipulative bulletin board to help your kids learn new vocabulary words. On a light-colored background, place a construction-paper cutout of a boy or girl sitting on a tree stump with a fishing pole in hand. Now place several paper fish in a "pond" cut from dark blue construction paper. Print one new vocabulary word on each paper fish. As your kids master a word, remove the corresponding fish from the pond until every one has been "caught." Label the display "Fishing for New Words."

TERESA CHURCHILL

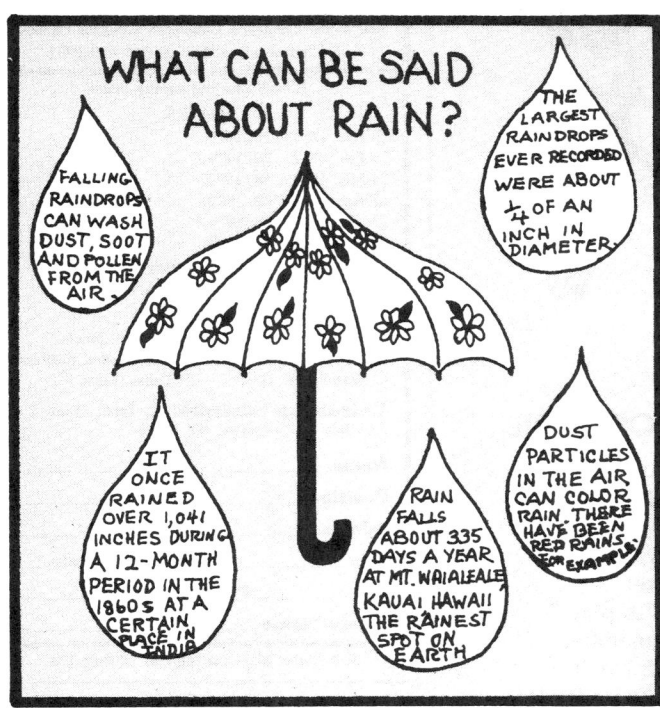

THERE'S more to rain than water! Let middle and upper graders research the facts. Challenge them, for example, with: Where and when did the most rain fall in one month? What is the rainiest spot in the world? What makes rain red? Have students write facts on raindrop-shaped cutouts and attach them to board around a colored-paper umbrella you've decorated. **Sandra J. Frey**

PRIMARIES work individually with "Math Magic." Make bulletin board from colored-paper shapes—labeled hats, bunny. Cut slits in brims and staple hats to board. Place flash cards in hats. During free time, students take cards and solve problems, orally or written, and check answers with card backs. Adapt to other subjects—spelling, color, and so on. **Lynda Gayle Merrell**

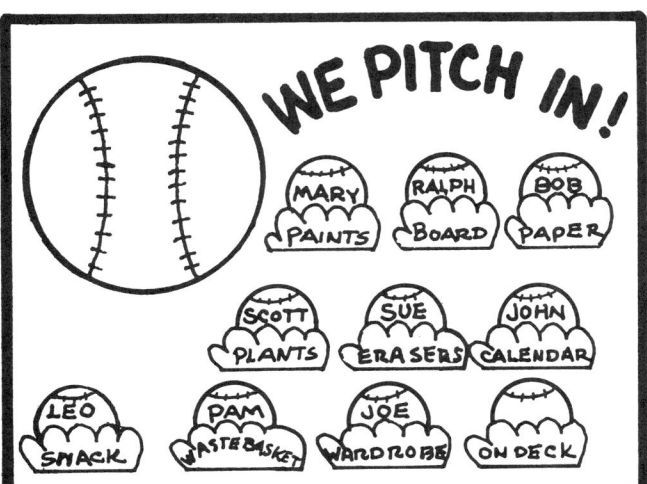

PEP up your classroom-helpers bulletin board. On a blue background, attach a paper-plate baseball. Staple replica mitts (scallop-cut, job labeled envelopes) across board. Kids draw ball stitching and their names on colored-paper circles. Those assigned jobs have balls in mitts, others wait in on-deck mitt. **Eleanor Schiano**

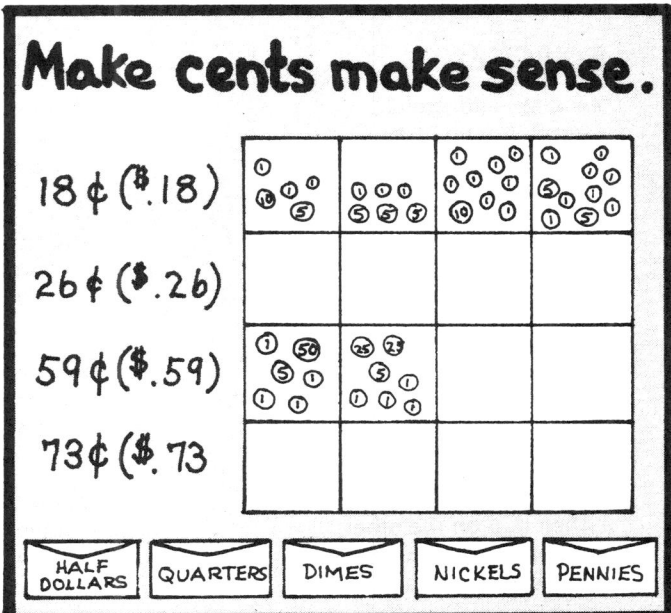

SPARE-TIME math. On one side of bulletin board, write amounts less than a dollar with four colored blocks after each. Place envelopes below for paper coins. Students choose coins to make amounts shown, tacking them in the blocks. Allow no repeat combination of coins. Students check each other's answers. **Sandra J. Frey**

MAY

Yes, we know. You're *weary.* It's been a long, hard year—and it's not over yet. You've still got another month of lesson plans to fill, you're running short on ideas, and your kids would rather be any place else but school.

May is a difficult month for teachers and students alike; but we've got some ideas that can change all that. In this special chapter, you'll find lots of unusual, amusing, and downright zany activities that will keep your class going all month long. Most of them are educational—but don't worry. They're cleverly disguised so no one will notice unles *you* spill the beans!

So go ahead. It's alright to be a little crazy. Try some of these activities, and turn this month into a marvelous, magical, May!

MAY: Make it a month-long festival

1 Today is the first day of AMERICAN BIKE MONTH. Have your kids research different styles of bicycles and ask student volunteers to bring in their own bikes for examples. Then, if possible, plan a bicycle field trip to local points of interest. Some kids may have to borrow bicycles and the activity will require close supervision for safety's sake, but the resulting enthusiasm and exhilaration will be worth it!

This is LEI DAY in Honolulu. Spread the spirit of goodwill in your class by having kids make paper leis for one another.

2 May is NATIONAL RADIO MONTH. Have your kids read up on radio shows from the forties or fifties like The Shadow or The Green Hornet, then write a program of their own to be broadcast over the school's loudspeaker system. You might want them to work in small groups to create several "radio shows."

Today is ROBERT'S RULES DAY, to commemorate the birthday of Henry M. Robert, author of Robert's Rules of Order. Acquaint your kids with some of the major points of parliamentary procedure; then let them debate a really "hot" issue like, "Are girls smarter than boys?" The debate must be waged strictly by the rules.

Smile! It's NATIONAL HUMOR MONTH and this is a perfect day to tickle your students' funny bones with some silly activities. Have a joke-telling session and give a prize to the child who draws the most laughs. Or hold a contest and see who can laugh the longest.

No one knows why, but the great artist Leonardo da Vinci wrote backwards in all his notebooks. Today-- BACKWARDS DAY--marks the anniversary of his death in 1519. Have your kids try writing stories backwards, or hold a contest to see who can be the first to transpose a full sentence. For a real twist, let the winner attempt to read the sentence aloud--backwards!

3 Celebrate the birthday of L. FRANK BAUM, author of The Wizard of Oz. Plan an honorary birthday party for him. Decorate the room in an Oz motif, and encourage kids to come dressed like favorite characters. Sing songs from the movie version of the book, dramatize favorite scenes, and end by discussing the following ideas: Should Dorothy have stayed in Oz? What if the twister had never whisked her away in the first place? What if Toto had been left behind in Kansas?

4 On this day in 1776, INVISIBLE INK was first used in diplomatic correspondence. Your kids can make their own invisible ink for writing secret messages with this simple recipe.
1. Use citrus juice or milk for the ink.
2. Use a toothpick or clean drawing pen for writing, dipping it in the "ink" frequently.
3. Let the ink dry thoroughly on unglossed paper.
4. Now hold the message up to a light bulb...and watch the words appear!

5 NELLIE BLY, pioneer American newspaper woman and crusader for women's rights and social reform, was born in 1867. Have kids assemble a class newspaper in her honor. Include an editorial page for children to write essays on social problems and issues that are making waves in your school.

Today is CHILDREN'S DAY in Japan, and families across that country fly red and black flags outside their homes-- one for every boy in the family. The tradition seems to be changing, though, and we hope that flags will soon be flown for girls, too! Make your own Children's Day banners and hang them in the hallway outside your classroom. The kids can decorate their banners with pictures from old magazines and portray personality characteristics, favorite foods, hobbies, and so on.

Happy birthday, GWENDOLYN BROOKS-- first black person to win a Pulitzer Prize (for her book of poetry, Annie Allen). Read her work, then have kids

MAY: Make it a month-long festival

write birthday poems for Gwendolyn.

The FIRST SPACE FLIGHT BY AN AMERICAN ASTRONAUT took place this day in 1961, with Alan B. Shepard aboard. Have kids dramatize the exchange between the spacecraft and Mission Control at the time of lift-off and splashdown. Then choose kids to portray newscasters commenting on the dramatic event.

6 "Penny Black," the WORLD'S FIRST POSTAGE STAMP, was issued in 1840. Since then, countless stamps have been designed by artists the world over. Your kids will enjoy designing their own postage stamps on special subjects like animals, outer space, and music. Then put all the "stamps" together in a class album. You may also wish to get your class interested in stamp collecting. Write to your local post office for information.

Today is RUDOLPH VALENTINO'S BIRTHDAY. He was the sensational romantic star of silent movies, and is well known for performances in The Sheik and Blood and Sand. Let your kids have fun today creating their own "silent movie." You supply the plot outline, and let them take it from there. Background music is allowed, but remember--no talking!

SIR RABINDRANATH TAGORE was born this day in 1861. An Indian poet known for advocating freedom for India, he gave a new sense of pride to fellow Hindus and wrote poems that dealt with the beauty of nature. Have your kids write their own nature poems (outdoors, if possible, where the mood is right!). Haiku is an especially effective form for this type of writing--and simple, too!

7 Today is the anniversary of the FIRST PRESIDENTIAL INAUGURAL BALL, held in New York City in honor of the inauguration of George Washington. Ask your kids to imagine that they've been invited to serve on the first Inaugural Ball Committee. What food will be served? What entertainment will they have? What attire will be required? What arrangements would they make for a contemporary Inaugural Ball?

Sing "Happy Birthday" to ROBERT BROWNING today, the famous poet who brought the Pied Piper of Hamelin to life. The poem is also a fable about the unfortunate things that happen when people fail to keep their promises. Have your kids work in small groups to write contemporary versions of the Pied Piper.

Today is also the birthday of PETER ILYICH TCHAIKOVSKY, composer of operas, symphonies, and ballets. Play some of Tchaikovsky's music in class today, and let your kids do a little "mood drawing" while they listen. The famous Nutcracker Suite lends itself especially well to this kind of activity.

8 The FIRST U.S. PATENT FOR AN AUTOMOBILE was awarded to G. B. Selden in 1879. For every successful idea like Selden's there are dozens of others rejected every year by the U.S. Patent Office. Have your kids suggest inventions that might be patented. Then choose a group of kids to represent patent officers. Inventors describe their patents to the officers who will consider each invention in terms of originality, feasibility, and practicality and vote on whether or not it should be patented.

9 Tennis champ PANCHO GONZALES was born in 1928. It's the perfect time to talk about all kinds of athletes and what it takes to be a winner. Ask your class to name their favorite athletes. Does anyone want to train for the Olympics? Become a professional athlete? Why?

SIR JAMES M. BARRIE, creator of the ever popular Peter Pan, was born in 1860. If your children are off in a Never-Never Land, get them hooked on writing by having the whole class write a story together. Start with two lines on the top of a long, lined sheet of paper. You might write, "Once upon a time, I was sitting under a tree when suddenly...." Fold the top of the paper down to cover the first line, and pass it on to one of your children. He or she might continue, "a large hand came out and...." Have this child fold down the paper to cover the second line and pass it on. Only two lines of the story should show at any one time. When each child has had a turn, open it up and read it aloud. The result may not be exactly literature, but it'll be literally hilarious!

10 VICTORIA WOODHULL became a V.I.P. on this day in 1872 when she became the FIRST WOMAN EVER TO RUN FOR THE U.S. PRESIDENCY. And it was 50 years before women were allowed to vote! Is there a woman or girl running for office in your area, school, or class? Get children in on the fun and excitement by making campaign buttons for such a candidate or any candidate of their choice. Just have your kids collect old campaign buttons, paint out the message with typewrite correction fluid, and write their own message with marking pens. After the campaign, your kids can recycle the buttons and use them to advertise an upcoming school fair or just to tell the world they're number one--which they are, of course!

East is east and west is west and finally the twain met on GOLDEN SPIKE DAY in 1869. On this day, the first transcontinental railroad was completed and a golden spike was driven into the ground to celebrate. (It has since been removed for preservation.) Commemorate the day by making tracks-- hold a track race! Try a sack race, a three-legged race, or a relay race. Or if possible, invite a railroad engineer or conductor to talk to your class about his or her job.

11 Choreographer and dancer MARTHA GRAHAM was born today. What does it take to become a professional dancer? Have your kids research the facts by studying her life. Later, interested students might want to produce a dance festival for other classmates or the rest of the school.

12 FLORENCE NIGHTINGALE, the famous nurse who founded nursing as a profession, was born today in 1820. In the spirit of this great woman, have your children make brightly colored posters, get together some songs or even a play, and play Florence Nightingale to the dozens of sick or elderly people in institutions in your area. One visit is sure to brighten their day--and yours!

EDWARD LEAR, lord of the limerick, born in 1846. Find a limerick from a book and leave off the last word in each line. Have your children fill in the blanks after you explain how a limerick works. When they are done, read the different variations on the same limerick and then let them try their hands at making up their own silly rhymes.

The FIRST WOMAN NEWS REPORTER AT A POLITICAL CONVENTION exercised her right to write and report this day in 1860. Mary Ashton Rice Livermore, an editor with the New Covenant, covered the Chicago Republican National Convention where Abraham Lincoln was nominated for the presidency. Discuss the First Amendment's guarantee of freedom of speech and a newpaper's responsibility to report the facts as objectively as possible. Give your kids firsthand experience by publishing your own Grade School Gazette!

Three cheers for NONCOMMERCIAL EDUCATIONAL TV which first flashed across our screens in 1953. After all, it's educational TV that first brought us the Muppets on "Sesame Street." What could be more fun for children than to make and name their own Muppet? Use socks, felt mouths, ping-pong ball eyes, and discarded or outgrown clothes. Stuff the clothes with newspaper; then on with the show!

13 The FIRST CROSS-COUNTRY HELICOPTER FLIGHT took place in 1942. Kids will love making their own helicopters out of paper cups. Hold the cup upside down and cut slits in the sides from the rim, to about ½ inch from the base of the cup. Fold each strip up. Then snip another small slit a third of the way across each strip near the base of the cup. Starting at this snip, make a

MAY: Make it a month-long festival

crease down the length of the strip. Punch a hole in the bottom of the cup and tie a string through the hole. Attach a paper clip to the other end of the string under the flaps and drop from any height.

SIR ARTHUR SULLIVAN of the musical team Gilbert and Sullivan, was born in 1842. Sing his praises with your own classroom opera. Any favorite story makes good opera material. If kids are shy, have them use the Muppet they made as the opera singer or have them draw a face on their hand. When you put your index finger together with your thumb it forms a circle that makes a perfect mouth. Draw eyes and nose above on the side of the index finger and lips around the hole. Soon you'll have a whole chorus of altos and sopranos right in your hands!

Here's a date fit to print! In 1821 on the day, AMERICA'S FIRST PRINTING PRESS was patented by Samuel Rust in New York City. Use potatoes and thick tempera paints to teach your children how it's done. Use plenty of newspapers under the paper you want to print on. Have your children cut an initial or a design in the potato, dip it in a pan of paint and press down on the paper. You can make great wrapping paper or wall hangings for your class.

14 LEWIS AND CLARK started their famous expedition up the Missouri River and on to the Pacific Coast on this day in 1804. The diaries and maps they made during their two-year trip did much to dispel the myth of the long-sought Northwest Passage. In honor of this historic journey, send your kids on an exploration of their own. Hold a scavenger hunt right in your classroom! Place small objects such as a coin, a nail, a safety pin, a stamp, a button, and so on, around the room so they are in plain sight, but camouflaged. For instance, pin the safety pin to the outside of a coat or smock hanging in the room. Hand out a list of the objects to each child. He or she walks around the room, quietly checking off the things on the list he or she sees. The first child to check them all off wins and points them out to the other students. You can play again and again by simply finding new hiding places.

As the temperature is warming up outside, it's the perfect day to teach your children the use of a thermometer. In 1714, GABRIEL DANIEL FAHRENHEIT, the German physicist who invented the thermometer and the Fahrenheit scale that bears his name, was born. Explain the difference between Fahrenheit and Celsius scales. Discuss why the U.S. and England still use the Fahrenheit scale while most other countries use the Celsius scale, invented in 1742.

ROBERT OWEN, 19th-century proponent of a Utopian society, was born in 1771. He proposed a system of cooperative communities in which the work and the rewards would be equally shared by all, and several experimental communities were formed based on his ideas. Discuss with students how you could apply these theories to the classroom. Ask them to imagine an ideal day at school. What would they wear? What would they do? What would they eat? Who, if anyone, would be in charge? If you're feeling adventurous you might try it for an hour, or a day, or a few minutes. What problems come up? How would your kids deal with the problem?

15 On this day in 1948, the STATE OF ISRAEL was established for the first time in 2,000 years. following the United Nations decision to partition Palestine. This action represented the fulfillment of the Jewish people's belief in God's promise of their holy land. It's the perfect opportunity to discuss Jewish traditions and customs with your children. If someone has a Menorah, ask him or her to bring it in. Research the history and customs that are associated with the Menorah, the Star of David, Hanukkah, the dreidel, Yom Kippur, Rosh Hashanna, and so on. Or, ask parent volunteers to supply their favorite dishes for a Jewish feast.

ELLEN CHURCH, the FIRST AIRLINE

STEWARDESS (now called flight attendent) was hired today in 1930. Use this occasion to introduce your children to new countries and cultures from far and wide. Send for travel brochures and travel posters to hang up in your room.

16 Lights, camera, action! The very first ACADEMY AWARDS got rolling on this day in 1929. As the children come in the room today, pin the name of a well-known movie star on each child's back. Then, by asking the other kids yes or no questions, each child must guess his or her movie star's identity. Sample questions are: "Am I female?" "Did I win an Oscar this year?" and so on. Then have your own Academy Awards ceremony by having kids nominate and select film stars they think should have won the categories of Best Actor, Best Actress, Best Supporting Actor, Best Supporting Actress, and Best Picture this year. They can also practice their letter-writing skills by writing to a favorite film star c/o the studio that produced his or her latest film.

What this country needs is a good five-cent nickel! That's what the U.S. Government decided on this date in 1866 when they authorized THE FIRST U.S. NICKEL. Did your students know that before that time there was a silver coin worth five cents that was called half a dime? Or that there was once a twenty-cent coin and a half-cent coin? Start a class coin collection. Try to collect the different kinds of nickels depicting Thomas Jefferson, a Buffalo Head, and the Liberty Head.

Today must be your lucky day! It's the day the HORSESHOE PITCHERS ASSOCIATION was formed back in 1914. It's a good day to discuss why the horseshoe is considered a good luck symbol. What other good luck charms can your children think of? What things are considered bad luck? Why? You'll find there's often a very good reason behind the origins of these beliefs. For example, the expression "knock on wood" came from an ancient belief that

gods lived inside the trees of forests. When people were in trouble, they would knock on the tree, appealing to the god for help. When your children understand the origins of superstitions, it should help dispel fears they may have about these things.

17 The landmark SUPREME COURT decision in the case of Brown v. Board of Education of Topeka, Kansas, was made in 1954. The Supreme Court ruled that racial segregation in public schools was unconstitutional. Discuss that decision and why it was made.

18 BIRTHDAY OF MOTHER'S WHISTLER doesn't have anything to do with Whistler or his famous mother. The day is sponsored by a group in Huntington Valley, Pennsylvania, and is intended to encourage people to whistle. So hold a "Birthday of Mother's Whistler World Champion Whistling Contest." First prize, a box of crackers--after all, the rest of the class can use the handicap! (And just to set the record straight, find a picture of the real Whistler's Mother to grace the competition.

19 It's MAY RAY DAY, time to applaud warm outside days. Plan a picnic, a softball game, a walk through a park--anything to get you outside. Other activities include making a sundial. Draw a circle on a large piece of paper. Make a line from the center to just outside the circle, and label this line "north." Tape the clock face to a piece of cardboard, and glue an empty thread spool to center of the circle. Sharpen a pencil at both ends and stick one end into the spool. (The pencil, which will cast a shadow, must be straight up and down.) Put the sun dial outside, facing north. At each hour trace the shadow the pencil makes on the paper. Write the hour at the place where the shadow crosses the circle.

In 1932, Congressman Claude Fuller of Arkansas introduced a new resolution in the House of Representatives that called for all civil service employees to

MAY: Make it a month-long festival

memorize the national anthem. The resolution died, but Fuller's intention didn't. NATIONAL ANTHEM MEMORIZATION RESOLUTION DAY, held today, commemorates Fuller's patriotic spirit. Sponsor a contest today to learn the "Star Spangled Banner" by heart.

This was not a lucky day in 1911 for burglar Caesar Cella. CELLA WAS THE FIRST PERSON TO BE CONVICTED OF A CRIME ON THE BASIS OF FINGERPRINTS found at the scene. Let your students try their "fingers" at being amateur sleuths by lifting fingerprints. Press fingers to a dark surface. Sprinkle the surface lightly with talcum powder, and brush carefully with a feather. (The powder should stick to the prints and make them visible.) Place a small piece of clear tape over the prints, and lift them off the surface. Mount the tape on a dark piece of paper to make the prints distinguishable.

20 DOLLEY PAYNE MADISON, wife of the fourth president of the United States, was born in 1768. She is famous for saving the portrait of George Washington when the British burned the capital in 1812, and for her gracious parties. But a little-known fact about Dolley is that she started the custom of rolling colored eggs on the White House lawn. Honor Dolley by having a May egg rolling contest. Older kids can race each other while attempting to push an egg with their nose.

How good are your pupils at guessing the weight of an object? Find out today on WEIGHTS AND MEASURES DAY. (It's the anniversary of the International Bureau of Weights and Measures.) Bring in a number of objects of varying size and mass. Ask students to guess the weight of each object on the basis of the type of material it's made of.

21 THE FIRST BICYCLE MADE ITS APPEARANCE IN NEW YORK CITY IN 1819. Students will be interested in the history of this early model, called a velocipede, or "swift walker." To

celebrate the day, sponsor a bike-decorating contest. Have kids use their imaginations to create a costume for their "wheels."

HOW FAR WILL A BALLOON TRAVEL? Jane Dorst, Atherton, California, found that one can go pretty far. In 1972 she released a balloon with her name and address attached to it, and received word 20 days later that the balloon had reached Pietermaritzburg, South Africa. Try this with your students. Give each a balloon and a 3" x 5" card to attach with a string. Have kids print their name and address on the card, along with the message that whoever finds the balloon should contact the child. Keep a record on a classroom map of where each balloon ends up.

CLARA BARTON, founder of the American Red Cross, was born in 1821. Find out more about the Red Cross and the important work it does. And have your students contact your local chapter to learn the ways in which they can help by raising money, volunteering time, and so on.

22 GEORGE BAKER, creator of the "Sad Sack" cartoon character (that little GI), was born this day in 1915. Use this day to give students a shot at drawing cartoons. Have each originate a comic-strip personality and tell a story about the character. Or display an example of a serious cartoon and explain what a caricature is. Suggest children design a cartoon expressing their views on an issue in the school, community, or the world.

There's another famous birthday today that will interest your students. SIR ARTHUR CONAN DOYLE, author of Sherlock Holmes, was born in 1859. To honor this great storyteller test your kids' skill and imagination at solving mysteries. Supply pupils with a plot for a story, several characters, and clues; then have each write a solution the the puzzle.

You may not think your kids are opera buffs, but put on a recording of music composed by RICHARD WAGNER--such as the "Wedding March" from Lohengrin, the "Ride of the Valkyries," or the overture to The Flying Dutchman--and just watch their reaction. The German composer was born in 1813.

23 HAPPY BIRTHDAY TO MARY CASSATT, born in 1844. An American artist who painted in the style of the French impressionists, Cassatt is noted for her scenes of family life. Display books on the impressionists for pupils to browse through, then have them try painting a scene from their family life in this style.

24 SAMUEL MORSE FIRST SENT HIS CODE over the wires in 1844. Locate a copy of the code in an encyclopedia and use it to devise some code exercises for your class. Give each a list of words or sentences written in Morse Code to decipher, along with a list of the code dots and dashes. To make the exercises more challenging, give only a partial list of the symbols so missing letters must be determined from the context of the sentence. Encourage kids to develop their own code for sending secret messages to friends.

JAMES PEALE, a member of the family of American artists, died in 1749. Peale is noted for his portraits, still lifes, and landscapes, so celebrate his birthday by making shadow portraits. Place a piece of paper on a wall, and have a child sit with his profile against it. Shine a light to achieve a shadow, and have another child trace around the seated child. Try funny poses or facial expressions for humorous effects.

25 Today is the birthday of BILL (BOJANGLES) ROBINSON, who is known as "the king of tap dancers." Arrange a student dance concert in your classroom as a birthday celebration.

In 1977, the movie "Star Wars" was released. Help students mount a puppet production using their own science-fiction script. You might want to begin with a narrator--who is a computer.

Golf in America--the FIRST HOW-TO GOLF BOOK--was published in 1895. Have kids write their own one-page how-to "book" on any goofy topic of their choice: how to do a swan dive, speak pig Latin, make mud pies, and so on. Remind kids of the rules for writing clear directions: Each step must be accurately and clearly stated, and the steps must be in proper order.

26 On this day in 1906, the ARCHAEOLOGICAL INSTITUTE OF AMERICA was founded. Ask students to "dig up" all the facts they can about one of the following famous archaeologists: Howard Carter, Sir Arthur J. Evans, Sir Petrie Flinders, Heinrich Schliemann.

JOHN WAYNE was born in 1907--so why not declare it "Wild West Day" in honor of the many western films in which he appeared. Western "duds" are required, of course, and sometime during the day discuss what life was like in the Old West.

27 ROBERT RIPLEY--creator of the famous cartoon strip "Believe It or Not"--died in 1949. If possible, obtain a copy of one of the Ripley anthologies. Share some of the oddities with kids. Then go on a "Believe-It-or-Not-Wild-Animal" safari. Ask kids to make drawings or paintings or write short descriptions of imaginary wild animals. Encourage kids to be wild and crazy! Have them share their creations and compile their own "Believe-It-or-Not."

On this day in 1878, famous American dancer ISADORA DUNCAN was born. Influenced by Greek art, she often performed her modern dances barefoot and wearing a loose, flowing Greek tunic. Read aloud an ancient Greek myth and have students interpret it in mime and dance.

Today is also the birthday of RACHEL CARSON, American environmentalist who wrote Silent Spring--a book that condemned the irresponsible use of

MAY: Make it a month-long festival

pesticides. Help kids interview the building-and-grounds person to find out the kind of pesticide used on the school's lawn or plants. Then contact your local health department for a report on the safety of that pesticide.

28 On May 28, 1929, Warner Brothers' film "On with the Show" was first shown at the Winter Garden Theater in New York. It was the FIRST TALKING PICTURE ENTIRELY IN COLOR! To help kids appreciate this development, have them draw or paint a landscape using colored crayons, chalk, or paints, then do another one in black and white. Discuss the different effects of the color and black and white versions.

In 1892, the SIERRA CLUB, an American organization that works to protect the environment, was founded by naturalist John Muir. Encourage interested kids to form their own "nature" club and formulate the rules and goals of their organization.

Today is the birthday of JIM THORPE (1886-1953)--one of the greatest all-around athletes in history. Among his many athletic accomplishments, Thorpe played major-league baseball, pro football, and excelled at track and field events. Devote your physical education period to one or all of those sports as a birthday salute to Jim Thorpe--all-American.

29 On May 29, 1917, JOHN F. KENNEDY was born. In his inaugural address, he told Americans, "Ask not what your country can do for you--ask what you can do for your country." Discuss things kids can do to improve their neighborhood or community.

On this day in 1916, the OFFICIAL FLAG OF THE PRESIDENT OF THE UNITED STATES was adopted. Ask each student to design his or her very own personal flag.

Today is the BIRTHDAY OF BOB HOPE, the witty and talented entertainer who is best known for his efforts on behalf of the USO. Mr. Hope's birthday is celebrated today at different USO headquarters around the world. Have

your kids research the history of the USO, then plan their own show in honor of the man who has done so much for members of the armed forces. You might want to invite the whole school to participate.

30 On May 30, 1901, the HALL OF FAME FOR GREAT AMERICANS was dedicated at New York University in New York City. Students can create their own "Hall of Fame" bulletin board by drawing or painting portraits of famous people.

In 1943, the ICE CREAM FREEZER WAS PATENTED. Hurray! Do some research on the history of ice cream and have your class create a time line or mural depicting the major events. Top it off with ice cream for dessert at lunch.

The famous LINCOLN MEMORIAL in Washington, D.C. was dedicated in 1922. Kids will enjoy reenacting the dedication ceremony. First, have a committee write a dedication speech, listing some of Lincoln's contributions to our country's history. Another committee might draw a likeness of the famous memorial. And the whole class can choose someone to rehearse the speech and deliver it.

31 Today is the birthday of famous American poet, WALT WHITMAN, born in 1819. His book of poetry, Leaves of Grass, is considered one of our major literary works. Read aloud a portion of the poem "Song of Myself." Then encourage pupils to write their own "Song"--describing themselves.

On May 31, 1790, the first U.S. COPYRIGHT LAW was passed. Discuss the importance of such laws by asking these questions: How would you feel if someone else were given credit for a project you had created yourself? How would you react if someone else were paid for a job you had performed?

In 1964, the LONGEST BASEBALL GAME in history was played. It lasted seven hours and 23 minutes for a total of 23 innings. Have kids find out where and when that record was broken.